THE GHOSTS OF BIGGIN HILL

When the RAF quit Biggin Hill in the early 1990s they left behind sprawling blocks of anonymous-looking buildings, a chapel which bears witness to the station's great engagements, memories of the greatest aerial combat the world has ever known and many, many ghosts.

The ghosts materialise frequently. They have appeared from within the redundant administrative buildings and near the old runway. They have been seen running to and from the dispersal shelters. They have been spotted, in full flying gear, walking the country lanes and, of course, they regularly mingle with the visitors to the Chapel of St George's. On occasions, the evocative sound of a Merlin engine has filled the air.

The Ghosts of Biggin Hill is not just about the friendly spirits which inhabit the old fighter station. It's also about the heroes and heroines and, by selecting a story here and a picture there from his superb archives, Bob Ogley has completed a splendid follow-up to his highly-acclaimed book, *Biggin on The Bump*, the story of the most famous fighter station in the world.

Froglets Publications

Brasted Chart,
Westerham, Kent
TN16 1LY
Tel: 01959 562972
Fax: 01959 565365

ISBN
Paperback 1 872337 41 4

Hardback 1 872337 46 5

© Bob Ogley

Front cover shows a pilot 'ghost' of 133 Eagle Squadron with the airfield in the background. The Hurricanes are taken from Kenneth McDonough's painting 'Battle for Biggin'.

Back cover : ' Returning Home' A Spitfire of 72 Squadron returns to Biggin Hill. Copyright Trevor Lay/Spitfire Art , Ditchling.

This book was originated by Froglets Publications Ltd, printed and slot bound by Thanet Press, Margate. Hardbound by Green Street Bindery, Oxford.

Jacket design by Sally Marshall

Supporting the RAF Benevolent Fund and Demelza House

A former WAAF, stationed at Biggin Hill in 1941, came up to my bookstall during a special event to celebrate the 60th anniversary of the Battle of Britain and told me that *Biggin On The Bump* was the best book she had ever read. "I still have it by my bedside", she said. "And I read it over and over again". Implying that there must be many untold stories about Biggin, she asked: "Are you going to write a follow-up?"

Well, here it is. *The Ghosts of Biggin Hill* — dedicated to Lorraine Balmforth and all the WAAFs and airmen who worked on the ground, or flew from RAF Biggin Hill during the war years.

Many of the photographs came from the Biggin Hill archives which I inherited when the station closed in 1992. The majority had been taken by individuals but some, I am certain, come from official sources such as the Imperial War Museum or the RAF Museum at Hendon.

Because of this uncertainty and because they need funds urgently it is my desire that part of the royalties should — like those from the sale of *Biggin on The Bump* — go to the RAF Benevolent Fund. Additionally, I would like to support a charity close to home — Demelza House, a hospice in Kent for children with terminal illness.

I have many people to thank for making this book possible. Peter Halliday from High Wycombe, who lived at Biggin Hill during the war, for his schoolboy's perspective, Canon O'Hanlon, padre in 1940-41, for his emotive experiences, Nick Gilman for his extraordinary spiritual tale, Dave Witherspoon from Downe for his encouragement throughout, Valerie Preston for her mother's story, Mike and Sheila Blundell for organising a get-together of residents with fantastic memories, Ian Piper for showing me where 1940 still survives and members of many proud Squadron associations for their special contributions about Biggin Hill.

There are several others but I would particularly like to thank the following: Aviation Art, Ted Williams, Bill Langley, John Nelson, Joe Merchant, Jack Lancaster, George Blundell, Peter Martin and Bromley Borough Council, John Tann, Jim Barton, Graeme Gillard, Tom Docherty, Terry Smith, Dennis Chambers, Alan Morris, David Duval, Ian Douglas, Jackie Stillman, Eric Weeks, Gordon Clarke, Robert Burkin, Dave Adams, Laurie Chester, Richard Geiger, Dot Beavers, Tracey Williams, Kim Cross, Barbara Robbins, Peter Richardson, Susanne Harrison, Roberta Single, Les Lyne, Ken Stanley, Mike Beale, Nicole Whittle, Helen Edmunds, John Potts, Ray Phillips, Lesley Kingcome, Brian Petch, Trevor Lay, and Group Captain Hugh O'Neill.

As ever, thanks to Fern Flynn who has been involved in all stages of production, Avril Oswald who read the text and made many sound suggestions, Francesca Wade who helped with the research and Alan Killen, Robin Brooks and Mo Dyke who checked the text. May I remind readers and booksellers that *Biggin on The Bump* is still available and details can be found on the back page along with other titles from Froglets Publications.

Please let is know if you recognise any of the characters featured in this book. We can include their names in the reprint. *Bob Ogley*

Contents

The Ghosts of Biggin Hill was made possible by those who came forward with tales of incidents, experiences and events. A few of the stories have been told before but many have never been revealed. I thank these people especially. They have helped me to commit to the folklore and to the wonderful history of Biggin Hill what may have been lost for ever. Don't forget, it is the most famous fighter station in the world; no-one knows that better than the ghosts who inhabit it.

The first chapter contains the ghost stories. It is followed by chapters dealing with specific periods at Biggin Hill with an emphasis on those who gave their lives, either by 'careless' flying, through an unfortunate accident, as a result of bombing or in tragic combat.

Each chapter is preceded by a chronology of events — to guide the reader through Biggin Hill's historic role in the ongoing theatre of war. .

Bob Ogley

Photographic credits

The majority of photographs in this book, where not otherwise credited, come from **Bob Ogley's "Biggin Hill Collection"** which was donated to him when the RAF left the station in 1992. The collection includes scores of personal photographs donated by WAAFs and airmen which have never been published. We are grateful to them and to the following: **Fern Flynn** (pages) 11, 13, 19, 21 (bottom), 22, 23, 39, 55, 186, 187, 188, 189 and 190. **Alex Watson** 27. **Philip Lane** 31. **Tracey Williams** 15, 17. **Valerie Preston** 33, 75, 179 (both). **Kentish Times** 34. **RAF Museum, Hendon** 40, 41. **Brian Petch** 77, 197. **Bill Blundell (part of the Ted Williams collection)** 108. **Peter Halliday sketches** 111. **Imperial War Museum** 99, 114, 145, 146, 158, 148, 162, 166, 172, 173, 174, 195. **Nick Gilman** 78. **David Witherspoon** 125 (top), **L. Smith (part of the Ted Williams collection)** 125 (bottom). **Margaret Marfell** 127, **Associated Kent Newspapers** 104. **Canon O'Hanlon** 133. **Mary Wells** 150. **Lorraine Balmforth** 153. **Group Captain Hugh O'Neill** 173. **Vernon Dadd** 183. **Sevenoaks Chronicle** 184, 185. **Trevor Lay/Spitfire Art,** 191. In some cases we have been unable to trace the copyright holder but have made every effort to do so.

The first gate guardians were placed on the concrete apron near the main hangar in September 1954 and dedicated by the Bishop of Rochester as a permanent memorial to The Few. When the new Chapel of Remembrance was completed the following year they were transferred to the lawn outside. In 1987 the two precious veterans were removed and replaced by the fibre-glass models which remain today.

Foreword

IN September 1989 I was invited by the chaplain of St George's Chapel, Biggin Hill, the Rev Eric Mantle to give an illustrated talk about the Great Storm which had devastated south-east England two years earlier.

Having written a (best-selling) book about the never-to-be-forgotten night of October 16, 1987 when hurricane-force winds tore up a million trees, crippled communications and changed the face of our landscape for ever, I was considered to be reasonably knowledgeable on the subject — and certainly in demand to tell my story.

The Biggin Hill talk went well. Rev Eric Mantle introduced me to the Commanding Officer of the RAF Station, Wing Commander Alan Jones and a few senior officers. He showed me round the St George's Chapel of Remembrance and I was immediately moved for here was the clearest reminder I had ever experienced of the spirit and selfless dedication that took Britain through its most crucial years in history.

The twelve beautiful stained glass windows each tell a story of Biggin Hill. There are badges of the seven squadrons who served there during the Battle of Britain and at the rear of the chapel is an oaken reredos containing the names of the 453 aircrew who were killed while flying with the Biggin Hill Wing between 1939 and 1945. Mr Mantle showed me the gilded wooden eagle on the lectern, the altar crosses and the book of remembrance. He said that in the whole of the free world there was possibly no better memorial to The Few.

I drove home that night thinking about aviation aces, the four years of front-line fighting and how lucky I was to have Britain's former premier fighter station so close to my home at Brasted. As a journalist I had already met the WAAFs who carried on working when the station was bombed in 1940. I knew a couple of the former fighter pilots, including the incomparable Brian Kingcome and I had been privileged to meet and enjoy a drink with Kath Preston, landlady of the White Hart, Brasted, the pub that many of the squadrons used as their local during the war years.

A few days later I received a letter from one of Biggin Hill's senior officers. He reminded me that the 50th anniversary of the Battle of Britain was fast approaching and suggested that a well-illustrated book about Biggin Hill would possibly raise a bob or two as part of the station's contribution towards the RAF Benevolent Fund. It is possible, he wrote, that the RAF will pull out of the station altogether within a few years presenting a final opportunity to tell the story of the "most famous fighter station in the world". The letter concluded: "Can you help?".

As I read I felt a warm glow; a kind of special satisfaction. I had only just made the decision to leave my post as editor of the local newspaper in Sevenoaks and see if I could make a living out of writing books. Although I was a director of a tiny publishing company run by my partner, Fern, I had no definite plans in the pipeline. But here was a special challenge. More important I could meet the pilots, WAAFs, technicians and all those who made a vital contribution to the defence of our country in 1940 and beyond. A great adventure was just beginning.

Some months later *Biggin on The Bump* was published and the critics were more than generous. "A glorious story" said the Aviation News. "From the first page the story and illustrations give a fascinating insight into the men and machines from the days of World War One. "A remarkable account of Biggin Hill's history", said the Royal Air Force News. "It will bring back many memories". "A glorious tribute to gallantry", wrote Flypast. "From the brilliantly-named Froglets Publications comes the equally brilliant *Biggin on The Bump*". And so on...

I was bowled over by the reaction and certainly by the decision of TV South to meet some of my heroes and feature the book on one of their Battle of Britain anniversary programmes. The first print run of 5,000 sold out in four weeks and a reprint was organised. Two more reprints followed. By 1994 *Biggin on The Bump* had generated more than £15,000 for the RAF Benevolent Fund.

On October 4, 1992 the officers of the Aircrew Selection Centre, which had made its home at Biggin Hill some years after the war, gathered in St George's Chapel once more — not to remember the finest hour — but to pay homage to their saddest hour. The RAF were leaving Biggin Hill and the last rites to the famous old fighter station had to be observed with the solemnity, dignity and respect that it had earned during its lifespan of 76 years. The decommissioning service was followed by the lowering of the flag. The Last Post was to commemorate the final act in the life of the station. Station Commander Les Palmer then locked the gates of the guardhouse and handed Biggin Hill over to RAF Uxbridge as a detached site.

Several years have passed since that sad occasion. After completing the necessary formal details, RAF Uxbridge handed Biggin Hill to the Central Disposal Unit of the Ministry of Defence whose responsibility it was to part with the famous agglomeration of hangars, offices, workshops, administrative buildings and houses. Aviation enthusiasts were soon on the site haggling for souvenirs. The flagpole was saved for the yet-to-be-finalised Battle of Britain memorial site at Capel-le-Ferne overlooking the English Channel. Other than that sentiment seemed to be of no value to the CDU. Biggin Hill was systematically stripped.

As author of *Biggin on The Bump* and the proud holder of a Certificate of Merit presented to me by Air Chief Marshal Sir Roger Palin, Controller of the RAF Benevolent Fund, I also received a small "farewell" present which, as a historian, I considered to be of far more value than a souvenir. Les Palmer gave me the Biggin Hill photographic collection which the station had accumulated over the years. It went back to the days of the Royal Flying Corps and the Wireless Testing Station. It included pictures taken after the bombing of the station in the grim days of August 1940 and, of course, featured many heroes and heroines.

I promised the officers that, one day, I would write a follow-up to *Biggin on The Bump* and told them that I had many more stories of the men, women, machines and indomitable spirit which still pervades their old airfield. Spirit? Spirits? I remember now Squadron Leader Brian Kingcome's well chosen words: "I walk with ghosts when I revisit my old station but they are friendly ones....."

Here they are — *The Ghosts of Biggin Hill.*

1

Who are the ghosts of Biggin Hill?

Ever since Biggin Hill became an operational fighter station back in 1917 there have been strange sightings and perplexing events which defy all rational explanation. The ghosts — if that is what they are — have been seen in the Chapel, near the guardroom and on the airfield. They have caused havoc in the old telephone exchange, terrified the residents of Vincent Square and caused confusion in the village. They have comforted distinguished aviators but have terrified mothers and held conversations with bemused custodians of St George's Chapel. A grave prelate has given advice and a local cleric has managed to send one back to her spiritual world. As brave as they were the aviators of Biggin Hill were frightened by death. And as long as man fears death there will be ghosts.

The Sun is sweet on rose and wheat
And on the eyes of children;
Quiet the street for old men's feet
And gardens for the children

The soil is safe, for widow and waif,
And for the soul of England,
Because their bodies men vouchsafe
To save the soul of England.

Fair days are yet left for the old,
And children's cheeks are ruddy.
Because the good lads limbs lie cold
And their brave cheeks are bloody.

From *Storm* by Wilfred Owen

This aerial photograph of RAF Biggin Hill was taken just after the war when two Auxiliary Squadrons, 600 and 615 flew a mix of modern Spitfires. By then the rebuilding of the aerodrome, following the devastating attacks of 1940, had been completed and the station was in good trim. The Officers' Mess with its swimming pool, the airmens' quarters and the married quarters to the west of the Bromley Road are clearly shown along with the aircraft on the ground. The hangars, two main runways, the road that runs around the perimeter of the airfield, the dispersal pens to the east and the busy area on the South Camp are also shown.

Ghost Station

IT was the late Squadron Leader Brian Kingcome who first drew my attention to the ghosts of Biggin Hill. "When I revisit my old station", he said," I walk with ghosts but they are friendly ones. I mourn them, but they had counted the cost and they died with regret but without surprise. They were typical of their generation and their generation was typical of all others. The young of all generations are the same. They may dress differently and have different rites and rituals, but give them a crisis and they are all the same. I salute them".

Pressed to define exactly what he meant by "ghosts" and the identification of those who still haunted Biggin Hill, Brian Kingcome, (Kingpin to his old friends of 92 Squadron) said he had experienced no particular strange encounters apart from an uncanny, phantasmal feeling that they were there — outside the old mess, in the now-dilapidated dispersal pens, walking across the tarmac and, who knows, possibly airborne at angels one-five behind a thin sheet of perspex.

"I imagine them", he said, "back in that unreal world of twisting smoke trails, spiralling to earth on the end of a parachute, in the hangar, in the mess, walking down the lane to The Jail pub. RAF squadron historians will know their names. There are hundreds of ghosts at Biggin Hill".

Kingcome is now dead and so are many of his old friends. But those who are left still return to Biggin Hill to peer into the past. Rather like the pull of invisible chains they find their memories easily drawn to events of long ago. Before their eyes they see a modern airfield with executive jets lined up for take off and smart customs officers and security teams mingling with the airport staff, but in their mind they can still see a bustling, thundering combat airfield, scarred and mauled but still defiant. The emotions are mixed; the ghosts are real.

On the basis that a ghost is the spirit of a dead person capable of making itself seen or heard by the living, I decided to see if there was any evidence to support this strong belief in the supernatural. I quickly discovered that Biggin Hill is saturated with unexplained incidents such as the sight and sound of fighter planes returning from combat. The ghosts appear in different forms — the solid or transparent likeness of the deceased or a disembodied voice. There is no evidence of the existence of disruptive poltergeists who move or break objects. The ghosts of Biggin Hill are well behaved, proud perhaps to still serve at the famous old station!

Belief in, and the worship of, ghosts dates back to the Middle Ages. The belief declined in the ensuing centuries but was revived in the 19th century when spiritualism came into vogue. By the beginning of the 20th century it was much easier to believe in ghosts than it was to accept that one day man would be cocooned in the cockpit of a flying machine as he climbed full throttle into the lower heavens for an hour's fighting with a hostile enemy. It was even harder to believe that, some 70 years hence, man would jump, sing and dance his way across the surface of the moon.

So, for the sake of those young men (and women) who gave their lives in two world wars (and beyond) let me explain that most of the people involved in this book lived and worked at, or flew from Biggin Hill.

The ghosts of airmen have certainly been inside the Chapel of St George's which is situated on the main road opposite the old mess and slightly to the south of the guardroom. Only by speculating wildly can a total be placed on the frequency of their visits but, of all the buildings associated with Biggin Hill, the Chapel remains inviolate. Built in a rich red brick with a large barn-style roof in heavy terracotta tiles it is one of the best memorials in Britain to *The Few*. The atmosphere inside is one of tranquillity — severe but simple. It is a place of worship but it is also a small museum surrounded, on the outside, by consecrated land on which no-one can build for 100 years or so.

Visitors from all over the world have walked through the doors of St George's to experience the deeply moving reminder of the men who took us through the most crucial five years of our history. The ghosts of airmen of all ranks have slipped in with them, some to pray but the majority to study the reredos, situated at the back of this unique place of worship.

These oaken panels contain the names of 453 aircrew who were killed in operations while flying from the Biggin Hill Sector between 1939 and 1945. They come from 52 squadrons and their names are inscribed on the panels to each side of the altar. The gilded wooden eagle on the lectern, the altar crosses, the alms dish and the candlesticks were gifts from the friends of Biggin Hill when the Chapel opened on July 25, 1951.

A visitors' book contains the names of the visitors who care to sign. Most people leave a message. "A humbling experience" — "My seventh visit. I'll be back" — "Goose pimples again" — "What better place to come on the 80th birthday of the RAF" — "I owe my freedom to them , I'm 10 years old" — "A prayer for my heroes" —"A fitting memorial to all brave men".

The officer in charge of St George's Chapel from 1983 was Wing Commander (Retired) David Duval and one of his first tasks was to supervise the refurbishment of the reredos and check the personal details of all the aircrew from the Biggin Hill Sector whose names were listed. Squadron, rank, forenames, surnames and medals were all checked against the official records to ensure completeness and accuracy and the details were then passed to the draughtsman who was reworking the lettering.

"When the boards came back", said David, "they were again checked against the updated information and a few errors were corrected. We were satisfied eventually that the panels were accurate".

Late one afternoon David was working in the vestry which is beside the entrance door to the Chapel. The door was then spring-loaded and had an annoying squeak whenever it was opened so David always knew if a visitor had walked into the Chapel. Imagine his surprise when he went to check the building prior to locking up and found a rather scruffy and unkempt man in a dirty trenchcoat standing beside the reredos.

"I asked if I could help him as I was about to lock up", said David. "The man said he was looking for Wing Commander Slater on the reredos. I pointed out the name and, thinking he might like a few minutes on his own, I returned to the vestry. I waited for a few minutes and, having heard no-one leave the Chapel, went to escort him out. He

CHAPEL OF REMEMBRANCE: The hands of Richard Geiger, Chapel engraver, are seen putting the finishing touches to a small alteration on the reredos in the St George's Chapel at Biggin Hill.
"The ghosts" he said "have helped to keep me busy".

was not there. He had just vanished.

"The same thing happened on at least two other occasions. After one of his visits I found a rather strange entry in the visitors' book written in German.

"Sometime after the third event I was in my usual work office when the telephone rang. A rather agitated WRAF girl from the guardroom was on the other end and asked me to go down to the guardroom straight away. There, the duty personnel told me that a few minutes earlier, a rather scruffy man with staring eyes, unshaven and wearing a dirty trenchcoat had come in and asked a question to which no-one present knew the answer off the top of their head. They had turned round to consult papers or books to find the answer but on turning round to speak to the visitor no-one was there. They all said that the guardroom had suddenly and quite inexplicably turned very cold. The man was nowhere to be seen, inside or outside the guardroom".

Soon after this incident one of the Chapel caretakers said he had found an error on the reredos. Wing Commander Slater's AFC (Air Force Cross) had been omitted. David Duval could not believe that such a major error had been missed by three people who had checked the board, particularly as the AFC was relatively uncommon for wartime pilots. "I had the error corrected at once by a local draughtsman", said David. "I never saw the man in the trenchcoat again".

Wing Commander James Hogarth-Slater of 611 (West Lancs) Squadron died on March 14, 1943 — a tragic date in the combative history of Biggin Hill. A newcomer to 611 Squadron, and to the station, this experienced pilot had borrowed a Spitfire and was "bounced" off Le Touquet together with Commandant Reilhac, the new CO of the first Free French unit, 330 Squadron, to be stationed there. In the same Rodeo — as these surprise attacks were known — Squadron Leader Dickie Milne developed engine trouble and was shot down by Focke Wulf 190s. He spent the next two years as a prisoner of war.

A few days earlier Squadron Leader Hugo Armstrong, CO of 611 had also lost his life. Setting off on a routine practice flight he was surprised by eight Huns off Boulogne. As he went down in flames he was heard to say: "This is it, chaps, I'm baling out". He was never seen again.

Two Squadron Leaders and two Wing Commanders killed or lost within a few days of each other, a costly toll for Biggin Hill and one in line with the blackest days of the Battle of Britain. The four "veterans" (average age 25) had been looking forward to their return to base and a show that evening by the Windmill Girls. It was called off. No-one wanted a party.

Is it possible that James Hogarth-Slater, Eugene Reilhac and Hugo Armstrong still visit their old station hoping perhaps that the girls of the Windmill Theatre troupe may be performing at Biggin Hill? And what is the significance of the German message in the Chapel visitors' book? Perhaps it refers to the original memorial chapel which was opened by 'Sailor' Malan in 1943 and was then destroyed by fire in 1946. From March 1943 'Sailor' was the station's Commanding Officer.

Chapel attendant Dave Adams of Orpington remembers a visit some years ago from three ladies, one of whom was related to a Free French pilot. She said he was a member of 340 (*le Groupe Ile-de-France)* Squadron and was delighted to have the honour of flying from Britain's premier fighter station in 1942. She pointed to the name of Squadron Leader Charles de Beaumont on the Reredos and said the proper family name, d'Autichamp, was missing. "That died", she said, "when we left the country in 1940. Could it it now be rectified?".

At that moment Dave noticed that a man had joined the little group. "Charles de Beaumont d'Autichamp is standing with us", he said, "and I should know. My name is Olly McPike and I am chairman of the Medium Society of New Zealand. I have the ability to speak on behalf of dead pilots. I would like you to know that our squadron is still flying — still flying the skies of Kent". Dave Adams remembered how the room suddenly became very cold and goose pimples appeared on his arm as the man carried on talking. Said Dave: "Before he left he asked me if I had recovered from my recent operation. He then signed the visitors book and I nipped home for a double Scotch!"

Within a few days the chapel engraver was busy again.

A one-time Biggin Hill security guard Les Dixon firmly believes that one airman has haunted the airfield since the war years. Mr Dixon, a former policeman, said the apparition was first seen by a friend's wife many years ago. "She worked up here and used to cycle

No. 340 (FRENCH) SQUADRON
P/O MARCEL RENAUD
F/LT EUGENE REILHAC
S/LT JACQUES MOREAC
F/SGT PAUL HUBIDOS
F/O EMILE CLAUDE HELIES
S/LT CHARLES DE BEAUMONT D'AUTICHAMP

No. 605 (COUNTY OF WARWICK) SQUADRON
F/LT ARNOLD JOHN CRAVEN D·F·C
F/LT RICHARD MAITLAND SINGER
F/SGT LEONARD WILLIAM WOODA...

No. 322 (DUTCH) S...
W/O JUSTIN ALBERT...
F/O BARON EG... NAGELL
F/SGT CORN...
F/O RUI... GWAL
F/LT ... ESMAN
CORNELIUS DE NEVE
... WES·WOLTERS

...F) SQUADRON
(BARNEY) WALLIS

229 SQUADRON
...LT PATRICK EDGAR SEMPHILL FAIRFAX MONTEAGLE BROWNE
P/O GEORGES LOUIS JOSEPH DOUTREPONT
F/O MALCOLM RAVENHILL
F/O GEOFFREY MERVYN SIMPSON
F/LT GEORGE MAINS
LT ROBERT ALEXANDER CUMMING
W/O HAROLD GORE HEAD
F/LT WALTER DOORNINK IDEMA

No. 56 (PUNJAB) SQUADRON
P/O ROSS·CARROCK RICHARD LEAN
F/O THOMAS GUY ATKINSON
F/SGT ANTHONY CLAYTON DREW

No. 79 (MADRAS PRESIDENCY) SQUADRON
P/O JAMES JOSEPH TARLINTON
P/O STANISLAW PIATKOWSKI
F/O GEORGE CHARLES BOYCE PETERS
F/O EDWARD WILLIAM MITCHELL
SGT RONALD REVAN McQUEEN
S/LDR JOHN DAVIES CLEMENT JOSLIN
F/LT RICHARD WILLOUGHBY REYNOLDS
P/O JOHN EDWARD RANDELL WOOD
P/O LIONEL ROGER DORRIEN-SMITH
F/LT JAMES WILLIAM ELIAS DAVIES D·F·C
SGT HENRY CARTWRIGHT D·F·M
SGT HENRY ALBERT BOLTON
P/O LLEWELLYN LISTER APPLETON

No. 410 (R·C·A·F) SQUADRON
...LT RALPH HENRY BURGESS JACKSON
...O MURDOCH CAMPBELL MURRAY

...DRON
...DWARD KOSH
W· DOMANSKI
...HN MACKERRAS
ALBERT WIGGLESWORTH D·F·C

...DRON
...WHITMORE
...ASER
...ER
...IRBAIRN
...NNINGH
...HALI...
...SON

...REL...
...WY...

...Y...
...ART...

...UN...
...SQ...
...CC...
...SDI...
...EN...

Chapel attendant, Dave Adams points to the name of Squadron Leader Charles de Beaumont d'Autichamp who flew with 340 (le Groupe Ile-de-France) Squadron at Biggin Hill from September 1942 to March 1943. He was one of six pilots from the Squadron to die while flying from the Biggin Wing.

from Shirley. One evening, when returning home, she saw this figure on Hayes Common in full RAF uniform. He just appeared out of the mist walking in such a way that his feet were off the ground. I think he wanted to chat but my friend hastily cycled away with the figure in pursuit. The same ghost", said Les, "has also been seen moving across the airfield. Several people have mentioned that to me".

Workmen, employed to help with repairs to the runway, have also experienced strange feelings. No actual sightings have been reported but many have sensed an extra presence and that tell-tale chill in the air.

One man who definitely believes that Biggin Hill is haunted is ex-soldier, John Levy who was delivering newspapers and magazines in the area at 3 am on a misty morning in 1963. When he got to the junction of the road leading to Tatsfield his van was flagged down by an airman in flying kit waving his leather flying helmet. John stopped the van and opened the door — but the airman had disappeared.

"At first", he told a reporter from the *Kentish Times*, "I thought the man had fallen under the front wheel but there was no-one there. I looked around. There was no sound, not even of a person walking away quietly. I was so badly shaken that I drove straight to the local police station and reported my strange experience".

John's story was not dismissed. The local bobby quietly told him that the figure who stopped his van was possibly that of a pilot, a Flight Lieutenant, who had been seen before in the vicinity. "During the Battle of Britain", he said "a fighter crashed into the hillside and the pilot died. His ghost has been seen on a number of occasions. He is quite friendly. We all know him".

The late Gilbert Wild, Tempest pilot in the later years of the war and a founder member of the Biggin Hill Aircrew Association, also met that particular ghost. During the 50th anniversary of the Battle of Britain in the summer of 1990 he mentioned it to the then Commanding Officer at Biggin Hill, Wing Commander Alan Jones and was told the ghost was still around. "About two years ago in the early morning", said Alan, "a Sergeant in the officers' mess checked one of the empty bedrooms and saw our ghost, in flying kit, sitting in a chair. He disappeared almost immediately!"

In his book *Ghosts of Kent* Peter Underwood tells how a couple of RAF officers became so interested in the many stories of apparent paranormal activities in the area that they decided to investigate further. "They found a surprising amount of good evidence", he writes, "and even succeeded in recording sounds of aircraft and of people that they were satisfied had no rational explanation.

"If such things are possible then surely Biggin Hill, in the very front line during the Battle of Britain and arguably the most famous fighter station in the world, is likely to be among the haunted airfields. Indeed it does seem that the ghostly sound of a Spitfire has been heard again at this place".

Many residents living round the airfield say there is no mistaking the sound of a Merlin engine as it changes pitch in preparation to land. And January 19th each year is the date when the sounds are most often heard. Peter Underwood takes up the story again. "Some say", he writes, "that the long-dead pilot signals his return with a low victory roll before coming in to land; others say that men's voices are heard, glasses clink together and sounds are heard that would have followed the return of a victorious RAF pilot during the war. But then, as suddenly and as inexplicably as it began, the sound fades and Biggin Hill resumes its peaceful atmosphere".

So what is special about January 19 and what year does it commemorate? Certainly not 1940 because Biggin Hill was then more like a building site than a fighter station. All three resident squadrons were on deployment elsewhere while workmen laid a short but substantial runway and excavated deep air-raid shelters.

It was more likely to be January 1941 when the the two squadrons billeted at 'The Bump' were No 74 and No 66 with Spitfires, while the formidable 92 Squadron were briefly based at Manston. They all had reason to celebrate.

First, Biggin Hill had just become the first station in Fighter Command to shoot down 600 enemy aircraft. Secondly, and of far greater significance, was the fact that one pilot, Flight Lieutenant "Pancho" Villa had shot down an enemy aircraft by cannon fire. The new 20 mm cannon had replaced the .303 Browning machine guns which had served so well during the Battle of Britain.

Thirdly, 'Sailor' Malan, the charismatic Commanding Officer of 74 Squadron and Flight Lieutenant H.M.Stephen had just been awarded the DSO for "outstanding success over an

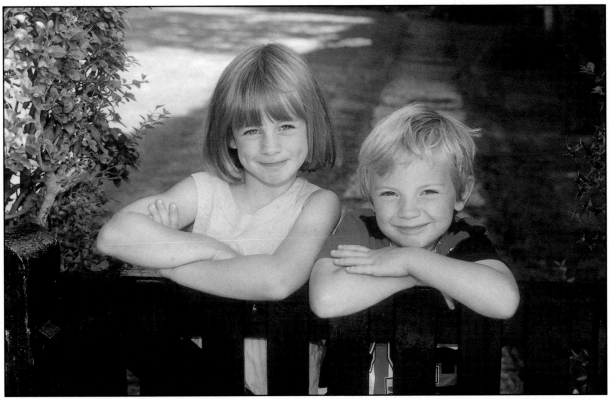

"Dear America", wrote Sophie Williams, aged six, "here is a picture of a necklace we found in our garden at Biggin Hill. Please can you help us find the owner". "Dear Sophie and Thomas", replied the Natchez Town Clerk after a little research, "we are awarding you honorary citizenship of our town".

extended period of air operations".

In addition to all this the station had only recently said goodbye to its Commanding Officer for more than a year, Group Captain Dick Grice. By January 1941 the pilots would have perfected "victory rolls" on their return to base and the "clinking of glasses" was not an unfamiliar sound during that second phase of the war in the air.

It is said that the ghosts of Biggin Hill represent all nationalities and men from every corner of Britain. Who are the tall upright figures whose ghostly silhouettes have been spotted on a few occasions on misty evenings standing motionless on the old parade ground? Is it possible that one of them could be Jimmy Davies, the young American who was the first Biggin Hill pilot to shoot down an enemy aircraft during the second world war? He died on the day King George VI came to Biggin to present him and others with the Distinguished Flying Cross. Could another be that of Flying Officer and Winter Olympic hero, Billy Fiske who flew from The Bump with 601 Squadron during the first few months of the war and died during the Battle of Britain? And could a third be Lieutenant Sam Junkin who flew with the 31st Group USAAF and was assigned to No 401

Canadian Squadron in1942?

Sam, who was 23 at the time, had made history by becoming the first member of the 31st group to shoot down an enemy aircraft — an act which won him a DFC and a Purple Heart for gallantry. He was wounded during the disastrous raid over Dieppe in August 1942, baled out over the English Channel and recovered in hospital where he met a Canadian nurse, Evelyn.

Sam married his nurse and survived the war but died of a heart attack in Natchez, Mississippi in 1966 aged 47. He never forgot his brief tour of duty at Britain's premier fighter station and often told his American friends of the occasion his Squadron flew from Biggin Hill to give cover during the Dieppe raid when 106 aircraft were lost, including many from the Biggin Wing.

Perhaps it is a little far fetched to speculate that Sam's ghost is one of the shadowy figures at Biggin Hill but he did leave behind something a little more tangible. In August 1997 seven year old Sophie Williams and her brother Thomas, four, unearthed in their garden in Hanbury Drive a pair of rusty identification tags on a chain. On them was a military service number, an address in Mississippi and the name Lieutenant Samuel F. Junkin.

Sophie's mother, Tracey wrote to the local newspaper in Natchez appealing for help in tracing the owner of the tags and soon discovered they belonged to the American hero. Sam's wife Evelyn wrote to Sophie and Thomas thanking them for finding the tags and letters followed from an old school friend of Sam and from the Mississippi chapter of the Eighth Air Force Historical Society.

But why were Sam Junkin's identity tags buried in the garden of the house at Hanbury Drive which had been built for RAF personnel? "Perhaps he buried it there himself", said Mrs Williams, "hoping one day to retrieve it. Perhaps it fell onto the ground during a party and stayed there for half a century. It's a real mystery. A puzzle unsolved".

Ian Cross also has a puzzling moment which occurred in 1981. Why was his wife of just a few months standing motionless with her face against the drawn curtains of the bedroom window in the dead of night? Was she still asleep or had she spotted a flaw in the curtain material that needed immediate attention?

Kim Cross remained in that position for about five minutes and then returned to the bed. The next morning she told Ian that she had woken up in the night and couldn't remember who, or where she was. There was no carpet in the floor, no curtains hanging at the window, no street lights outside, no parked cars and no houses. Looking out of the window she saw bright moonlight, a large field and some big army huts. There were no figures lurking in the shadows and no voices to alarm her. "In fact", said Kim, there was no special aura or atmosphere. It just happened and it was very real".

Kim and Ian were living in Crossley Close, a road of houses built between the wars off Jail Lane and later re-named after the charismatic Commanding Officer of 32 Squadron. For some unexplained reason she had been transported back to the period at the end of the Great War and was seeing the South Camp, Biggin Hill exactly as it had looked then.

Kim Cross, 42, described her strange experience in the lounge bar of the Biggin Hill

This photograph of Sam Junkin receiving the Purple Heart appeared in the: Natchez Democrat, Mississippi during the war. Sam died in 1966. When his tags were found in the garden at Biggin Hill his widow, Evelyn wrote to Thomas and Sophie Williams: "It is hard that all this has happened to me because of you both and I am very proud of you. One day I hope I can thank you personally. Sadly, Evelyn Junkin died later in 1997, shortly after her own picture had appeared in the Natchez Democrat with the dog tags. The Williams family then received another letter from Sam Junkin's childhood friend, Henry Charles Doherty. He wrote: "You should rejoice that your darling children brought so much pleasure and brightness into Evelyn's life in her last weeks on earth".

Squash Club during a special "tell your ghost story" evening organised by her parents, Mike and Sheila Blundell. With the reminder that ghosts leave no documentary evidence of their activities and are recorded only in the narratives of those who claim to see them, Sheila had arranged for a succession of Old Biggonians to reveal what can only be described as an infinite treasure of ghost lore — mostly with strong connections to the RAF station.

Barbara Robbins told a grim story about the day she took her two Collie dogs for their usual walk down Polesteeple Hill and into The Grove, a road almost at the foot of the valley. "Here", she said, "I sensed a strange feeling, a coldness and then a presence. The dogs stiffened and their hackles rose but they didn't bark or growl or run away. They went down on their bellies and just whimpered quietly. I realised they were literally scared stiff".

For several days thereafter Barbara took a different route but when she returned to The Grove it happened again and this time the dogs disappeared. "I had this feeling I was being enclosed by arms. Someone was drawing me close and I actually saw a cloak being placed around me. Then a voice said quietly: 'Don't be afraid'. And the cloak opened revealing the dogs".

Barbara is convinced the area is haunted but she is uncertain why. She has heard of a murder at Hermitage House nearby and she knows that scores of pilots have crashed and died in the valley below the airfield but why should they want to have fun at her expense?

Peter Richardson also knows The Grove well. "A Messerschmitt 109 crashed in the woods nearby in 1940", he said, "and us kids went to look for souvenirs. I got the rudder with the swastika on it but eventually had to surrender it to the British pilot who had shot it down". Could the pilot of the 109 possibly be Barbara's ghost?

Just as strange was the personal experience of Suzanne Harrison, 47, another lady born and bred in Biggin Hill and now living at Ricketts Hill Road, Tatsfield. In 1972 she and her husband Gerald were married and bought a bungalow in Hawthorn Avenue that backed onto the airfield. It was in a poor state and needed urgent attention so Gerald started pulling floorboards out in preparation for the restoration work.

Suzanne remembers clearly seeing through a partly-opened doorway the figure of an airman standing in one of the rooms. He was talking amiably, although the words were indistinguishable and there were lots of other voices followed by a succession of thuds. Plop, plop, plop. "I was curious rather than frightened", she said and I stood there watching and listening for about five minutes. Then the airman disappeared and the noises stopped".

Some time later Suzanne and Gerald were taking a door off its hinges and they discovered lots of small holes in the woodwork. A neighbour solved the mystery. Airmen had been billeted in that house during the war and the dartboard had hung on that door. Suzanne had somehow been an unsuspecting spectator of a darts game (circa 1940) and that was the reason for the thuds.

Roberta Single, 69, also knows about the RAF occupation of Hawthorn Avenue. She lives at *Pasadena*, her bungalow home, in fact, for more than 40 years. "When I first moved in with my husband, Frank, the hatch had been left off the area which led into the roof space and I saw a woman in white standing there above me. In the house I smelt tobacco, a rich, beautiful smell wafting from one of the rooms. I did wonder who lived there and who was the woman?"

Homes for bombed-out airmen and WAAFs were found all over Biggin Hill and district after the bombing in 1940 and some of the squadrons were housed in large houses which were infinitely more comfortable than the vulnerable billets on the airfield. One such mansion was *Southwood* in Buckhurst Road whose occupants for several months were the silk-shirted playboys of 92 Squadron — famous for their high party spirit, infamous for the number of casualties they suffered.

Les Lyne of Main Road, Biggin Hill remembers a day in 1958 when he attended the Farnborough Air Show with a friend, Pete Emmerson. They borrowed a Mini Minor from Les' grandfather for the trip leaving their old van at his home in Gray's Lane. "When we returned to exchange vehicles", said Les, "it was getting dark and very misty but I could see clearly about 20 yards in front a ghostly figure of a man all in white but perfect in shape. He came out of a hedge and walked across the road. It was eerie and quite scary. Pete said 'let's get out of here". *Southwood*, the former home of 92 Squadron, was just down the road.

Between August 18 and August 31 1940, Biggin Hill was systematically attacked on eight occasions. While the Spitfires were scrapping many miles from home every available man and woman was filling in the craters knowing that the Luftwaffe's work was not yet over. And the WAAFs, who had remained defiantly at the switchboard when the Ops Room was bombed, had moved into an emergency set-up in the village. The story appears in full in a later chapter.

The courageous action of those 1940 WAAFs, who defied death and injury in order to maintain the vital telephone connection with Fighter Command and give information to the defence posts, was a talking point at Biggin Hill long after the war ended.

Eric Weeks, who now lives in Bourne End, Buckinghamshire, remembers his pride in being an ordinary National Service aircraftsman stationed at Biggin Hill and trained to be one of the station's telephonists. But he is haunted still by the memory of an unexplained

FRIENDLY: A fighter crashed into the hillside near the airfield. The pilot died but his ghost has been seen on many occasions. "We know him well", said the local policeman. "He is quite friendly".

incident which took place in the winter of 1948.

"I was on night duty during the Christmas period with my colleague, Geoff Syrett", he said. "The switchboard was then in a building across the road from the airfield to the right of the Officers' Mess. The main building was surrounded by a perimeter wall and in the centre of that wall was a big iron sliding door which we closed always for security purposes.

"Geoff and I were not alone; keeping us company in the hallway was an Alsatian dog and her puppies, belonging to another airman".

Although the fury of war had long abated, Biggin Hill was not yet back in the hands of Fighter Command. It was then controlled by Reserve Command and two squadrons of the Royal Auxiliary Air Force, Nos 600 and 615 remained the sole flying units equipped with the new Spitfires. Many hundreds of personnel worked at the famous old station and because of the shift system the nights were far from sleepy affairs. As individual lights began to light up on their PBX board Aircraftsmen Weeks and Syrett knew they were in for a fairly busy night.

"Towards midnight on this particular evening", said Eric, "and totally without warning the PBX board began to assume a mind of its own and go berserk. Lights flashed and high-pitched blips drowned the urgency of our voices. As the dog in the hallway became agitated we noticed the firmly-locked metal door on the perimeter wall was sliding open and the shadow of a figure was clearly visible. We sat almost rooted to the spot. Then just as quickly as it started the switchboard stopped flashing and we gingerly went outside the room. The door was jammed open and the dog was still cowering".

The same procedure continued on the two following nights while Eric and Geoff were on duty. On the fourth night nothing happened — normality had returned.

Eric has no explanation for the experience but it dominated his mind until his National Service days were over. As we enter the early years of a new millennium the memory of that incident remains crystal clear.

Is there some eerie connection with that terrible day in August 1940 when Sergeant Helen Turner, a WRAF veteran of 1918, remained at her telephone switchboard alone in a little cubicle room outside the Operations Room when a bomb fell directly on the box of cables and lines outside severing everything but the direct line to Group headquarters? Helen ignored the bomb preferring to try and establish contact with the rest of Biggin Hill. It was an act that was to earn her the Military Medal.

Helen Turner, like the other heroic WAAFs at Biggin Hill, had a road renamed after her. On the 30th anniversary of the Battle of Britain, brass hats from the Ministry of Defence, along with a smattering of former pilots and senior WRAF officers, officiated at the re-naming ceremony and spoke of Miss Turner's incredible bravery, her resourcefulness and devotion to duty. Sadly, she wasn't present having died a few years after the war.

Another National Servicemen who has never forgotten his posting at Biggin Hill is Ken Stanley whose family lived at nearby Eltham. Like Eric Weeks, Ken served at the old station during the time when the Auxiliary Squadrons, 600 and 615 were flying alone with a mix of FR14s, F14s and F21s.

Ken was a military policeman with the RAF, charged with maintaining security and discipline at this front-line fighter station and used to patrolling the base alone with his Alsatian dog. He was billeted with other MPs in a large house near the South Camp not far from the main road to Bromley.

One evening during the summer of 1948 Ken was alone in his billet and noticed his dog was becoming rather restless and agitated. His ears were fully pricked as if anticipating the arrival of unexpected company. No-one knocked at the door but the dog suddenly jumped up, ran into the kitchen and began to bark furiously at a blank wall.

Ken made enquiries and discovered that noises had been heard before beyond this blanked up kitchen wall and decided that perhaps it was time to solve the mystery. The RAF invited two para-psychologists to talk to the "veteran airmen" at Biggin Hill. They quickly discovered that an old meat store was once attached to the kitchen of this large house and that, during the war, a Polish airman was found hanging there. As that store was then in disuse the Squadron Commanding Officer ordered it be bricked off.

Ken Stanley, now 71, has never forgotten that incident. Today he lives in Port Dover, Toronto, Canada but makes an annual pilgrimage to Biggin Hill to visit the Chapel and then regale his nephew, Roger Watts, at Brasted with stories of his days at the most famous fighter station in the world. His tale of the ghost, trapped in the bricked-up meat store, is always on the agenda.

Who was this Polish airman who took his own life and what Squadron did he belong to? Sadly, it remains a mystery because hundreds of Poles made their way to England from 1939 and by the following summer there were a few thousand dispersed among the fighter stations and active in every sphere of RAF life.

VINCENT SQUARE, Biggin Hill was built between 1929 and 1932 during the major reconstruction of the station. The house, demolished after the bombing of 1940, is marked with an 'X'. Below: Vincent Square today and the area which the bombed house once occupied. One couple, at least, believe the house next door is haunted.

32 Squadron   *79 Squadron*   *72 Squadron*

Stained glass windows show the winged spirit...

INSPIRED by Padre Cecil King, the St George's Chapel of Remembrance was built in memory of the pilots who died on the site of an old hangar near the main Westerham to Bromley Road. It replaced a little memorial chapel nearby which burnt down in a mystery fire in 1946.

The chapel contains 12 stained glass windows each telling a story about Biggin Hill. These contain badges

of the seven Squadrons who served there during the Battle of Britain. The theme is a cloud of witnesses — and each depicts the winged spirit of a young pilot embracing a badge in his arms.

The designer was Hugh Easton, best known for his Battle of Britain Memorial Window in Westminster Abbey. The Chapel itself remains as a permanent memorial to the 453 aircrew who were killed while

141 Squadron

92 Squadron

74 Squadron

..of a young pilot embracing his squadron crest

flying from the Biggin Hill Sector between 1939 and 1945 and they came from 45 Squadrons.

Their names are inscribed on the reredos. Flags of the Commonwealth and Allied countries, whose pilots served in the Biggin Hill Sector, are each side of the altar. The altar frontal is embroidered with emblems of the British Isles and Allied countries and bears the quotation from Psalm 63 — *In the Shadow of Thy Wings*

Will I Rejoice.

The foundation stone was laid by the Air Chief Marshal The Lord Dowding on July 25, 1951 and the service of Dedication conducted by the Bishop of Rochester on November 10, 1951. For many years this unique chapel was a regular place of worship for the airmen and their families who lived and worked at RAF Biggin Hill. *See pages 186 and 187.*

Polish Squadrons — most notably No 315 — fought with the Biggin Wing but none were billeted on the Bump. However, there were Polish pilots and Polish ground crew and technicians with almost every other Biggin Hill squadron. More than 7,000 of them arrived in Britain after the capitulation of France and more than 50 fought with British units during the Battle of Britain.

The homes in Turner Road provided married quarters for senior RAF personnel. They were built between 1927 and 1932 during the reconstruction of Biggin Hill. All the original huts and hangars had been situated on the strip of land between the Bromley to Westerham Road and the grass runways but in 1927 Air Defence Staff insisted that all new non-operational buildings, such as married quarters and barracks, be built on the other side of the main road. By doing this, they pointed out, the southern flying approaches to the runways would not be endangered.

The RAF building committee opposed this idea at the time. They wanted the new living quarters to be erected some two miles north of the working area but, with pressure from the ADS, reluctantly agreed to compulsory purchase land on the western side and suffer the inconvenience of having a highway through the station.

So 29 acres of land were purchased with difficulty and the first roads laid out. One of them was Vincent Square, named after Squadron Leader F.J.Vincent DFC, commanding officer of the incomparable 56 Squadron who memorably fought on the Western Front in 1916. The terraced homes were built in blocks of four round a grassy square and were considered to be among the most attractive of all the new houses

By the time the Battle of Britain began in1940 the homes in Vincent Square were showing signs of wear and tear. All except one block of four were occupied by married couples but numbers 25 to 28 had been converted into a Waafery. Three of these four homes were destroyed during the two attacks made on the station on August 30, 1940. On that day 16 1,000 pounders fell. It was to be the most tragic day in the history of Biggin Hill *(see page 115)*.

Peter Stillman, a mechanical engineer employed by RAF Biggin Hill and his wife Jackie, lived at No 28 Vincent Square between 1982 and 1984. By then the house stood on its own as a single unit with an area of open land where the neighbouring homes had once stood. There had been no time to rebuild after the devastating raid of 1940.

Jackie Stillman remembers the house well. "In one upstairs room", she said, "there was a bricked-up door which once gave the WAAFs access to the accommodation in the next house but we rarely went in; it was a spare bedroom.

"In 1983 my husband was posted to the Falklands and my sister Gina came to live with me to keep me company. I told her she would be very comfortable in the spare bedroom. Unfortunately, she wasn't. After a few terrifying minutes on the first night she came into my bedroom and said someone had been knocking on the wall where the door used to be.

"We returned quietly to the room and the knocking continued — not in any frantic way — just a gentle but continuous knocking. After a while it stopped but then began again. There was no pattern, entirely inconsistent."

SMILING: A photograph found in the Biggin Hill archives of a group of WAAFs who served at the station during the war. Sadly, no names are given but if readers can identify anyone in this picture — or any of the other pictures in this book — please write to the publishers, whose address is on page two.

Jackie said that her sister never returned to that room. She noticed later that her Labrador dog also refused to go in.

"Some time later", said Jackie, "after Peter had returned there was another strange incident when a clock on the mantlepiece at No 28 Vincent Square started to chime. The trouble was I didn't have a clock and I didn't have a mantlepiece!"

The non-existent chiming clock on the non-existent mantlepiece continued to strike the hours on many more occasions. It was heard by visitors to the house; in fact Peter and Jackie used to set their watches in time with the chimes but neither them ever found an explanation.

Is the home haunted by the WAAFs of Vincent Road? Jackie is convinced that is the case. "When I lived there", she said, "RAF wives used to exchange stories about the things that went bump in the night. Some of them were so incredible that they could not possibly have been invented.

"On one occasion late at night", she said, "a number of girls came out of the Naafi and stood talking near the car park which stands opposite the main guard room. In the mist they saw some WAAFs, visible only from the waist up, apparently hovering over the grassy area nearby. After a while they disappeared."

That was in the early 1980s when the RAF were in residence. Today the homes in Vincent Square are privately owned having been sensitively refurbished by a development company. Mike Beale, who lives in No 28, has not yet heard the knocking noise or the chimes of a non-existent chiming clock. He is not frightened of ghosts but says he is prepared to be calm and friendly when they next call.

Are the ghosts calm and friendly? Nicole Whittle thinks not. In 1995 she was living in a caravan with her husband Keith who worked for Artesians — the company redeveloping the houses on the old North Camp. "Keith was — and still is — the caretaker", she said, "and one of his duties was to make sure that no trespassers wandered onto the site.

"Towards dusk on one evening my dog started barking and I saw in the gloom a tall figure dressed in RAF uniform. When I asked him what he was doing on the building site he wanted to know who I was. He was extremely well-spoken but had an abrupt manner. In fact he was rude.

"I asked him to leave and saw him walk towards the back of the houses. He then just disappeared."

Some weeks later Nicole put her clothes into the washing machine, turned it on and went shopping. When she returned the machine was empty. Everything had been taken out, folded up neatly and placed into the washing basket ready to iron.

Today the couple live in a small home by the entrance to Vincent Square. Keith is still the caretaker and cares deeply about the memory of those who lost their lives when the station was so badly mauled by the Luftwaffe.

It was to the Officers' Mess at Biggin Hill that pilots sought salvation from the tedium of flying, the daily strain of trying to stay alive and the short, cryptic sentence that always made the goose pimples stand higher than before — 'have you heard the news, Bill's bought it!' To those who stood at the bar or were slumped in the easy chair with glass in hand this was a world under constant assault by the legions of the dead. It required a great deal of faith to live with it. Little wonder then that the old place, with its memories, its superstitions and its demons should be haunted.

Peter Halliday, whose Battle of Britain story is told later, remembers how his dad came out of the air force in 1946 and found a civilian job with the Works and Bricks department of the civil organisation still repairing the aerodrome. "Dad was a chippy", said Peter, "and as a 14-year-old I often helped him. We were working on the second floor of the Officers' Mess on one occasion when dad suddenly said: 'Who's upstairs? Someone is moving around. I bet it's the governor, the cunning little sod, checking my work. He's always snooping around. Go and have a look'.

Peter went up to the top floor. It was empty and forlorn. The Mess was then occupied by the Auxiliary pilots and although they drank and ate there the rooms once occupied by the pilots were vacant and bare. Peter looked into the bedrooms one by one and then moved through the tank room onto the balcony where a machine gun post had once been established. There was no-one to be seen.

He went back downstairs and immediately heard footsteps once more going across the floor above. It was later confirmed that others had heard the same thing. There was, it seems, a regular visitor.

Helen Edmunds, who worked in the Officers' Mess as a stewardess from 1984 to 1989, always wondered why the television room next to an ante room at the far end of the lounge

FIVE ACES: Wing Commander Ian Cosby (second left) is pictured here with Battle of Britain colleagues at a dinner near Sevenoaks in 1990. 'Cos' served with 610 and 72 Squadrons in 1940 and enjoyed a distinguished career in the RAF before retiring in 1974 and returning to live at Biggin Hill. With him from the left are 'Beacon' Rose (32 Squadron in 1940), Col James Goodson, (American Eagle pilot, 133 Squadron), Dennis Thomas, president of the Sevenoaks Rotary Club, Squadron Leader Henryk Szczesny (74 Squadron) and Wing Commander Donald Stones (79 Squadron). The stories of all these pilots are featured in this book.

was so cold and rarely used. Assuming that RAF officers and their guests preferred to chat in the bar she gave it not another thought until Jack Archer, a former pilot, told her that it had been used as a temporary morgue in August 1940. "I saw no ghosts" she said, "but the atmosphere was decidedly inhospitable".

One former Battle of Britain pilot who regularly enjoyed a drink in the Officers' Mess until its closure in 1992 was the late Wing Commander Ian Cosby. Describing it as his "intensive care unit" he always looked forward to those reunions with old pilots who so frequently returned to their former station. It took very little time to evoke the memories. The breakfasts of lukewarm baked beans and tepid tea, the dawn scramble, the lunches at noon, the second scramble and then the desserts at 3pm, the evenings off at a night club, returning in the early hours for two or three hours sleep. "A crazy life", said Ian, "and an exhausting one".

"The waiting 'at readiness' felt like ten years" said Brian Kingcome once. "And then came the inevitable stomach-turning telephone ring and the voice from Ops: '92 Squadron scramble'. I've never believed in the theory that some people don't know fear. You felt quite sick and some chaps used to be sick, physically sick".

Kingcome's description of the wave of blind panic that washed all over him as death became a terrifying reality in the cockpit of his Spitfire is contained later in this book. In his case he miraculously escaped but hundreds of airmen, flying from the Biggin Wing, didn't. The old station may be renowned for its heroic status and for the part it played in winning the war but it is also known as a charnel-house of pilots burned, maimed, wounded, torn limb from limb — and of many who died.

We know who they are. We know they were young, eager and bright and represented many nationalities and religions and backgrounds. We know their souls were laid to rest but we don't know the names of those restless few whose spirits still hang around.

Take, for example, the traumatic events facing the Reverend Alan Morris, vicar of St Marks, Biggin Hill from 1974 to 1982. St Marks is the parish church, known locally as "the moving church". It was built brick-by-brick, timber-by-timber from materials salvaged from the ruins of All Saints in North-East Peckham. The inspiration behind the remarkable feat was the Reverend Vivian Symons who organised the lorries and spent many months instructing volunteers on what to take from the derelict site. Not long after the new building was dedicated Symons became emotionally involved with a young girl and had to leave the parish and the church that he built.

By 1974 Alan Morris was the man in charge and, as with all incumbents of the Biggin Hill parish, he was closely linked with the airfield and the personnel who lived and worked there.

Two of his parishioners were Colin and Joan Ryan who lived in number 14 Main Road, a bungalow close to the married quarters, opposite the main entrance to the airfield and next door but one to Robinsons, the dry cleaners, which have occupied the site for many years.

In 1981 Joan was admitted to Bromley Hospital for a major hip operation, followed by a long period of recuperation. As the parish priest, Alan visited her regularly and forged a good relationship. "She was an easy-going, brave and likeable young woman", he said, "but she had a problem that she thought I might be able to sort out and said she would be grateful if I visited her husband Colin who would give me the details."

Colin explained that for several months peculiar things had been happening in the bungalow but there had always been a rational explanation. On one occasion, however, soon after Joan had gone into hospital and her sister had come to stay to look after their daughter Claire, he came home from work and found the house icy cold. He turned up the central heating but the cold persisted. Colin, concerned about his daughter, put Claire to bed and left a light shining in the passage as he always did.

In the early hours Claire woke up coughing so Colin comforted her with a warm drink and she eventually went to sleep. Aunty in the next bedroom never woke up. Colin went back to bed and was now aware that his room was even colder. He then saw the figure of a woman in the doorway silhouetted by the light behind. "Go back to bed, Aunty", he said. "I've settled Claire. She's asleep".

Aunty didn't move so Colin again said: "Go back to bed". She still didn't move so Colin got up to talk to her and to his astonishment the figure just faded into the distance and disappeared. Colin, quite frightened by the experience, looked into Aunty's bedroom and there she was — fast asleep!

Had he seen a female burglar? Colin searched the house but there was no sign of anyone

EXPELLED: The bungalow at No 14 Main Road, Biggin Hill where the local vicar held a communion service in order to evict a worrying spirit.

breaking and entering.

This incident, coupled with earlier phantasmal experiences, prompted Joan Ryan to ask the Rev Alan Morris for help. By now she realised the bungalow was haunted. The apparition her husband had seen was visible, obvious and certainly not in the category of hallucination. Colin said he could not live in the house with a wife and child and a ghost. Perhaps the vicar would know what to do.

Alan Morris certainly believed the story but explained to Joan and Colin that his experience in dealing with the paranormal was non-existent so he would need guidance. He contacted Canon Pearce-Higgins, vice-provost of Southwark Cathedral who was then making plans to set up a Diocesan Advice Centre on paranormal activities. Known by readers of tabloid newspapers as the Church of England's 'chief ghost buster' he was keen to help.

The Canon said the church was rather ill-informed on spiritual matters concerning phantoms or apparitions but suggested the best method was for Alan to hold a church service in the bungalow. "I'll send over a copy of an appropriate communion service", he said. "It will not be necessary to carry out an exorcism. This is not an evil spirit that needs expelling but a departed one who, for reasons we do not know, is unable to move away entirely from her earthly existence. She may be over-related to someone or something in Biggin Hill".

Explaining that Alan must claim the power of Christ's resurrection, turn the spirit round and send her back, the Canon suggested that he be accompanied by some of the congregation of St Marks. "Don't worry about upsetting the spirit. People on the other side will help to settle her down".

Alan took the advice of his superior on all aspects of the matter except the presence of a large congregation as he was worried by the reaction and the rumours that would inevitably sweep through the village. He took with him Valerie Herd, parish office secretary at St Marks and Paul Francis who was training for the ministry. He chose a time when Claire was at school and Joan had been discharged from hospital.

"I felt rather silly" he said. "I wondered if this lady spirit would misbehave and throw things around the house but I addressed her in the language of King James from the copy of the service I had been sent. I told her to be off, that she had no right worrying this family. I did the Eucharist and added a few more appropriate words. It was a little bit like a scene from a Dennis Wheatley novel. Keeping my cassock on, I then toured the house making the sign of the Celtic Cross over every doorway and keyhole."

It did the trick. Neither Colin nor Joan saw their ghost again. Encouraged by the vicar's demands she had obediently slipped back to her spiritual world leaving two very relieved human beings reflecting on the purpose of her frequent visits to their home. Was she a WAAF who died in the summer of 1940? Was that particular bungalow among the buildings hit by the Luftwaffe bombs?

We know that most of the bombs in August and September 1940 fell on the North Camp and caused damage to the runway and most of the buildings. A few, however, fell on the South Camp where the Army personnel were billeted. Before the war a few flying clubs operated from this area and it was here that famous aviation pioneers such as Alan Cobham took local people on joy rides in the skies above the Downs. It cost 'a mere five shillings a go'.

There were no flying clubs at Biggin Hill during the war and the buildings they left behind were requisitioned and strengthened — but not sufficiently to withstand the 1,000 pounders which fell among them in the summer of 1940.

Roy Savage, now 81, of Slades Drive, Chislehurst knows the area well. In 1980, having retired from his job as production controller with a large company, he answered an advertisement for someone familiar with aircraft parts to work in a large hangar belonging to Artecs. Apparently the Civil Aviation Authority had advised the company to tidy up the huge pile of spares in the middle of the hangar and Roy was well qualified for the job.

"It was a full-time task" said Roy, "and it took me a year. I used to go there in the evenings and work all night but I hated every moment. Doors constantly opened and shut but there was never anyone around. As soon as I walked in one door I heard the sound of another closing. The only heat came from a small paraffin stove and I remember going outside whenever it needed refilling. The icy cold wind would hit me broadside as it whistled across the airfield, sending even more shivers up my spine. It was eerie and spooky. I knew that building had received a direct hit during the war and I was convinced it was haunted and whoever was in there didn't like me being around."

That feeling was confirmed in the most painful way. One night late in 1980 Roy placed an aluminium ladder against the wall in order to reach some shelves above. As always he ensured it was steady and climbed towards the upper rungs. There was no-one else around.

FROM THE AIR — ***The South Camp ghost is still around*** — ***alarming those who work in this area.***

"Suddenly", said Roy, "the ladder was pulled away and I fell heavily to the ground and was quite badly hurt. I managed to ring for an ambulance and I was taken to Farnborough Hospital. I never went into that hangar again".

More than 20 years later the South Camp ghost is still in residence and is well known to scores of people who work there. "We see him often" said Joe Merchant of Pilots' Pals. "He hangs around usually at night, threatens no-one but occasionally scares the living daylights out of those who do not know him". One of his latest 'victims' was Debbie, daughter of Jill Minter, who runs the bar of Pilots' Pals. Debbie left the club at 11.10pm and saw him just standing in the car park wearing a long trenchcoat. He "swam" in the vicinity for several minutes while Debbie, frozen with terror, fumbled for her car keys and drove off. The popular theory is that he is the spirit of a person deceased who is either under commission to return for some special errand or is someone who committed an injustice while living and cannot rest until that is redressed.

Joe Merchant probably knows Biggin Hill airfield better than anyone else alive. Back in 1954 he was attached to 615 Squadron as an apprentice fitter. "It was a schoolboy's dream job", he said, "but it turned into a nightmare when the Auxiliaries were disbanded in 1957 and a year later operational flying at Biggin came to an end". Four years later he obtained his flying licence and enjoyed a new view of the airfield — birds' eye from his Chipmunk.

In 1979 Joe and his family came to live at Koonowla Close and from there he formed his company Pilots' Pals. His aviation calendars, enhanced by femine charm and glamour, achieved world-wide fame but were overtaken in time by what he calls the demands of 'political correctness'.

Two years after moving in Joe and his wife Valerie heard what sounded like the cracking of a whip. The noise, right outside the house, was extraordinary for its volume. Three times it sounded and then stopped. Next night it happened again — then again and again — but as time went on the goose pimples, which had once crawled over their bodies, slowly disappeared. "One night", said Joe, "we were sitting up late and the whipping noises started again. This time I counted 15 cracks, more violent than ever, followed by the sight of smoke drifting past the kitchen window. Fearing an explosion I 'phoned the police. They found nothing. No fire, no smoke, no whips, no guns, no footprints, no body and no explanation. Nothing".

The tragic events that occurred at Biggin Hill before, during and after the war have come in many forms. In 1918, when a Royal Flying Corps pilot crashed and died in the valley below the aerodrome it was discovered that a pigeon had caused the accident. In 1927, a parachute instructor attempted to beat the world record for a delayed drop. His parachute never opened. In 1939, in the last month before the outbreak of war, a Hurricane pilot, on blackout patrol, flew into the side of Tatsfield Hill. A colleague, who flew out with a marker flare, did the same thing. They both perished. Between May 1940 and June 1945 tragedies at Biggin Hill were almost daily occurrences. And since the war ended there have been scores of unexplained crashes at Biggin Hill involving loss of life. Why, for example, did two highly experienced pilots die during the annual Air Fair of 2001?

WHITE HART INN: This is the original bar of the pilots' favourite pub in Brasted a few miles south of Biggin Hill. Landlady Kath Preston said that as the war progressed she began to notice the missing faces. "If one of the blue uniforms was sitting by himself we would join him, talk about films and shows and try to take his mind off his pal who had 'bought' it that day.

The RAF may have left Biggin Hill but unlike other airfields in its sector it has never been allowed to become an empty graveyard or unwanted eyesore with buildings condemned to be demolished. That fate, however, has befallen Hawkinge, Detling and West Malling — and, of course, all of them have ghosts.

In the summer of 1954 three resident squadrons were based at RAF West Malling, flying first Mosquitos and then Meteors and the Commanding Officer was Group Captain Hamley. LAC Norman Skinner remembers how the Officers' Mess ante-room had a pair of glazed 'french window' type doors leading to the outside. "One particular evening", he said, "a group of officers were sitting in the ante-room talking when suddenly one of them noticed a figure, clad in 1940s-type flying gear, peering through the glass. The figure was sighted many times and each time people rushed to investigate but no-one could be found. The phantom airman was the subject of considerable barrack room conversation".

In his book *Ghost Stations* air historian, Bruce Barrymore Halpenny, mentions this West Malling ghost. He also tells of another who liked to activate intruder alarms in the early hours of the morning and then hurl house bricks at security patrol vans. Twice this occurred in situations that human hands would have found impossible. Those investigating the incident later learned that a Spitfire pilot had once force-landed on the airfield, hit a low brick wall

MARCH PAST: RAF Biggin Hill said goodbye to the Borough of Bromley with a march past through the town centre in October 1992. Thousands of residents lined the streets in honour of an association which had existed since the men of the Royal Flying Corps moved into the district in 1917.

and was killed by a blow from a single brick which entered the cockpit.

One man who flew from Lympne in September 1942 and never returned was Pilot Officer Arthur Donahue who earlier had given his definition of exhaustion.. "I didn't want to sleep", he said, "but I didn't want to move, or talk, or fly or anything else either, just relax. It's a feeling that always pervaded me after a fight or a nerve-racking patrol. It is a sensation of being drained completely, in every part of your body, but I don't know what of ".

This exhaustion led to hallucinations similar to those experienced by battle weary, exhausted, retreating British soldiers of 1914 who saw before them the Angel of Mons on the traditional white horse, clad all in white with flaming sword, facing the advancing German army and forbidding their further progress. A famous but fictitious legend.

During the second world war there were many angels in the sky to guide the pilots home but the fact remains that 453 of them, flying from the Biggin Wing, were killed. It is the most famous of all the fighter stations and the memory of its role is etched deeply in our history. This book contains chapters highlighting the ordeal facing the Squadrons and of those pilots who could not find a guardian angel. It also gives a blow-by-blow account of the bombing of Biggin Hill in the summer of 1940 through the memories of people who recall what it was like to be there.

From the days of the Royal Flying Corps, when aviation pioneers were enjoying their dangerous role in the cause of scientific advancement to the daredevil entertainers of today who manoeuvre their modern machines in such spectacular formations, there has always been a risk of death most macabre. There is no doubt that the story of Biggin Hill is intertwined with the existence of spirits and that is why it is destined for ever to remain Britain's premier Ghost Station.

2
Operational: 1917 — 1939

The station was born in the days of the Royal Flying Corps when the pioneer airmen lived in bell tents in the corner of a great wide 80-acre pasture and their frail bi-planes were housed in one Bessoneau hangar. Operational during the last days of the Great War there were many casualties as well as loss of life; in fact the first aviator to die crashed in the valley to the west of the airfield — a scene of many later tragedies. Some years after the war Biggin Hill welcomed members of the celebrated 56 Squadron. They came from the Western Front and were accompanied by many, many ghosts whose deeds in France were already legendary. They, too, suffered casualties. Nos 32 and 23 Squadrons followed in the 1930s, witnessed the total reconstruction of the airfield but lost many experienced peacetime pilots.
They sang their battle song:—

Stand by your glasses steady
This is a life of woe.
Here's a toast to the dead already,
Three cheers for the next to go.

Battle Song of the Royal Flying Corps — anon

1916 - 1918

May 1916: Major Orme, officer commanding Wireless Testing Park at Joyce Green, Dartford is instructed by Signals Experimental Establishment at Woolwich to move his unit to a better location.

August 1916: Lieutenants Hanzard and Furnival discover ideal site on farmland in open country south of Bromley. They find the field already scheduled as a night emergency landing ground by the War Office.

December 1916: Official sanction given for re-siting of Wireless Testing Park at Biggin Hill. The new land, comprising of 80 acres, formed part of Cudham Lodge, a Georgian mansion owned by the Earl of Stanhope.

December 1916: A large house, Koonowla, used as a hospital for sick children, is requisitioned by the War Office for a Mess.

January 2 1917: Lieutenant Dickie with Air Mechanic Chadwick as passenger become first men to land at Biggin Hill. Having taxied their RE7 to a halt in front of the newly erected canvas hangar they kiss the ground in mock ritual.

July 1917: Two airmen flying separately in Sopwith 1.5 Strutters speak to each other using air-to air-wireless technology. A great achievement for Biggin Hill.

November 1917: Some 36 officers a week now passing through the school of technology at Biggin Hill. King George V offers his congratulations.

November 1917: Biggin Hill earmarked as ideal site for defence of London against Gotha bombers. Pilot from Penshurst aerodrome, in Sopwith 1.5 Strutter, makes several experimental landings on north end of airfield

before it is accepted as suitable home for fighter squadron.

December 1917: Wireless site renamed the Wireless Experimental Establishment (WEE). Home defence squadrons equipped with this new technology for battle against Gotha bombers.

December 1917: Biggin Hill becomes operational fighter station. Two Bessoneau hangars erected behind a cottage called Salt Box. D. Flight of 39 Squadron flies in with B.E. 2es and B.E. 12s. Crown Ash cottage hastily requisitioned as a Mess.

February 1918: Newly-formed home defence squadron, 141, joins detached flight at Biggin Hill. CO Major P. Babington.

March 1918: Royal Flying Corps and Royal Naval Air Service incorporated under the title RAF (Royal Air Force). All wireless research now concentrated at Biggin Hill South Camp.

March 1918: Work starts on the permanent buildings of the South Camp. New officers' mess, barrack blocks and steel and concrete hangars erected. 600 men involved in construction work. It will take two years to complete.

May 18, 1918: Lieutenants Turner and Barwise, pilot and observer of 141 Squadron, flying Bristol Fighter shoot down Gotha bomber which crashes at Frinstead in Kent. Both men awarded DFC for Biggin Hill's first "kill".

August 1918: Station roll now up to 593 persons - 68 officers, 297 men and 228 women. Handley Page 0/400s and DH 10s now being used. Runways are lengthened.

One Four One — or All for All!

IT would be wrong to assume that the ghosts of Biggin Hill belong exclusively to the pilots and aircrew of the second world war. From the moment that a detached flight of 39 Squadron set up camp at the north end of the airfield in 1917 to defend London against the threat of Gotha bomber attacks till the famous party in March 1919 when the boys of One Four One (141 Squadron) said their sad farewells, Biggin Hill lost many friends. Others died later during missions never completed.

The first fighter unit to make its home at Biggin Hill was 49 Wing of 39 Squadron whose pilots landed on a hurriedly-prepared grass runway which lay directly behind a well-known but rather isolated landmark called Salt Box cottage. The date was December 1, 1917. Although the deep snow had been pushed aside it was a bumpy arrival and the spartan conditions of this wintry wilderness added to the discomfort of these confused airmen. Could this bleak, vast area of weeds and mole hills be transformed into a front-line fighter base? The doubts lingered on for many weeks.

With single seater B.E.2s and B.E.12s, all housed in one Bessoneau hangar, the pilots lived in bell tents in another. Oil lamps supplied little warmth so many slept, or tried to sleep, in flying suits pulled over pyjamas. For two months the detached Wing held the fort at Biggin Hill and constantly patrolled the Thames, hoping to see in the moonlight, that unmistakable snake of silver that was the Gotha bomber.

The silhouettes evaded them. One exasperated pilot returning from yet another night's hunt over London famously said: "I was like a blind bastard in a dark room looking for a nigger who isn't bloody well there".

Such frustration contrasted greatly to the strain and stresses of the Western Front where 39 Squadron had flown repeatedly into the heat of battle. Although their average age was just 21 and their average life expectancy barely 11 days, those that came back were determined to live their lives to the full. In February 1918 they joined forces with 141 Squadron as the first full operational squadron at Biggin Hill and were given a mixed bag of B.E.2s and 12s, a Sopwith Pup, a Vickers Vampire 3-gun pusher and a flight of Dolphins?

Although the boys of One Four One were recent volunteers to the Royal Flying Corps they quickly settled down at Biggin Hill and were delighted to be re-equipped with the new two-seater Bristol Fighter. This had a 250 hp Rolls-Royce Falcon engine, could fly at 120 m.p.h and climb to 20,000 feet. The "Brisfits" carried wireless telephony and information on enemy movements was given to the pilots by coastguard stations, observer post searchlight and gun sites via the newly-opened Operations Room at the North Camp.

Life at Biggin Hill in those early days was tedious — endless hours of flying formation by day and serious patrols by night over the Thames. To enliven these uneventful days One Four One indulged in uninhibited, mischievous merry-making. They collected various trophies from public places including signs saying 'Trains Up', 'Ladies' and 'Players Please'. On one occasion they removed a large wooden teapot (six-foot high) hanging over the entrance to the Salt Box cafe and smuggled it into the North Camp. The next night it was abducted by officers of the WEE and for several days the teapot went back and forth between the two camps until the local policeman demanded a truce.

Within this efficient, happy, carefree but rapidly maturing unit were the almost inevitable tragedies and almost weekly came the news of another wrecked aircraft and loss of life. By the time the Royal Air Force had been created from a merger of the Royal Flying Corps and the Royal Naval Air Service. 141 Squadron was divided into three flights of Bristol Fighters commanded by Captains Dimmock, Rawson and Slingsby — and they were fully operational with wireless telephony.

The station's first Commanding Officer was Major Philip Babington MC who spent six months in charge at Biggin Hill and flew his Bristol Fighters whenever the opportunity arose. In June 1918, returning from a patrol he crash-landed in the fog and was taken to hospital. Although he recovered from his injuries and rose through the ranks to the position of Air Marshal, Babington never returned to Biggin Hill and Major Brian Baker took command.

Here was a great leader who had flown in France with 48 Squadron and experienced many air-to-air battles with the Richthofen Circus. He was on duty on the night that Lieutenant Pownall took off in a BE2e for a routine searchlight exercise. It was close to the longest day, a clear warm night and perfect for flying.

Pownall flew north and returned low over the North Camp. His chums below took little notice of the lone aircraft until the familiar sound of the engine suddenly changed in tone. They looked up in alarm. The engine was stuttering and the beat was becoming more and more irregular. Then suddenly it stopped. For a while there was silence and then a loud explosion echoed from deep in the valley to the west of the aerodrome.

Some men climbed on top of a low brick building and saw a plume of black smoke rise ominously from behind a clump of trees. Pownall was dead among the mangled remains of his BE2e — and so was the small pigeon who had caused the tragedy.

The brave aviator's funeral was one of many held at the station during the last few months of the Great War. Pownall was buried in the little church graveyard on the road to Keston beneath a four-bladed wooden propeller and a small plaque gave his name and rank. In the years to come many ghosts were reported flitting in and out of Keston churchyard. Few people mentioned the name of Lieutenant Pownall but is it possible this pioneer airman was also a pioneer ghost of Biggin Hill?

More tragedies were followed by more funerals and all too frequently selected members of 141 Squadron bore a coffin on their shoulders and marched slowly along the Bromley Road to the churchyard holding up the traffic. There, they said prayers and a bugler played the Last Post. They marched back to camp singing their own requiem to the dead.

Major General Seeley was the Under Secretary of State for Air and he instigated enquiries to find the cause of these sickeningly regular accidents none of which occurred in combat.

On May 20 1918 a congratulatory message from the Lord Mayor of London arrived at the

FIRST TO GO: *Lieutenant Pownall of 141 Squadron is buried in the churchyard at Keston along with many more of Biggin Hill's pioneer airmen of the Royal Flying Corps. For many years this was the station's graveyard.*

A brave aviator lay dying
And as on his death bed he lay
To his swearing mechanics around him
These last dying words did he say

Take the cylinder out of my kidneys
The connecting rod out of my brain
From the small of my back take the gear box
And assemble the engine again.

So gather up quickly the fragments
And when you've returned them to store

Write a letter to Seely and tell him
His 141st is no more

When the Court of Enquiry assembles
Please tell them the reason I died
Was because I forgot twice iota
Was the maximum angle of glide

So when I am dead I'll be joining
The Flying Corps up in the sky
Let's hope that they've studied iota
And the wings that they give me will fly!

SPARTAN: The bleakness of Biggin: This Bristol F2B fighter (Brisfit) belonging to 141 Squadron landed in deep snow in the winter of 1918.

Officer's Mess: "The citizens of London are filled with admiration and gratitude for the splendid defensive measures taken by the Air Services against the enemy's attack and will be glad if their appreciation and thanks may be conveyed to those who gallantly and successfully protected the capital on that occasion."

His Worship was referring to 141 Squadron's destruction of a Gotha the previous evening. The bomber — part of an attacking force of 38 intent on dropping their bombs on London — was intercepted by a Bristol Fighter piloted by Lieutenant E.E.Turner with Lieutenant H.B.Barwise as Observer. As Turner poured incendiary tracer bullets into the Gotha, Barwise sprayed it furiously from nose to tail with his Lewis gun. It crashed at Frinstead in Kent. The German pilot and navigator died but the rear gunner escaped with a broken arm.

One Four One celebrated their first "kill" wildly in the Mess that night not knowing that it was also to be their last "kill" of the Great War. The Germans had lost too many night raiders to attempt any more attacks on England. The war in the air was over.

Not so the tragedies. Shortly after winning a Concours d'Elegance, which culminated in a test for proficiency in wireless telephony and gaining the coveted title of "Cock" Squadron, 141 left Sutton Park in Essex — the scene of their triumph — for the short journey back to Biggin Hill. They landed expecting a cheering, welcoming party but were met instead by a lone sergeant with the news that one Bristol Fighter had crashed on the return flight and the pilot and observer were dead.

On March 1, 1919 the "Cock" Squadron as they were now known said goodbye to Biggin

COCK SQUADRON: Members of 141 Squadron at Biggin Hill in 1918 standing in front of a Bristol Fighter with a cockerel painted on the fuselage. Pilots and observers in this photograph include Major Philip Babington MC (with white scarf), the first senior officer at Biggin Hill, Lieutenants Turner and Barwise, who achieved the first "kill" in August 1918, Lieutenant F.S.Mockford, Wireless Operator transferred from 39 Squadron, Lieutenant Hardit Singh Malik, a Sikh from Rawalpindi and former Oxford Blue at golf and Lieutenant R.A.Langford-Sainsbury, the Squadron's ace marksman. It was the latter's expertise in a proficiency contest that helped 141 Squadron win the title of Cock Squadron. Malik became the British Air Attaché for Paris and Washington, Babington an Air Marshal KCB, MC, AFC and Langford-Sainsbury an Air Vice Marshal CB, OBE, DFC, AFC.

Hill and flew in their Avro 504Ks for Tallaght in Ireland wearing their "lucky" khaki Royal Flying Corps uniforms. Some were still hung over after the previous evening's memorable farewell party but they were not sad to quit their role with London's slender fighter defences and meet the new challenges in Ireland. The popular Lieutenant Hetherington never made it. He was lost in the Irish Sea alongside his Observer.

Turner, the first real hero of Biggin Hill, took his newly-earned DFC and a Spandau gun taken from the Gotha to Ireland with him. He lived only a few more years. In 1922 he was posted to India and died on the North West Frontier. Other members of 141 Squadron to perish included A. Bamber, a test pilot and E.Chater, who was killed flying for Guinea Airways.

By the early 1920s One Four One could muster almost a squadron of ghosts — and Biggin Hill was only five years old!

1919 - 1939

January 1919: Mutiny at Biggin Hill. Some 500 men living under canvas on the South Camp with no heating and nowhere to wash or dry, refuse to report for duty and present a list of demands. The Air Ministry eventually agrees to introduce improvements.

January 1919: Wing Commander Grenfell DSO replaces Colonel Blandy as commanding officer of the WEE.

March 1919: 141 "Cock" Squadron leaves for Ireland. 39 Squadron flies in with Sopwith Camels. They are greeted on arrival by officers from the South Camp who drench them with foam from fire extinguishers.

August 1919: Greetings by wireless telephony exchanged between a wireless operator at Aperfield Court and an assembly of VIPs in the House of Lords in a bid to dramatise the value of work being carried out at Biggin Hill.

January 1922: 39 Squadron transferred to Kenley leaving Biggin Hill without a fighter squadron.

January 1923: The Instrument Design Establishment set up to research and develop every branch of aviation is amalgamated with the Royal Aircraft Establishment at Farnborough. Staff at Biggin Hill slashed from 600 to 346.

March 1923: An anti-aircraft school, searchlight experimental station and special Night Flying Flight replaces the IDE on the South Camp. Army are now in control at Biggin Hill.

May 1923: Fighters return. 56 Squadron flies in from Hawkinge with Sopwith Snipes.

July 1923: Night Flying Flight equipped with three Vickers Vimys. Great consternation among people of Biggin Hill, Cudham and Downe as these giants roar over their homes.

1926: General strike in Britain. Vimys from Biggin Hill drop the *British Gazette* over the towns and villages of the south.

1929: 29 acres to the west of the main Bromley road opposite the North Camp purchased for the reconstruction of Biggin Hill. 56 Squadron moves to North Weald.

1932: Building work completed. New Messes, barrack blocks, married quarters ready for occupation. Wing Commander Grenfell remains station commander of some 300 personnel.

1932: Two squadron station. Biggin Hill welcomes Nos 23 and 32 Squadrons with Bristol Bulldogs and Hawker Demons.

1935: 23 Squadron leaves for Middle East. 32 Squadron re-equipped with Gloster Gauntlets.

1936: Home Defence Force reorganised into four functional commands — Bomber, Fighter, Coastal and Training. Biggin Hill becomes sector station with HQ at Uxbridge.

1937: B Flight of 32 Squadron separated to form nucleus of 79 Squadron. Air Chief Marshal Sir Hugh Dowding makes frequent visits to Biggin Hill.

1937: 20,000 visitors to Biggin Hill see the Empire Day flying display.

August 1938: Operation Diabolo. Wing Commander Lock, new station Commanding Officer brings his station to a state of immediate readiness for war.

The legendary 56

WHEN the seasoned pilots of 56 Squadron took up occupation of the North Camp in 1923 an excited buzz filled the air. Biggin Hill had been without a front-line fighter squadron for two years and now they welcomed the most celebrated squadron in the Royal Air Force. Their deeds on the Western Front were legendary but only a handful of young men had survived the war to fly again in peacetime.

For many weeks after their arrival the talk in the Mess and the pubs concerned tales of gallant deeds and especially of the prowess of a young fellow called Captain Albert Ball who destroyed 43 Boche fighters — many before he reached the age of 20. Ball was killed in action in May 1917 and awarded a posthumous Victoria Cross for "his conspicuous bravery during the previous 11 days". on many occasions he had flown alone.

From Captain Ball the conversation would switch to Captain McCudden whose intelligent tactics, skilful flying and acute marksmanship gave him an even greater tally. Jimmy McCudden came from Gillingham and had been credited with 52 'kills'. He was also gazetted and presented, not only with the VC, but also the DSO and bar to accompany his MC and Croix de Guerre. Jimmy McCudden was killed at Aux-le-Chateau just four months before Armistice Day.

The stories told by the pilots of 56 Squadron inevitably included the grim, dark exploits of the most famous aviator of them all — but this one was on the other side. Baron Manfred Freiherr von Richthofen was known as the Red Baron. Credited with the destruction of 80 Allied planes in dogfights he was killed when his famous red Fokker triplane was shot down by 56 Squadron in April 1918.

So comprehensively had von Richthofen and his red bandits upset the ambitions of the Allies that many of those former Royal Flying Corps squadrons (including 56 Squadron) were disbanded immediately after the war. Now, with the expansion of the RAF sanctioned by the War Office, they were reformed to be part of nine single-seater fighter squadrons in two Wings under the auspices of the Home Defence Unit. Biggin Hill became headquarters of No 5 Wing.

From their valour and dexterity in the air over France, the pilots now had a new challenge — to master the complexities of Radio Telephony. Equipped with the latest fighter, the Gloster Grebe, the peacetime pilots of 56 Squadron , in time became the masters of R/T tactics. They also continued to show little regard for their own lives and, on one occasion, actually shot down a Vickers Vimy killing the two occupants of the front cockpit.

The incident occurred in the winter of 1924 when a film unit visited the station, with Air Ministry consent, and invited 56 Squadron to re-enact a typical dog fight in mock aerial combat. This was the sort of mission that the pilots loved; it made a change from the tedious grind of the daily training routine and the pioneering work with radio telephony so elaborate plans were made to make the spectacle as realistic as possible. As it turned out it was too realistic.

A Vimy, disguised as an enemy bomber, flew towards Biggin Hill followed by a cameraman

UNDER CANVAS: Photographs of Biggin Hill before the great reconstruction of 1929-1932 are rare. This Leopard Moth belonging to 56 Squadron was often seen on the airfield between 1923 and 1927. There are few people alive today who remember the canvas hangars.

in a second Vimy. As it approached the airfield the fighters of 56 Squadron took off, swarmed around the "enemy" and pumped it with round after round. The pilots were delighted with the mock action and so was the cameraman, especially when the rear gunner threw up his arms, clutched his heart and then hung 'dead' over the side.

The fighters and the cameraman were still 'shooting' as the pilot lit the flares and dived steeply down towards the village of Cudham. The Vimy crash-landed in a wood, slid along the ground, hit a tree and came to halt with black smoke still belching from the engines and the fuselage. Above in the second Vimy the cameraman filmed this astonishing piece of 'realism' unaware that the occupants of the front cockpit were dead. The pilot, in attempting to skim the tree tops, had misjudged the height and lost control.

This sobering incident did not stop the daring, some say irresponsible, pilots of 56 Squadron from showing off their skills in the air. In their wonderfully manoeuvrable Gloster Grebe, with a top speed of 150mph and a ceiling of 23,000 feet, the young men would wait for their Commanding Officer to leave the station on business, before performing aerobatics and establishing new records for consecutive loops. One fine day Flying Officer Luxmore set out to beat the squadron record thinking that Squadron Leader Frederick Vincent was safely away. He looped the first loop with ease and picked up speed for a second as the C.O appeared on the grass below and released a Very signal ordering him to land immediately. Luxmore ignored the order, completed his second loop and prepared for a third. He was in deep trouble, he faced a court martial perhaps but the squadron championship was now within sight.

As the pilots below looked up in bewilderment, anxiety and even admiration the Grebe came into sight again, zoomed up into a vertical position, then flipped over on its back, fell to the ground and burst into flames.

Another flying accident. Another pilot lost and more to come. The days of grieving were not over yet for the young men of 56 Squadron.

Although the parachute was first used in an emergency to save a human life as far back as 1808 it did not become standard equipment in the RAF until 1927 and it was in that year that a Parachute Circus turned up at Biggin Hill to give the young fighters of 56 Squadron practice in pull offs and drops.

Two small platforms had been built around a strut on each wing of a Vickers Vimy and an expert, experienced parachutist, Corporal East and his colleagues were assigned to show the pilots how and when to jump and the right technique in pulling the ripcord.

The pilots, used to flying by the feel in their buttocks, were not too pleased about this new safety device but agreed to join hundreds of spectators and watch Corporal East attempt to beat the world record for a delayed drop. All the station personnel were present and so, it seemed, was the entire population of Biggin Hill for the event had been well publicised.

The Vimy took off, climbed to 6,000 feet and swung back home for Biggin Hill. At the right moment Corporal East clambered out of the cockpit, edged his way along the wing and stood on the platform. The pressure of the airstream held him in place.

As Biggin Hill held its breath the spectators watched the would-be record breaker as he fell through the air at a fantastic speed. He struck the road by the Salt Box and died immediately, his parachute only half opened. The passengers on a bus which had drawn up by the side of the road saw the whole episode in its gruesome entirety and many fainted. The driver was so overcome that he could not continue his journey.

Another tragedy. Another ghost for Biggin Hill.

A Siskin of 56 Squadron. Later the pilots graduated to the Gloster Grebe.

READY FOR ACTION: Biggin Hill on Empire Day, 1936 and the Avro Tutors are lined up ready for a display in which the resident squadrons are keen to show their strength and ability in aerobatics. Some two or three months earlier (March) Adolf Hitler, Chancellor and Führer of the Third Reich had sent a handful of battalions to occupy the 9,000 square miles of the demilitarised Rhineland in defiance of the 1919 Treaty of Versailles. In Britain this display of naked aggression was tacitly accepted. The key word was 'appeasement'.

Three cheers for the next to go!

WHEN the great reconstruction of Biggin Hill had been finally completed in 1932, the North Camp was ready to welcome, not one, but two fighter squadrons. Within four days of each other Nos 23 and 32 flew in with a mix of Bulldogs, Harts, Siskins and Demons — pleased to be able to show off their aeronautical skills to the 300 RAF personnel now billeted there.

23 Squadron arrived first. They had already performed synchronised aerobatics at the Hendon Air Pageant and other shows and were still talking about the tragic crash suffered by one of their number a few months earlier. Douglas Bader, a young promising pilot, should have been with them at Biggin Hill but was learning to walk again after having both his legs amputated.

The Great Depression which was afflicting much of the country had little effect on the lives of the pilots who were enjoying the good life — games of rugger and cricket against other units, outings to night clubs in London and the theatre, challenges at cards, snooker and chess, pub crawls and some memorable, roisterous tricks with officers from the South Camp as the victims.

More serious was the constant round of training and exercises and the practice of total mobilisation with the entire personnel involved. Turmoil was building up in Europe and Biggin Hill, as a key sector station in the air defence of London, needed to be at maximum efficiency in the unlikely event of a war!

That feeling had escalated by 1935 and when Mussolini and his Fascists invaded Abyssinia the Demons of 23 Squadron were given major inspections, dismantled and shipped to the Middle East. The pilots of 23 Squadron did not go with them — their beloved Demons were wanted for strategic reserve in case hostilities spread but the boys were not part of that plan. Gradually they were transferred to other units leaving 32 Squadron as Biggin Hill's only operational unit.

They also remained at full strength. By now Winston Churchill, out of office, was warning against the persecution of the Jews, the gathering storm and Hitler's cynical repudiation of the Treaty of Versailles. He spoke also against Neville Chamberlain's policy of appeasement and, on one trip to meet the officers at Biggin Hill, said he sometimes couldn't sleep at night, thinking of all our dangers and how the Empire could be dissipated in a minute.

By now Germany had introduced the Luftwaffe and were building bombers in large numbers. As a counter measure the Home Defence Force was reorganised into four functional commands — Bomber, Fighter, Coastal and Training. Biggin Hill was a fighter station, the headquarters were at Bentley Priory, Stanmore and the AOC was Air Chief Marshal Sir Hugh Dowding.

The activity in the air was immense. When the international airport at Croydon was fog bound, as it often was, great airliners would be diverted to Biggin Hill. In 1938 an Imperial Airways Hannibal flew in with the American Olympic Games team including Jesse Owens, fresh from his triumphs in Berlin.

Attendance figures at flying displays were now breaking all records. On Empire Day 1937 nearly 20,000 people had turned up. The Bristol Bulldogs had been replaced by Gloster

The Operations Room was the nerve centre of Biggin Hill and its personnel had operational control of the Sector and also of the army searchlight units in the area. Some of the Volunteer Reservists are pictured here with the Officers' Mess in the background.

Gauntlets and on March 27 'B' Flight of 32 Squadron was split off as the nucleus of a new fighter Squadron, No 79. Their pilots were also equipped with Gauntlets — and so began, not only a fierce rivalry, but a fighting partnership that was to continue long into the darkest days of 1940.

The "local" for the two squadrons was the White Hart Inn at Brasted, some six miles south of Biggin Hill. One of the first to find the pub was Squadron Leader Beatty, known as 'The Admiral', who arrived on his own and enjoyed himself so much that he returned with some of his boys, including Flight Lieutenant Mike Crossley. Gradually more and more pilots of 32 and 79 Squadrons found the White Hart. Crossley, a great saxophonist, joined the dance band with the well-known Paddy Roberts on the piano.

There had been no tragedies associated with Biggin Hill for more than 10 years but that was all about to end. In 1937 Squadron Leader Beatty and a Wing Commander volunteered to take two flying boats to Messina. At one of the stops en route the two pilots were introduced to the two pretty daughters of a government official and romance immediately flourished. With plans for the future clearly mapped out the pilots took off on the last stage of their journey, hit the side of a mountain and were killed. Weeks later the two young sisters came over to England, hired an aircraft and threw themselves out. Four more lives wasted.

Kath Preston, landlady of the White Hart, remembered the names of those pre-war pilots. "We were on Christian name terms with Bob Roberts, Jimmy Davies, Lance Bowler, Oscar Train, Freddie Shute, Wimpy Wade, Desmond McEwan, Pete Brothers, Guy Harris, Grubby

Flying Officer Robin Buchanan-Woolaston (second left in this group) was killed in August 1939 just before the outbreak of war. On the left is Flight Lieutenant (and Squadron saxophonist) Michael Crossley who joined 32 Squadron at Biggin Hill in 1936. On the right are Pilot Officers John Milner and John White.
Pilot Officer C.W. Fry is in the Hurricane.

Grice and Chiggy Chignell. Only a handful survived the war".

As both Squadrons put in many hours of flying so the days wore on with increasing uncertainty. In April 1938, 79 Squadron made the first formation flight at night to be carried out in Fighter Command. It was such a great success that more nocturnal outings were planned but then cancelled as the code word 'Diabolo' was flashed to Biggin Hill. Wing Commander Lock took the cue; he was to bring his station to a state of 'immediate readiness for war'.

Theese were grim days. The only good news for the pilots came in September 1938 when a single Hawker Hurricane was delivered to the station. Suspicious at first of this sleek new fighter the pilots were soon bowled over by its manoeuvrability and ability to exceed 300 mph in level flight. A few days later the Prime Minister returned from Munich, waved a piece of paper from outside 10 Downing Street and said "there would be peace in our time".

The crisis, however, dragged on into 1939. In August, the last full month of peace, there was a trial black-out of the London area and the new station commander at Biggin Hill, Wing Commander Richard Grice DFC, was instructed to send up an aircraft to see the effect.

It was an unpleasant night and Biggin Hill was shrouded in low cloud and poor visibility. Flying Officer Olding, the man who volunteered for the black-out patrol, took off, circled the station and strained his eyes as the mist gathered around his Hurricane. Without warning the Merlin engine cut out and was followed by a deafening explosion.

Wing Commander Grice now instructed another pilot, Flying Officer Robin Buchanan-Woolaston to drop a marker flare by the side of Olding's Hurricane and at the same time ordered a crash tender to watch out for the glare of burning magnesium. They didn't see a thing but they heard another explosion. 'Wooly' Woolaston had flown into the side of Tatsfield hill — less than 100 yards from Olding's mangled wreck.

Biggin Hill could ill afford to lose such valuable pilots on the eve of war but the old first world war fighter station had already experienced much tragedy and the aircrew knew that accidents were almost par for the course. As they sang the old battle song, with the words from the chorus handed down from the Royal Flying Corps, they wondered who would be next.

The Millionaire Mob

AS the turmoil in Europe grew during the summer of 1938 the decision was made to round up the Auxiliary pilots. Hundreds of telegrams were sent to offices and clubs and especially to holiday spots all over the world urging the "weekend flyers" to return to their squadrons. Among them were the passionate, aristocratic young men who flew with 601 (County of London) Squadron. They were delighted to learn that Biggin Hill would be their first wartime base.

The pilots arrived in Hawker Demons and included Max Aitken, son of Lord Beaverbrook, Loel Guinness, of the brewing family, Whitney Straight, later to become managing director of BOAC, Sir Archibald Hope, son of the 16th Baronet of Craighall, Michael Peacock a barrister and the South African Roger Bushell, also a barrister, British ski champion and a man destined to mastermind, as 'Big X', the Great Escape from Stalag Luft III. They wore big brass AAs on the lapels of their tunics. The regulars insisted that the As stood for Amateur Airmen or even Argue and Answerback. Of course they stood for Auxiliary Airmen.

These lawyers and farmers, stockbrokers and journalists, landowners and artisans, serious minded accountants and unrepentant playboys had one thing in common with the boys of 32 Squadron — a passion for flying but also a determination that anything the regulars could do they could do better.

Because of this rivalry was fierce and many competitions between the two squadrons were instigated. One involved a game of polo played on old motorbikes. 601 Squadron appeared on the "battlefield" with a stable of brand new Brough Superiors and were easy victors.

The Auxiliary spirit was born in White's Club in the 1920s and fathered by Lord Edward Grosvenor, the aristocratic seventh son of the first Duke of Westminster, whose greatest joy in life was flying.

He had been one of the first Englishmen to own an aeroplane — a Bleriot — with which he offered himself to the Royal Naval Air Service in 1914. He had flown throughout the 1914-18 war and in peacetime he supported Lord Trenchard's idea of creating an Auxiliary Air Force.

It was in the back dining room at Whites that Lord Edward began to recruit pilots among his friends and old time comrades and by 1925 he had raised and was commanding the celebrated County of London Squadron. Both 600 and 601 Squadrons were formed at Northolt and moved to Hendon in January 1927, where they shared the flying field.

As new auxiliary squadrons were raised in various parts of the country during the 1930s they looked at Hendon for their tradition. Here was a group of enthusiastic, well-heeled young men of great wealth giving every moment of their spare time to their squadrons. One of 601 Squadron's commanding officers (1948-1950) Group Captain Hugh Dundas later wrote that they affected an approach which was so light hearted as to appear almost frivolous, yet they achieved a standard of efficiency in the air which surpassed many regular squadrons.

"Thus in an atmosphere combining outrageous light-heartedness with an underlying determination to excel at operational flying was born, and so developed, the auxiliary spirit".

601 Squadron left Biggin Hill after a few months but returned on the eve of war bringing new Blenheims to join the Hurricanes of 32 and 79 Squadrons. They also renewed their acquaintance with Teddy and Kath Preston, mine hosts at the White Hart Inn, Brasted which the 601 boys had always used as their local.

One night the local policeman found them in the pub after hours. As Roger Bushell, Michael Peacock and their friends hurriedly pushed their beer mugs under chairs and cushions, Teddy yelled out: "You have met your match now, Giles. We have two King's Counsellors in our midst". 601 Squadron stayed until December when they were transferred to Tangmere.

Today, the auxiliary spirit is more applicable to the ghosts who haunt the airfields of England for many of them died in the battles which were to follow. 601 Squadron lost many of the pilots who served at Biggin Hill during those early months of the war. In fact a great number were killed before the Battle of Britain had started In June 1940 42 operational squadrons had been assigned to Dowding. Of these 12 were Auxiliary units. By the beginning of July 1940 there was not, on average, more than eight or nine Auxiliary pilots left in each Squadron of Fighter Command.

The losses continued. 120 auxiliary pilots went into the battle and 27 of them — nearly one in four — were killed between July 10 and the end of October. Many more were shot down and seriously wounded. But they scored more than their share of victories for Britain and no unit in the whole of Fighter Command excelled in 1940 more than the fighting aces of London's 601 Squadron.

One of the charismatic pilots of 601 Squadron who died in the Battle of Britain was the American Flying Officer Billy Fiske, the son of an international banker and a brilliant sportsman. Fiske set a record for the Cresta Run at St Moritz and captained the US Olympic team that won the bobsled event in 1932. He drove the first Stutz car to be entered at Le Mans 24 hour race when he was just 19.

The American authorities did not approve of foreign enlistment but Fiske had many influential friends among the stockbroker fraternity and that enabled him to join 601 Squadron in September 1939. It attracted enormous publicity especially as his wife was the ex-Countess of Warwick and a noted society figure.

On August 16, 1940 he crash-landed in flames at Tangmere, grievously burned and died of shock and injuries the following day. A bronze memorial plaque later unveiled at St Paul's Cathedral reads: "An American citizen who died that England might live".

Was he the only American to die in the Battle of Britain? Contemporary reports say he was but later researchers believe several other Americans enlisted under the guise of Canadians to avoid the displeasure of the US State Department.

Another 601 Squadron pilot who died during the Battle of Britain was Pilot Officer William Doulton, a mechanical engineer and renowned as the then tallest pilot in the RAF. Doulton was shot down on August 30, 1940 and reported missing. The whereabouts of his Hurricane remained a mystery until 1984 when it was excavated near Wennington Church, south of Romford. Doulton's remains were still in the cockpit.

Flying Officer Humphrey Gilbert, a Cheltenham College schoolboy, known as a prankster, twice survived crashes during the Battle of Britain. In May 1942 as a Flight Commander then with 71 Squadron he attempted to take off in his Spitfire from Debden with his Controller sitting on his lap. They were going to a party. Both men were killed.

Another to die later in the war was Australian Pilot Officer Howard Mayers who gave up his job as a

Billy Fiske with his wife, the former Countess of Warwick.

successful company managing director to join his pals in 601 Squadron. Despite many hair-raising moments the auxiliary spirit never deserted him.

Leading an attack in Egypt in December 1941, Mayers saw one of his pilots shot down by flak. Although enemy vehicles were approaching he landed near the crashed aircraft, led the pilot to his seat, got on his lap and took off safely reaching his base.

Three months later Mayers radioed that he was in trouble near the Qattara Depression. His aircraft was found in the desert but there was no trace of him and he was never heard of again.

Biggin Hill had the honour of knowing these men and many others of the first Auxiliary squadron, including William Rhodes Moorhouse and Roger Bushell whose stirring but tragic stories are told elsewhere in this book.

Are these brave airmen among the ghosts who revisit their old airfield at Biggin Hill? Who knows!

3

Time to fuse all warheads

A few weeks after war was declared on September 3, 1939, the Commander-in-Chief of Fighter Command, Sir Hugh Dowding, a man of faultless generalship and great faith visited his so-called "chicks" at Biggin Hill. Solemn and unsmiling, he spoke to Group Captain Dick Grice about his anxiety for the lives of his fighter boys in defending the cause of civilisation. He gave no indication that he believed passionately that bodily death was not the end of all things. His spiritual thoughts were to emerge much later.

Two pilots from Biggin Hill died in the early months of the war but several of them, fighting alongside their French allies of the Armée de l'Air, inflicted serious losses on the Luftwaffe during the Battle of France — but at grievous cost. Eighteen were killed during the month of May alone and many valuable Hurricanes lost.

There were other important VIP visitors to Biggin Hill. One was the Prime Minister Winston Churchill who spoke to the pilots in the Officer's Mess and told them: "Remember, you're defending my house as well as your aerodrome". Another was Lord Trenchard, the father of the RAF whose nephew, Pilot Officer Lionel Roger Dorrien Smith was a brilliant pilot with 79 Squadron. Dorrien Smith was one of the first to die — shot down by German tanks on the western outskirts of Arras.

I have heard the sullen howl of madness
rising, falling from afar;
I see the desperate hate of nations
boiling up; it reeks of war.
I have dreamed of joy, unmeasured gladness,
planned my joys — for I am young;
England was weak, and dreams were broken
England meet the day — be strong!

Pilot Officer Archibald Weir DFC from Hythe, Kent was shot down and killed off the Isle of Wight on November 7, 1940. His father died in April 1941 when his ship was torpedoed and his younger brother died in February 1944 at Anzio while serving with the Scots Guards.

September 1939 - May 1940

Sept 3: Prime Minister announces war with Germany. Hurricanes of 32 and 79 Squadrons and Spitfires of 601 stand by - dispersed, fuelled and armed. 32 Squadron scrambled immediately. False alarm.

Sept 5: Bromley to Westerham road closed because of likely sabotage. Long diversion around aerodrome for private cars and pedestrians. Bus allowed through for passholders only.

Sept 10: Flight Lt R.W. Reynolds of 79 Squadron crashes in a wood on a night exercise — Biggin Hill's first casualty of the war.

Sept 30: Station Commander, Wing Commander Dick Grice, who won DFC as member of Royal Flying Corps, promoted to Group Captain.

Oct 4: 74 privates of the Queen's Own Royal West Regiment ordered to guard station against paratroops and saboteurs to complement the guns of the 90th Anti Aircraft Regiment. All searchlights in the area also come under the operational control of Biggin Hill. Searchlight HQ is at Knole Park, Sevenoaks.

October 10: Sound detectors pick up tell-tale blip but no enemy aircraft appears on plotting table. Sergeant 'Snow' White of 32 Squadron ordered to investigate but finds nothing. Mystery soon solved. Detectors had picked up the noise of an electric motor from the open door of an army refrigerator on the North Camp.

Nov 15: Deputy Company Commander Marie Petrie becomes first WAAF to be based at Biggin Hill. She is followed by scores of girls wearing blue berets and macs as uniform not yet ready. Airmens' wives told their married quarters will become new Waafery.

They are not pleased. Neither are they pleased with the cocktail party given by pilots to welcome the girls. Controllers in Ops Room sort their new assistants into three watches — 'first glamour', 'second glamour' and 'hags watch'.

Nov 21: Flying Officer Jimmy Davies of 79 Squadron makes Biggin Hill's first kill of the war, shooting down a Dornier 17 ('flying pencil') over the Channel.

Nov 29: Six Blenheims of 601 Squadron help destroy German seaplane base at Borkham, one of the Friesian Islands.

Dec 1: Squadron Leader Loel Guinness takes over command of 601 Squadron and Squadron Leader Chignell replaces Squadron Leader Prickman.

Dec 4: 79 Squadron escorts the royal destroyer carrying King George VI to France.

Jan 3 1940: Goodbye to 601 Squadron which has left for Tangmere. 79 and 32 Squadrons now billeted at Manston and Gravesend while construction firms excavate deep air raid shelters and lay short concrete runway.

January: Severe winter. Worst for many years. 15 foot snow drifts at Biggin Hill. Fighters kept airborne for 100 hours a week but no enemy activity reported.

March 31: Weather now improved. 79 and 32 Squadrons back at Biggin Hill where convoy patrols continue.

May 6: Squadron Leader Worrall replaces Squadron Leader Chignell.

May 10: Adolf Hitler invades Low Countries in his continuing Blitzkrieg. 79 Squadron ordered to France.

First casualties of the war

PICTURE the scene at Biggin Hill on the morning of Sunday September 3 1939. The day had dawned brightly and the tensions, felt by everyone and especially the pilots of the three resident squadrons, were relieved by the morning sunshine and the knowledge that the waiting was almost over.

At 11 o'clock came the voice of the man who had met Hitler at Munich, supported appeasement, tried to buy time, had many critics but still found himself Prime Minister of a united nation. "I am speaking to you from the Cabinet Room at No 10 Downing Street. This morning the British Ambassador in Berlin handed the German Government a final note stating that, unless we had heard from them by eleven o'clock that they were prepared at once to withdraw their troops from Poland, a state of war would exist between us....."

The majority of pilots were sitting in deck chairs in the sunshine listening to the Prime Minister. From one of the open windows of a dispersal hut the clear, resonant tones of Neville Chamberlain continued on the wireless. "I have to tell you that no such undertaking has been received and that consequently this country is at war with Germany..."

Around the perimeter, fuelled, armed, ready for instant take-off were the Hurricanes of 32 and 79 Squadrons and the Blenheims of 601 Squadron. In the Senior Operations Rooms, patient, tense and calm were the controllers and plotters.

All were alone with their thoughts and for a few moments no-one spoke. It was an 'erk on a bicycle with a made-up version of the hit tune *Pack Up Your Troubles* who broke the long silence. At last, Biggin Hill was at war. What lay in store for this senior sector station? How many airmen would die in the battles ahead? The answer was not long coming.

Eight days after the outbreak of war, Flight Lieutenant Richard Reynolds of 79 Squadron crashed his Hurricane in a wood near Biggin Hill after a night exercise. The 24-year-old son of Charles and Kate Reynolds of Bickley was the first Biggin Hill airman to die in the second world war. He was buried in the little churchyard at Cudham.

The Luftwaffe onslaught had failed to materialise but the inactivity or the Phoney War, as it was called, gave Group Captain Grice an opportunity to get Biggin Hill's defences into shape. All three squadrons were billeted elsewhere while construction gangs excavated deep air raid shelters and laid a short concrete runway. This was followed by the severest winter for 40 years with deep drifts making Biggin Hill unserviceable and it was the

MAY 10, 1940: Number One Grice Fighter Force. Back row (left to right): Squadron Leader Frankland, Flight Lieutenant Jackson, Flight Lieutenant Osmond, ? Front row: ACW2 Lonsdale, Wing Commander R. Grice, Squadron Leader Fowler. ACW2 Lonsdale was the driver to the Station Commander. Later commissioned as a cypher officer, in 1943 she left to marry Wing Commander S.G.Birch. Photograph taken by Squadron Leader John Worrall of 32 Squadron who was about to take over as senior controller.

expertise of the ground crews that kept the Hurricanes airborne at all. The snows had hardly melted when the station suffered its second wartime tragedy — the death of Flying Officer Lancelot Bowler.

Kath Preston, landlady of the White Hart, Brasted remembers the earnest tall young airman who visited her pub regularly with other members of the 32nd Pursuit. Flying Officer Bowler came from Wavertree, Liverpool and had joined the Royal Air Force a few years before the outbreak of war. Unlike his colleagues he did not complain too much about the lack of action and in February said to Kath: "I bet I don't come through this lot". He didn't. Lance Bowler, aged 22, was killed on Saturday March 23 — the second airman from Biggin Hill to die during the war.

Flying Officer Lancelot Bowler, son of Captain and Mrs Bowler of Wavertree, Liverpool. His grandfather was once captain of West Derby Golf Club.

Battle of France:
The Squadrons at Biggin Hill...

THE following squadrons were based at Biggin Hill or detached from one of the forward stations or from France in an attempt to stem the German advance and then to provide air cover for **Operation Dynamo.**

- **May 10 1940**: 79 Hurricane Squadron, based at Merville aerodrome (returned for a rest on May 20).

- **May 10 1940**: 32 Hurricane Squadron, based at Biggin Hill and then Abbeville as a forward base. Sent away for a brief rest on May 20th.

- **May 10 1940**: 610 Spitfire Squadron, based at Biggin Hill. Detached Gravesend May 25 — July 7)

- **May 18 1940**: 213 Hurricane Squadron, based at Biggin Hill for Dunkirk only. Left for Exeter in June.

- **May 21 1940**: 242 Hurricane Squadron, based at Biggin Hill for Dunkirk only. Left for Coltishall in June.

- **May 27 1940**: 229 Hurricane Squadron, led by Harold Maguire and based at Biggin Hill for Home Defence initially and then Dunkirk. Left for Digby in June.

SIX squadrons were based at Biggin Hill during the Dunkirk evacuation and, from these, 18 pilots were killed over the French port and the Channel. Only the long-time residents, 32 Squadron came out completely unscathed — and its turn was to come later in the war.

During those nine desperate days Fighter Command lost a precious 432 Hurricanes and Spitfires and scores of pilots killed, missing or wounded — the equivalent of 20 fighter squadrons. The RAF were badly mauled.

The greatest news about Dunkirk was that the British Expeditionary Force escaped. It lost virtually all its equipment in France but 338,226 Allied troops were brought back against the 45,000 estimated when *Operation Dynamo* was put in motion. But the young airmen at Biggin Hill did not see it as a great escape. They lost too many friends and, as Winston Churchill told them, victories are not won by evacuations. For most of these young pilots Biggin Hill was their first and last fighter base. When the great evacuation "the miracle of deliverance" had been completed the old station was licking its wounds and trying desperately to re-form its ranks.

Little wonder the spirits return today to see if the sacrifice has been worthwhile!

...And those who died

The Biggin Hill squadrons suffered the following casualties during the Battle of France and the Dunkirk evacuation:

79 Squadron

Pilot Officer Llewellyn Lister Appleton, son of Charles and Mary Appleton of Hartley, Kent who died on Tuesday May 14, 1940 aged 23. Runnymede Memorial Panel 71.

Pilot Officer Lionel Roger Dorrien-Smith, son of Major Arthur and Eleanor Dorrien-Smith of Tresco, Isles of Scilly who died on Monday May 20, 1940 aged 21. Runnymede Memorial Panel 8.

610 Squadron

Flying Officer Albert Rupert John Medcalf, son of Rupert and Florence Medcalf of Willaston, Cheshire who died on May 27, 1940 aged 26. Runnymede Memorial Panel 6.

Sergeant William Thomas Medway who died on Monday May 27, 1940. Oostduinkerke Communal Cemetery, Koksijde, West-Vlaanderen, Belgium.

Squadron Leader Alexander Lumsden Franks AFC, son of James and Margaret Franks who died on Wednesday May 29, 1940 aged 32. Sqn Ldr Franks is buried at Sage War Cemetery, Germany, 24 miles south of Oldenburg.

Flying Officer Gerald Malcolm Theodore Kerr, husband of Barbara Kerr of Frodsham, Cheshire, who died on Wednesday May 29, 1940 aged 30.Runnymede Memorial Panel 6.

Sergeant Peter Douglas Jenkins, son of Frederick and Dorothy Jenkins of Breage, Cornwall who died on Wednesday May 29, 1940 aged 20. Runnymede Memorial Panel 16.

Flying Officer Graham Lambert Chambers who died on May 31, 1940. Runnymede Memorial Panel 5.

Flying Officer John Kerr-Wilson died on May 29.

242 Squadron

Pilot Officer Dale Fred Jones, son of Luther and Vera Jones of Dinsmore, Saskatchewan, Canada who died on Tuesday May 28, 1940 aged 26. Oostduinkerke Communal Cemetery, Koksijde, Belgium.

Pilot Officer Gordon McKenzie Stewart who died on May 31, 1940. Runnymede Memorial Panel 10.

229 Squadron

Sergeant Stanley Albert Hillman, son of Tom and Lily Hillman of Exmouth, Devon who died on Tuesday May 28, 1940 aged 24. Sage War Cemetery, Germany.

Flight Lieutenant Falcon Nelson Clouston, son of Robert Edmund and Ruby Alexandra Clouston of Upper Moutere, Nelson, New Zealand who died on Wednesday May 29, 1940 aged 27.

Sergeant James Harrison who died on Wednesday May 29. Sage War Cemetery, Germany.

Flight Lieutenant Patrick Browne son of Patrick and Osra Browne, husband of Eileen who died on Wednesday May 29 aged 23. Runnymede Memorial Panel 4.

213 Squadron

Flight Lieutenant Edward George Winning who died on Tuesday May 28, 1940. Cement House Cemetery, Langemark-Poelkapelle, West-V, Belgium.

Flying Officer William Napier Gray, son of William and Jane Gray of Pollokshields, Glasgow, who died on Friday May 31, 1940 aged 22. The Hague General Cemetery, Zuid-Holland, Netherlands.

Sergeant Thomas Boyd, son of James and Ann Boyd of Bramhall, Cheshire who died on Friday May 31, 1940 aged 25. St-Joris Communal Cemetery, Nieuwpoort, West-Vlaanderen, Belgium.

Pilot Officer Stone who died on May 28. Buried at sea by the Royal Navy.

Operation Dynamo

WHEN Hitler invaded the Low Countries on May 10, 1940 he was immediately reprimanded by the diarist of 32 Squadron. "Naughty old Adolf", he wrote. "You know you said you wouldn't". The sentiments behind this delightful RAF flippancy — designed perhaps to defuse the most explosive news of the then fairly uneventful eight-month old war — was born of confidence. The young pilots, average age 22, were quite certain that British forces in France would easily withstand the German assault while the boys from Biggin would help provide protection from the air. Together they would push victoriously into Germany to teach the Hun a lesson. After many weeks of convoy patrols, air combat exercise and target practice the young pilots of the "32nd Pursuit" and their blood brothers, 79 Squadron, were about to meet the hitherto, elusive Luftwaffe. They were ready for a fight and they weren't going to lose their sense of humour.

The German invasion of France and the Low Countries was the signal for four more British fighter squadrons to reinforce the six already in France and, to the delight of the pilots, one of them was to be 79 Squadron — Biggin Hill residents since 1937. Their youngest member, Pilot Officer Donald 'Dimsie' Stones, recalled his exuberant mood on the morning of May 10, 1940 when he heard they were to face the enemy square on. "Having delivered my cases to a part of the aerodrome where all our luggage was to be collected and taken to France by transport aircraft, I made a careful inspection of my Hurricane, the oldest in the Squadron.....I gave it a silent lecture on what I expected from it in the forthcoming battles.... With great excitement I then joined the other pilots in the dispersal hut for a briefing by our Commanding Officer".

Dimsie's boyish exuberance was short-lived. "Have some regard for the pilots who are married and calm down" he was told by the wife of Flying Officer Edward Mitchell. He was not to know, of course, that she would be a Biggin Hill widow before the Battle of Britain began.

Pilot Officer Donald Stones
of 79 Squadron

79 Squadron were based at Merville, a grass aerodrome which looked more like a flying club than an operational base and pilots were billeted with local families in the village. Their place at Biggin Hill was taken by 610 Squadron with the first Spitfires to fly from 'The Bump'. 32 Squadron, under Squadron Leader John Worrall, had no cause to be envious of the Spitfires or of the "good fortune" of 79 Squadron. They were happy with their Hurricanes and the fact that they also were about to enter the fray. In RAF parlance the "balloon had gone up".

Pilot Officer Donald Stones, then just a few weeks short of his 19th birthday, was among the first to fire his guns in the heat of battle on May 14. "With Lew Appleton leading Sgt Cartwright and me we saw below us three Junker 88 bombers and I yelled 'bandits, bandits' on the R/T. They were in a wide V formation and I heard Lew shout "tally ho". Harry and I went after two of them and Lew disappeared presumably after the one which had broken formation. We never saw him again".

ACTION PACKED DAYS: Hurricanes in operations. Actually 73 Sq part of AASF in France. This is May 1940.

Pilot Officer Lew Appleton was the first Biggin Hill pilot to die in France. Within a few hours he had been joined by Pilot Officer Lionel Roger Dorrien-Smith, nephew of Lord Trenchard — the architect and founder of the RAF — whose Hurricane was shot down by German tanks on the Western outskirts of Arras. John Parker was also shot down but, not seriously injured, somehow managed to hitchhike from Arras to Merville.

The pilots of 79 Squadron would not have known that Air Chief Marshal Hugh Dowding was moving heaven and earth to prevent more fighter squadrons — other than those he had already committed — going to France. On that eventful day, May 14, he wrote to the Air Staff: "The Hurricane tap is now turned full on and you will not be able to resist the pressure to send more Hurricanes to France until I have been bled white and am in no condition to withstand the bombing attack which will inevitably be made upon this country as soon as our powers of resistance fall below a level to which we are already perilously close".

On May 15 Dowding attended a Chief of Staffs' meeting with Churchill in the chair in which he successfully pleaded to stem the flow of fighters to France. He also suggested that the bombing war against Germany should begin in order to draw retaliation on Britain and take the pressure off the French. That evening the War Cabinet agreed to send no more fighters to France and to bomb targets in the Ruhr. Historians agree that, with these strong convictions and forthright views, Dowding made it possible to win the Battle of Britain

Several desperate, action-packed days and combats later, the remnants of 79 Squadron were ordered back to Biggin Hill. "We had no more aircraft fit for combat", said PO Stones. "The seven which could make the short flight to England were patched up. The remainder were destroyed by our ground crews who quickly went to the evacuation ports after we left. The British Army now retreating towards Dunkirk had to be rescued or surrender. I remembered how Churchill had inspired us during his visit to the Mess some months earlier. Surely, I thought, he would rescue at least some of our forces from France".

Pilot Officers Donald Stones and Douglas Clift take it easy outside 79 dispersal. Flying Officer Mortimer, the adjutant is standing.

Enemy aircraft recognition was vital for the British pilots. Here, in the 32 Squadron dispersal at Biggin Hill, Group Captain Dick Grice and a young pilot officer meticulously study the latest poster issued by the War Office. The furniture in the hut includes the all-important wireless, wheelback and easy chairs, model aircraft and blinds for the windows.

By now no-one was being frivolous, not even the ebullient diarist of 32 Squadron whose pilots had witnessed a bird's eye view of the military disasters in France. Now using a field at Abbeville as a forward base they had seen the burnt-out Hurricanes of 79 Squadron on the abandoned airfield at Merville as they escorted Blenheim bombers over Northern France in a futile endeavour to stem the German advance. No pilot losses for 32 Squadron but their pilots had shot down nine enemy aircraft for the loss of one Hurricane. The diarist had this to say about the crisis in France. "Every day we land at Abbeville, refuel, hear dreadful stories and get very frightened. We do a patrol, see nothing, feel much better, do another, see nothing, feel much better, return to Biggin Hill, feel grand".

Biggin Hill was now like a giant railway terminus. During three hectic days in May more than 800 airmen were fed, clothed and given shelter and, they too, were made to feel grand. Squadron Leader Kingham and his staff in the Equipment Section stuffed hessian bags with straw donated by local farmers. The makeshift mattresses were then placed in hangars and air raid shelters where the airmen slept as best they could. Weatherwise it was a wonderful warm spring.

As the troops of the British Expeditionary Force and the French First Army pulled back towards the beaches of Dunkirk, Dowding made the controversial decision to send some of his squadrons away for a rest despite the protests from colleagues at Fighter Command. 32 and 79 Squadrons had been in action over France for 16 days. Some members of 79 had slept in barns and shaved in streams. Their dispersal had been little more than a field telephone and a ditch.

For the next few days the satellite airfield at Gravesend was to welcome the Spitfires of

610 Squadron in order to make way for three new Hurricane squadrons, 229 for Home Defence and 213 and 242 as reinforcements for the French campaign. They arrived in good time to learn that their role was to provide air cover for *Operation Dynamo*. As the three squadrons moved quickly into action, casualties, in terms of both men and machines, were to mount daily.

As the first of the troops were being evacuated from the beaches, Squadron Leader 'Bonzo' Franks led 610 Squadron into action on May 27. Flying at 18,000 feet he spotted the black crosses on the wing, the swastika on the tail and the unmistakable shape of a Heinkel squadron some feet below. As Franks and his pilots went in for the kill some 40 Messerschmitt's 109s appeared. Despite odds of more than three to one three 109s were sent spinning down in flames with another three 'probables'. With their ammunition spent the Spitfires returned to Gravesend only to learn that two popular pilots had been lost over the Channel — Flying Officer Albert Medcalf and Sergeant William Medway. The mood that evening at the old flying club, which served as a Mess for the Gravesend pilots, was grim. No-one felt like a party.

Three Biggin Hill squadrons were in the air patrolling the beaches on May 28. In the company of 213 came the mostly Canadian-manned 242 while flying as top cover was 229 — who had returned from a detachment to Kenley — led by Squadron Leader Harold Maguire, a former seaplane pilot. "I remember the excellent ground support given to the squadrons at Biggin", he said, "and the regular intelligence provided at briefings. They knew exactly how serious the situation was for the BEF".

He also remembered Pilot Officer Dale Jones who went down in flames when 242 was bounced by '60-plus 109s'. Pilot Officer Arthur Deacon also crash landed on the beach but, unlike his friend Dale, miraculously survived and was taken to a local hospital. By then Belgium had capitulated so Deacon discharged himself and made his way to the American Legation in Antwerp. They refused the necessary help so Deacon became a prisoner of war.

All three Biggin Hill squadrons suffered losses in the prolonged battles of this morning. 229 lost Sergeant Stanley Hillman who had been with Squadron Leader Maguire when they found themselves out of ammunition, low on fuel and being chased over the sea by a determined Messerschmitt pilot. The 110 pilot picked out Hillman.

213 Squadron lost three pilots. The squadron Adjutant, Flying Officer 'Tim' Winning, failed to get home from Dunkirk during a dawn patrol and was never seen again. Sergeant Lishman was rescued from the sea wounded in the arm and Pilot Officer Stone was picked up from the water and buried at sea by the Navy.

The blackest hour in the entire Dunkirk battle came at dawn on May 29 with two Biggin Hill squadrons in action. Flying lower down at 10,000 feet, 229 Squadron met the Germans first and found themselves heavily outnumbered. Five Hurricanes were shot down, only two pilots managing to bale out. Pilot Officer Patrick Edgar Sempill Browne, having chased and shot down a 109 at sea level, was the first to die. Moments later the squadron lost Sergeant James Harrison and Flight Lieutenant Falcon Clouston.

Flight Lieutenant Clouston's brother, a test pilot at Farnborough and famous before the

Happier days for the pilots and airmen of 610 Squadron. Seven of their dwindling numbers were killed during the Dunkirk evacuation.

war for his record breaking flights to the Cape, Australia and New Zealand, heard the news when the Squadron Leader Harold Maguire flew to Farnborough to say Falcon was missing. "It was a decent thing to do", he said. "I collected my brother's belongings from Biggin Hill a little later and was told that his body had been washed up on the island of Borkum".

As the struggle continued on this tragic morning 610 Squadron — on detachment at Gravesend — were also in trouble, bounced by a squadron of Me 109s. In the terrific dog fight which followed two Spitfires, flown by Flying Officers Gerald Kerr and John Kerr-Wilson, went down in flames. Both pilots were killed. The Biggin Hill squadrons had been joined by two other squadrons on this morning and as they finally disentangled themselves from the Messerschmitts the pilots all knew they had been in a fight. When the bullet-ridden planes finally arrived back at their respective bases ten of their number — one quarter of their force — were missing.

As early evening approached and Stuka dive-bombers continued to attack the ships off Dunkirk, 610 Squadron were turned round, re-fuelled, re-armed and were away again led by 'Bonzo' Franks. 242 Squadron was also in the air again but reduced to five pilots as Pilot Officer Jim Howitt crashed on take-off sustaining injuries which were to lead to his release from the RAF. 213 Squadron was also scrambled.

Flight Lieutenant John Ellis, a Flight Commander of 610 Squadron clearly remembers that terrible evening. "We had only just arrived over the beaches at 12,000 feet", he said, "when we were fired on either by the Royal Navy ships or from AA guns on shore. Sergeant Peter Jenkins, my number two, was immediately hit in the port wing, half of which was blown off. The aircraft went down inverted and I saw Jenkins bale out. He landed in the sea about two miles from a destroyer which I flew over towards the parachute in the sea. The only response of the destroyer was to open fire on me with Bofors guns. So I had to withdraw and leave Jenkins to his fate. He was never seen again".

Another outstanding pilot lost because the Army and the Navy did not know the difference between a Spitfire and a Ju87.

Squadron Leader Alexander Lumsden Franks was also missing after this sortie. Affectionately known as 'Bonzo' this large cheerful Irishman was a great character with a fund of marvellous Irish stories for the boys in the Mess. "No one saw him go down", said John Ellis, "but later on we heard that his body had been washed up on one of the small islands along the Dutch coast where he is buried".

The tragedy of losing a senior officer and a sergeant pilot brought down by "friendly" fire was further compounded by the news that Sergeant Wilson of 610 Squadron had also lost the wing of his Spitfire and was missing. Some days later he appeared in the Mess and apologised for his absence. "I splashed down in the Channel", he said "and was picked up by a destroyer". He disembarked at Dover and made his way to Gravesend.

Each day saw many more thousands of troops brought back to the Kentish ports but the number of Hurricanes and Spitfires was dwindling fast, a harsh fact that provoked much comment in the Mess. Talk also centred around the extraordinary scenes in the Channel. One pilot put it quite succinctly. "I saw", he said, "the Brighton Belle and the little paddle steamers and the sort of cheerful little boats you see calling at coastal towns on a Sunday. Hundreds of boats! Fishing boats and motor boats and Thames river craft and strings of dinghies being towed by bigger boats".

The reinforcement squadrons were decimated. No 242, the all-Canadian volunteer squadron, soon to become famous under Squadron Leader Douglas Bader, were in action in France from June 20. From early on Flying Officer Russ Wiens had noted; "The war in the air makes shows like Dawn Patrol seem like Sunday School". Between May and June every pilot of Flying Officer rank, all middle echelon officers were lost over enemy territory. Biggin Hill was the ultimate line of retreat for 242 Squadron and here Pilot Officer Don Howitt spent almost all his time re-addressing the letters and luggage of those who had gone missing.

For 213 Squadron the challenge was insurmountable. By May 31 a new Commanding Officer, Squadron Leader H.D.McGregor DSO from New Zealand was in charge. McGregor, who had been in the RAF since 1928, did not take over immediately as Humphrey Jones was reluctant to hand over his unit "until the Dunkirk show is over". On that morning they were soon heavily engaged by the Luftwaffe. Several were shot down including Flying Officer William Gray and Sergeant Thomas Boyd who may have parachuted inland into German-held territory. They were never seen again.

When the surviving pilots of 213 eventually returned to base they found Edward Jones in his office writing letters to next-of-kin. He was told that four or five more pilots were missing and one of them was Squadron Leader McGregor who had borrowed Jones' flying

CRASH COURSE: Jack 'Beacon' Rose of 32 Squadron with a few Polish pilots who flew from Biggin Hill. Among them were Pilot Officers Pfeiffer, Wlasnowalski and Pniak, better known as 'Fifi', 'Vodka' and Cognac', Janicki and Korber 'Cobra'. In white overalls is Jan Falowski. They arrived at Biggin having flown only the bi-planes of the Polish Air Force and had to be given a brief conversion course on Hurricanes. Picture taken at Acklington Oct. 1940.

helmet, parachute and Hurricane.

Some days later Biggin Hill heard that McGregor had been pulled out of the sea by a destroyer still clutching the parachute and helmet. He returned to The Bump and went on to command 213 in the Battle of Britain.

On this day (May 31) Blue Section of 610 Squadron lost Flying Officers Lambert Chambers and Peter Keighley who managed to get his crippled Spitfire two thirds of the way across the Channel before his engine packed up. Chambers was killed but Keighley was picked up by one of the "little boats".

The last Biggin Hill pilot to die at Dunkirk was Pilot Officer Gordon Stewart of 242 who was shot down in a dog-fight with 30 Messerschmitts. He had only just joined the squadron and that is possibly why his name is missing from the Reredos in the Chapel.

For nine long, exhausting days the young pilots of Biggin Hill had experienced the appalling noise of battle and seen their friends die in surroundings which, hitherto, had been totally unfamiliar. Scrambled at dawn they were back at Biggin Hill in time for breakfast and a quick nap. Scrambled again in the morning they saw the great pall of black smoke spiralling into the sky from the burning port of Dunkirk. Scrambled in the early evening they saw large numbers of Junkers and Heinkels drop their bombs on the beaches where the troops were waiting.

Between them the pilots of Biggin Hill engaged in *Operation Dynamo* claimed 56 enemy aircraft destroyed and 33 damaged. In one historic piece of action Sergeant Sammy Butterfield of 213 Squadron accounted for two 109s, one 110 and a Junkers 88 and, earlier in the

'John' Parker, the keeper and illustrator of 79 Squadron's unofficial diary, was shot down by German tanks near Arras. Uninjured he ran into the outskirts of Arras where he met British troops who had no idea the tanks were just minutes away. From there he hitch-hiked to the coast and found a ship for England. Back at Biggin Hill, and no worse for his hair-raising adventures in France, Parker decorated the walls of the dispersal hut with drawings in coloured chalk of near-nude chorus girls. One of them, which his fellow pilots thought a magnificent specimen with an "air cooled chest" wore only a short pair of French knickers attached by drawing pins to the wall. A visiting VIP of high rank fell into the trap when unendurable curiosity forced him to lift the knickers. There was a card bearing the message: "You have a dirty mind. Put 2s 6d in the beer kitty!".

morning a Heinkel III, before he too was shot down. He was still counting his tally when he was picked up by the paddle steamer, the *Sundown*, reaching the Kent coast by 1800 hours. Butterfield made it home to fly again two days later but for many pilots the war was over and the only future was long frustrating days in PoW camps in Germany. Sergeant Butterfield met his death in combat over Portland on August 11, 1940 at the age of 27.

By June 4 the great evacuation was over, the final patrol being provided by a single flight of 242 Squadron from Biggin Hill. Airborne over Dunkirk the pilots saw the abandoned, burnt-out vehicles littering the beaches and the promenades — thousands upon thousands of them. They saw smoke billowing from the still-burning port and they saw a lone yacht with a white sail moving towards the open sea. The streets of Dunkirk were deserted. No-one moved.

As the casualties, in terms of men and machines, mounted daily the news of old friends was similarly disquieting. The ill-fated B flight of 56 Squadron, detached from North Weald,. had been written off. 501 Squadron were left with three planes. The Hornchurch-based 92 Squadron, soon to be billeted at The Bump, was down to 14 out of 26 pilots. The dilemma was plain. The struggle in France followed by the evacuation had left Dowding with only 283 serviceable planes for the nation's defence. It prompted General Sir Hastings Ismay, assistant secretary to the War Cabinet, to give the understatement of the year. "The future of Western civilisation", he said, "rests on the shoulders of the Royal Navy and about 5,000 pink-cheeked young pilots".

But where is Jimmy Davies?

WHEN the young American airman, Pilot Officer Jimmy Davies, sighted a 'flying pencil'— a Dornier 17 — making a weather reconnaissance over the Channel on the morning of November 21, 1939 it may have fleetingly crossed his mind that here was an opportunity to make a significant personal contribution to the history of RAF Biggin Hill.

But any such thoughts would have been over in a flash as Davies and Flight Sergeant Brown, also of 79 Squadron in another Hurricane, switched on their gun sights, twisted the safety rings from 'safe' to 'fire' and closed on their quarry from the height advantage of 3,000 feet.

Firing the Browning machine guns from something like 600 yards Davies scored a direct hit and saw the Dornier twist onto its back as it spiralled out of control. He followed it to sea level where it struck the waves with an enormous explosion.

The party that night at the White Hart, Brasted was a riotous affair. After dreary weeks of idleness, cruising the skies between Hythe and Ramsgate like taxis looking for fares and stooging up and down the south coast in dirty weather, Biggin Hill had made a "kill" and the young American pilot was the hero to be toasted.

A little more than six months later, June 27, 1940, the same group of pilots — minus a few friends — were gathered in the White Hart once more for another celebration. King George VI had visited Biggin Hill that day to pin the DFC on Michael Crossley, Victor Daw and Grubby Grice of 32 Squadron and Donald Stones of 79 Squadron.

The King had decided that he would not command the pilots to attend the Palace but would take the unprecedented step of decorating them on the field of battle. He was more than an hour late. Delayed by air raids alert en route he eventually walked onto the parade ground where the award-winning pilots were at attention and the whole station standing by. "Dimsie" Stones remembers the hour. "Having pinned on the DFCs and presented a DFM to Sergeants Whitby and Cartwright, His Majesty asked why there was one DFC lying pathetically alone on the cushion. We told him that it belonged to Pilot Officer James Davies who had been shot

Flying Officer Jimmy Davies (with polo neck jumper) in France with French pilots. As acting A' Flight commander during the Dunkirk evacuation he saw much action. On June 27, while returning from escorting a formation of Blenheims to France, he was bounced by Me 109s and failed to return

HONOURED: King George VI presents a Distinguished Flying Cross during one of his visits to Biggin Hill. Identification of this pilot would be welcomed.

down that morning — missing, believed killed. The King was visibly moved".

Since making Biggin Hill's first kill Davies had added five more certainties to his score and had experienced a breathtaking time in France, fighting against grotesque odds, showing great qualities of leadership and exceptional courage. Right up to the end of the ceremony everyone hoped he would re-appear, apologising with his distinctive American stammer for being late on parade. It was not to be. Davies was dead. His best friend, 'Dimsie' Stones said: "After the King had left there was only a low-key celebration in the Mess but in the evening we cheered up a bit and went down to the White Hart where the wonderful landlords, Teddy and Kath Preston pushed out the boat. It was our refuge".

Kath Preston also remembers that party. "Dimsie was delighted to serve under Jimmy in France and so, on hearing the news of his demise, he joined other pilots in the saloon bar to drown his sorrows. He was a newcomer to us at the time but became, and remains, a great friend".

Acting Flight Lieutenant Davies was born in the USA of Welsh parents, Mr and Mrs Ashley Davies, residing in Bernardsville, New Jersey. He joined the RAF as a British citizen and joined 79 Squadron on the unit's formation in 1937. His parents later moved back to Wales and were living at Cwmoernant, Carmarthen in 1940 when they received the news that Jimmy was missing, believed killed on June 28, 1940. The tension was unbearable as they waited for the letter to say he was recovering in hospital from his wounds or that he was a prisoner in Germany or that he had made his own way back to Biggin Hill. The hope was in vain. Jimmy Davies was dead.

On July 12, 1940 the confirmation that a young pilot from the town was missing, believed killed, appeared in the *Carmarthen Gazette* which also said that his belongings had been sent by his Commanding Officer to his parents. The newspaper also published a letter from a young pilot to his mother written shortly before his death. It read:

"If I should die you must not grieve for me......I have no fear of death, only a queer elation. I would have it no other way. The universe is so vast and so ageless that the life of one man can only be justified by the measure of his sacrifice. We are sent into this world to acquire a personality and character to take with us. It can never be taken away from us. Those who just eat and sleep prosper and procreate, are no better than animals; if all their lives they are at peace".

This amazing letter so simple and direct in its wording and yet so uplifting in its outlook was typical of the reaction by so many young pilots to the prospect of death. Jimmy Davies was 23.

Having heard about the death of Davies, King George asked to be taken to 79 Squadron's dispersal point. Pilot Officer John Parker joined him in the royal car and showed him the aircraft in which he had been shot up. His Majesty then spent some time in the dispersal hut with the new CO, Squadron Leader John Joslin.

4

The Battle of Britain

Fifty four pilots from seven squadrons, based at Biggin Hill, died between July 10 and October 31, 1940 — the period which historians decreed should officially be known as *The Battle of Britain*. It was, without doubt, the greatest air battle in modern history and the battleground was the skies above Kent and the orchards, fields and villages below, where hundreds of aircraft crashed. The average age of the young pilots flying from Biggin Hill during that summer of 1940 was 24. The youngest to die was 19-year-old Keith Gillman of 32 Squadron whose story is told in this chapter. Six others, Pilot Officers Males, Williams, Hill, Sergeant Allton, Flight Lieutenant Paterson and Sub Lieutenant Bulmer — on loan by the Fleet Air Arm to 32 Squadron — were under 21. They were unmarried, interested in fast cars and girls and willing to die for their country.

The pages that follow briefly tell the story of those squadrons during the Battle with an emphasis on those who gave their lives. Little wonder that Brian Kingcome said he "walked with ghosts" when he revisited his old station.

Oh! I have slipped the surly bonds of earth
and danced the skies on laughter-silvered wings;
Sunward I've climbed and joined the tumbling mirth
of sun — split clouds and done a hundred things
you have not dreamed of — wheeled and soared
and swung high in the sunlit silence.
Hov'ring there I've chased the shouting wind along,
and flung my eager craft through footless halls of air.
Up, up the long delirious, burning blue,
I've topped the windswept heights with easy grace
where never lark or even eagle flew
— and while with silent lifting mind I've trod
the high untrespassed sanctity of space, put out my hand
and touched the face of God.

Pilot Officer Gillespie Magee Jnr 412 Squadron RCAF
killed December 11, 1941

The Squadrons at Biggin Hill...

RAF Biggin Hill was home to the Biggin Hill Sector Operations Room and staff and the following squadrons during the Battle of Britain. On occasions some were sent away for a brief rest or detached at the forward stations. Here are the principal dates:

- No 32 Hurricane Squadron - from September 1932 to August 31 1940 (with detachments to Manston, Gravesend, Wittering for rest.

- No 79 Hurricane Squadron - from March 1937 to September 8, 1940 (with detachments to Manston, Hawkinge, Merville & Digby).

- No 610 Spitfire Squadron - from May 10, 1940 to August 31, 1940 (with detachments to Gravesend).

- No 72 Spitfire Squadron - from August 31, 1940 to October 13, 1940 (with detachment to Croydon).

- No 92 Spitfire Squadron - from September 8, 1940 to September 25, 1941 (with detachment to Manston).

- No 141 Defiant Squadron - from September 13, 1940 to September 18, 1940.

- No 74 Spitfire Squadron - from October 13, 1940 to February 1941.

...And those who died

The RAF pilots who lost their lives while based at Biggin Hill during the Battle of Britain.

32 Squadron

Sub Lieutenant (FAA) Geoffrey Bulmer, aged 20 who was shot down in combat over Dover on July 20, 1940. Remembered on Fleet Air Arm Memorial at Lee-on-Solent.

Pilot Officer Keith Gillman of Dover. Failed to return from combat off Dover on August 25, 1940. Runnymede Memorial Panel 8.

79 Squadron

Sergeant Henry Bolton, 21, from West Hartlepool. Shot down in combat over Kenley on August 31, 1940. Buried in Stranton Cemetery, Hartlepool.

Sergeant John Wright, 24, wounded in action over Biggin Hill on September 4 and crashed at Surbiton. Died the next day. Buried in New Kilpatrick Cemetery.

Flying Officer George Peters, 27, and **Pilot Officer Stanislaw Piatkowski**, 28, were both killed during the Battle of Britain, soon after leaving Biggin Hill for Pembrey. Both of their names are on the reredos at St George's Chapel, Biggin Hill.

610 Squadron

Pilot Officer Kenneth Cox, 24, shot down and killed in combat with Me109s over Dover on August 28, 1940. His Spitfire crashed into a house at Stelling Minnis. His ashes were scattered at Old Castle Bromwich aerodrome.

Sergeant Sydney Ireland, 22, crashed during dog fight practice in Titsey Park, Surrey on July 12, 1940. Site excavated years later by London Air Museum.

Pilot Officer Peter Litchfield, 25, was shot down over the Channel and reported 'missing' on July 18, 1940. He is remembered on the Runnymede Memorial, Panel 9.

Sergeant Edward Manton, 25, of Bebington, Cheshire was shot down and killed in combat over Mayfield on August 28, 1940. His Spitfire crashed at the Great Wigsell Estate, Hurst Green. He is buried at Hawkhurst Cemetery.

Sergeant William Neville, 26, of Shepperton, Middlesex was reported 'missing' following a patrol off Calais on August 11, 1940. He is remembered on the Runnymede Memorial, Panel 17.

Squadron Leader Andrew Smith, 34, stalled attempting to land at Hawkinge on July 25, 1940 and crashed into a disused engine testing shed. He is buried in St Peter's Churchyard, Delamere, Cheshire.

Flight Sergeant John Tanner, 25, failed to return from a patrol over the Channel on August 11, 1940. He is buried in Calais Southern Cemetery, France.

Flight Lieutenant William Warner, 21, failed to return from combat over Dungeness on August 16, 1940. Remembered on the Runnymede Memorial, Panel 5.

Pilot Officer Frank Webster, 26, crashed in flames attempting to land at Hawkinge on July 28, 1940. He is buried in Sandown Cemetery, Isle of Wight.

92 Squadron

Sergeant Leslie Allton, 20, killed on October 19, 1940 when he crashed at Tuesnoad Farm, Smarden. The site of the crash was excavated in the late 1970s when the propeller, engine and other items were recovered. Allton is buried in the Oasten Road Cemetery, Nuneaton.

Pilot Officer John Bryson, 27, shot down and killed on September 24, 1940 near North Weald. He is buried at St Andrew's Churchyard, North Weald Bassett, Essex.

Flying Officer John Drummond DFC, 21, collided with Pilot Officer Williams over Tangmere on October 10, 1940. He baled out too low and was killed. He is buried in Thornton Garden of Rest, Lancashire.

Pilot Officer Harry Edwards, 24, was shot down and killed on September 11, 1940. His Spitfire crashed into a wood at Evegate Manor Farm, Smeeth. Edwards is buried in Folkestone New Cemetery.

Sergeant Peter Eyles, 24, was shot down into the Channel off Dungeness on September 20, 1940. He is remembered on the Runnymede Memorial, Panel 14.

Sergeant Eric Frith, 26, shot down on October 9, 1940, badly burned. His Spitfire crashed at The Ridgeway, Smeeth and he was admitted to Willesborough Hospital where he died from his injuries on October 17. He is buried in Oxford Cemetery, Botley, Berkshire.

Pilot Officer Frederick Hargreaves, 21, failed to return from a combat over Dungeness on September 11, 1940 and was reported 'missing'. His Spitfire crashed into the sea. He is remembered on Runnymede Memorial, Panel 8.

Pilot Officer Howard Hill, 20, crashed into high tree tops at West Houghton, Kent on September 20, 1940. His Spitfire remained undiscovered for a month. Hill is buried in Folkestone New Cemetery.

Sergeant Trevor Oldfield, 21, shot down and killed on September 27. His Spitfire crashed at Fullers House, Hesketh Park, Dartford and exploded on impact. Oldfield is buried in St Stephen's Churchyard, Chertsey, Surrey.

Sergeant Kenneth Parker, 25, shot down over the Thames Estuary on October 15, 1940. His Spitfire is believed to have crashed in the sea off Hoo Marina. He is buried in Terschelling General Cemetery, Netherlands.

The RAF pilots who lost their lives while based at Biggin Hill during the Battle of Britain.

Flight Lieutent J.A. Paterson MBE, 20, was shot down in flames on September 27, 1940. His Spitfire crashed and burned out in flames in Sparepenny Lane, Farningham. Paterson is buried in Star Lane Cemetery, St Mary Cray.

Flying Officer Aberconway Pattinson, 21, killed over Hawkinge on October 12, 1940. His Spitfire crashed and burned out in Bartholomews Wood, Postling Wents. He is buried in Parkstone Cemetery, Poole.

Pilot Officer Desmond Williams, 20, collided with Flying Officer Drummond on October 10, 1940 over Tangmere. Williams is buried in London Road Cemetery, Salisbury.

74 Squadron

Sergeant David Ayers, 26, baled into the sea during a routine patrol on September 23, 1940 over Southwold and was drowned. His body was recovered on October 4 and he was buried at Ipswich Cemetery.

Pilot Officer F.W. Buckland who collided with Pilot Officer Douglas Hastings during practice attacks on October 8 1940.

Pilot Officer Donald Cobden, 26, shot down and killed on August 11 some 12 miles east of Clacton. His body was recovered by the Germans and he was buried at Ostende Communal Cemetery.

Sergeant Frederick Eley, 21, shot down in flames off Folkestone Pier on July 31 Troops, sailors and boatmen pulled the Spitfire ashore and his body was recovered. His is buried in St Margeret's Churchyard, Wrenbury cum Frith, Cheshire.

Pilot Officer Harold Gunn, 27, also shot down on July 31, 1940 off Folkestone Pier.

Pilot Officer Douglas Hastings, 25, collided with Pilot Officer Buckland during practice attacks on October 9, 1940. His Spitfire crashed, inverted and he was killed south of Green Farm, Gillingham. He is

buried in Preston Cemetery, Tynemouth.

Sergeant Thomas Kirk, 22, shot down over Maidstone on October 20, 1940. Admitted to Preston Hall Hospital and died from his wounds on July 22, 1941. He is buried at St Oswald's churchyard, East Harlsey, Yorkshire.

Flying Officer Alan Ricalton, 26, shot down and killed over Maidstone on October 17, 1940. His Spitfire crashed near Hollingbourne. He is buried in Sittingbourne Cemetery.

Flying Officer Peter St John, 23, killed in combat on October 22, 1940. His Spitfire crashed at South Nutfield, Surrey. He is buried in St Mary's churchyard, Amersham, Bucks.

Sergeant John Scott, 22, killed in combat over Maidstone on October 27, 1940. His Spitfire crashed and exploded at Dundas Farm, Elsted. He is buried at Alperton Burial Ground, Wembley, Middlesex.

72 Squadron

Pilot Officer Herbert Case, 24, dropped out of formation and crashed at Capel-le-Ferne, Folkestone on October 12. Buried at St Nicholas Church, Withycombe, Somerset.

Pilot Officer Paul Davies-Cooke, 23, shot down over Sevenoaks on September 27. He baled out but fell dead near Hayes Station. His Spitfire crashed into Nos 70-72 Queensway, West Wickham. He is buried in Flintshire.

Sergeant Malcolm Gray, 20, shot down and killed on September 5. His Spitfire crashed into Elham Park Wood. He is buried at Fulford Cemetery, North Yorkshire.

Pilot Officer Dennis Holland, 23, shot down over Canterbury on September 20. Died soon after admission to hospital. His Spitfire crashed at Stiff Street, Sittingbourne. He is buried in St Andrew's Churchyard,

Chaddlesworth, Berkshire.

Pilot Officer Edward Males, 20, shot down and killed in combat over Sevenoaks on Sepember 27. His Spitfire crashed at Stepney. He is buried in Great Northern London Cemetery.

Flying Officer Oswald St John Pigg, 22. His Spitfire crashed and burned out on Elvey Farm, Pluckley on September 1. He is buried at Durham.

Flying Officer Edgar Wilcox, 23, shot down and killed over Dungeness on August 31. His Spitfire crashed at Checkenden Farm, Staplehurst. He is buried in Staplehurst.

Pilot Officer Douglas Winter, 26, killed when he attempted to bale out too low over Elham on September 5. He is buried in Harton Cemetery, South Shields.

141 Squadron

In an operation known as 'Slaughter of the Innocents' four pilots and six air gunners of 141 Squadron were killed on July 19, 1940. Flying from Hawkinge in the Biggin Hill sector they were in Boulton Paul two-seater Defiants and the Squadron had no operational experience. Assigned to patrol a line south of Folkestone at around 5,000 feet they were bounced by Bf 109s who came up underneath them and sent six aircraft crashing in flames into the sea. Those killed were **Pilot Officer John Kemp** and gunner **Crombie, Pilot Officer Howley** and gunner **Sgt Curley, Pilot Officer Kidson** and **Sergeant Atkins, Flight Lieutenant Donald** and **Pilot Officer Hamilton.** Pilot Officer Gardener managed to bale out but his gunner **Pilot Officer Dudley Slatter** was lost. Pilot Officer McDougal crash-landed at Hawkinge but **Sgt John Wise** drowned in the sea.

The 32nd Pursuit

WHEN the great air battle, later to be called the Battle of Britain, began in July 1940 the pilots of 32 Squadron were under no illusion as to the size of their task ahead. For the first time since the Napoleonic Wars an invasion was imminent. A few miles across the Channel the Germans were reorganising three immense Luftwaffeflotten, totalling some 3,500 aircraft on 400 aerodromes spread out from France to Norway. The Army was in disarray and the RAF outnumbered. The fiercest fighting would be borne by No 11 Group defending London and the South East. Biggin Hill, like all senior sector stations, desperately needed more Hurricanes and Spitfires.

In fact the aircraft factories were producing more fighters and fresh pilots were coming from the training units to replace those lost during the Battle of France and Dunkirk. A Belgian and two Poles were among those welcomed by the 32nd Pursuit. The former, Pilot Officer the Comte de Grunne, was an ex-Messerschmitt pilot who had flown with Hitler's Condor Legion in Spain. The Poles had only ever flown bi-planes of the Polish Air Force.

But the pilots were defiant and so were the people. Anthony Eden's 'broomstick army' was almost 500,000 strong. A memo to the War Cabinet by the thriller writer Dennis Wheatley had been adopted and country signposts, village signs and street names stored away to fool the potential invaders. They certainly foxed most of the 117,000 London evacuees, some of whom had been sent to 'safe havens' such as Dover and Folkestone!

As Hitler originally nominated August 10th — Eagle Day — in which to commence the annihilation of the Royal Air Force as a preliminary to the invasion, the Luftwaffe began to probe Britain's defences with tip and run raids on the Channel ports and coastal convoys. 32 Squadron were in action throughout July and on the 8th, before the Battle of Britain officially began, lost two Pilot Officers — Geoffrey Cherrington and New Zealander Kenneth Kirkcaldie who was 28. Cherrington was buried at Ste Marie Cemetery, Le Havre, Seine Maritime and Kirkcaldie at Houville-en-Vexin Churchyard in Eure, close to where they fell.

32 Squadron lost a third pilot on July 20. Their diary for that day reads: "...Later we intercepted, without any exaggeration a total of at least 20,000 assorted Huns. The following tipped stuff into the Drink: Hector, Pete B, Sgt Higgins, Humph and Red Knight. The Mandarin converted three non-smoking Ju 87s into smoking 87s but earned the attention of at least four squadrons of 109s to such an extent that he just couldn't make the drome. He force-landed in a field, 2532 caught fire and burnt out..."

The Red Knight was Flight Lieutenant Mike Crossley, the Mandarin was Squadron Leader John Worrall. The diary did not reveal that Sub Lieutenant Geoffrey Bulmer was missing after that interception and Sgt William Higgins injured.

Bulmer, in fact, was a naval pilot who had been loaned to 32 Squadron a month earlier. He had served on several battleships including HMS Pembroke before taking a fighter course, converting to Hurricanes and joining the boys at Biggin Hill. The 20-year-old pilot was shot down by Oberleutnant Priller in combat over Dover on July 20. He baled out in the sea but was drowned.

Geoffrey Bulmer's death, the intensity of the Luftwaffe attacks and the long hours of those sunny July days made the strain almost intolerable for the pilots of 32 Squadron.

Often scrambled three times a day they were usually woken at 3.45 am to 'be on readiness at Hawkinge 0500 hours'. At the dispersal area they would be greeted by the fitters and riggers who would report on the state of the Hurricanes. When the order came to scramble the pilot would sprint to his machine, clip on his parachute, lower himself into the constricted space of the cockpit and then roll across the field in a loose vic of three behind the Flight Commander. They could be airborne within two minutes.

The first real "blitzy day", as Squadron Leader Mike Crossley described it, came on August 12 when Hawkinge "copped a packet". The next was August 15 which saw some of the heaviest fighting of the entire battle. Apart from the loss of a few aircraft the greatest scare to those in the Ops Room came with a screaming announcement over the R/T — "Christ Almighty. They've got Grubby". Grubby Grice had baled into the sea off Harwich and was in the Shotley naval hospital suffering from burns much to the relief of his fiancée, Pam Beecroft— a WAAF cypher officer at Biggin Hill.

Three days later, some hours after the nasal crowings of Lord Haw Haw had claimed that "the mighty Luftwaffe would soon be turning its attention to Kenley and Biggin Hill" came the order that every pilot of 32 Squadron expected: "Jacko Squadron, scramble, scramble. Protect base".

Some 50 plus 'bandits' were approaching from the direction of Tunbridge Wells and opposing them were 12 Hurricanes of 32 Squadron, the faster Spitfires of 610 and, on his own, Pilot Officer 'Polly' Flinders in charge of the training Hurricane who was not going to miss the show.

Outnumbered five to one, the Red Knight took his Squadron into a head on attack over Sevenoaks. Dornier 215s, Junker 88s and Messerschmitt 109s scattered as the Hurricanes cut right through the middle in a classsic interception. As bombs dropped on the station revenge came in many forms. de Grunne, bagged two probables, Wlasnowalski, Pete Brothers and Flinders claimed a Dornier 215 each. A Junkers came down in flames at Ide Hill, a Dornier crash landed at Leaves Green and another one hit the earth at Hurst Green. Shag Eckford selected a Dornier and Crossley a Ju 88.

When the evening scramble came 32 Squadron were down to nine pilots but they still managed to shoot down five escorting 109s and Squadron Leader Crossley brought his own score to an incredible 21.

Since the great battle began they had still lost just one pilot in Geoffrey Bulmer but Pilot Officers Pain and de Grunne, Flight Lieutenant Russell, Sergeants Henson and Pearce were slightly wounded and the Red Knight Crossley was making his way home from Gillingham where he had baled out following a glycol leak.

There was to be just one last patrol before 32 Squadron said goodbye to its home of eight years. On August 25, with their nerves strained to a point where life and death seemed as one and desperately in need of that well-deserved rest at Acklington, Mike Crossley led his boys over Dover to intercept a dozen Dornier 215s escorted by 36 Me109s.

Two popular young pilots did not return, Pilot Officers Jack 'Beacon' Rose and Keith Gillman. Rose, who had just returned to 32 Squadron, was picked up alive from the Channel.

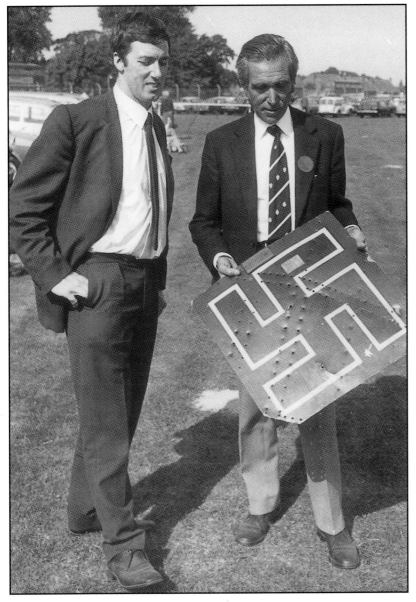

The German Luftwaffe pilot, Rudolph Lamberty, whose Dornier was shot down on August 18, 1940 — allegedly by the Home Guard but in reality by ground defences and air attacks — returned to Biggin Hill to be presented with the swastika from the aircraft. On the left is Alan Killen who, after acquiring pieces of Lamberty's aircraft, researched its history and traced the pilot.

Gillman, just 19 years old, was reported missing. He had died in the sea not far from the town where he was born and went to school — the fifth member of the 32nd Pursuit to give his life.

By now this Biggin Hill based Hurricane squadron had shot down 102 enemy aircraft — the most of any squadron in Fighter Command.

32 Squadron never returned to Biggin Hill after August 25 but they lost many more of the pilots who had flown during the Battle of Britain including the Belgian, Hemricourt de Grunne, Pilot Officers Boleslaw Wlasnowalski, John Humpherson and Herbert Black, who died in Ashford Hospital from burns with his wife by his side.

Before the Battle ended in October, Norman Heywood was hit by anti-aircraft fire at Folkestone and Sergeant Bernard Henson was shot down by Adolf Galland, who was to become a post-war visitor to the White Hart Inn at Brasted. Others to die were Jan Pfeiffer, who was lost in the sea with his Mosquito and Stanislaw Czternastek who collided with another aircraft while returning to Kenley.

The Squadron's fourth Polish pilot, Zbigniew Janicki survived until May 1944 when he was killed flying a Thunderbolt with 61 Squadron USAAF. In that year Belgian pilot Eugene Segers died trying to destroy a doodlebug over Uckfield.

Because of their length of service at Biggin Hill it is possible that the ghosts of 32 Squadron are the more frequent visitors to the station. Shall we ever know?

ONE OF THE FEW: This famous portrait of Keith Gillman was used on the front cover of the **Battle of Britain Then and Now** *as the epitome of The Few. The photograph was taken at Hawkinge in July, a little more than a month before he went missing over the Channel. Today members of the Life Guard Association compete for the Gillman Trophy in their annual swimming competition. The trophy was presented by Keith's mother and father who lived at Dover. Gillman is remembered on Panel 8 of the Runnymede Memorial.*

Pilot Officer is our constant companion

KEITH Gillman, the young pilot officer who ditched in the sea about 10 miles off Dover and drowned has become the pivotal figure in a spiritual experience that almost defies belief. According to a Kentish couple this brave young man who flew out of Hawkinge airfield and out of this world on the evening of August 25, 1940 is their constant companion. He is with them all the time — "materialising" they say "through extraordinary metaphysical encounters".

The couple are Nick Gilman and Thea Keeler. Nick shares the same surname as the young airman but spells it with one L rather than two. He says he is not conventionally related to Keith but believes he is spiritually part of him like fingers are to a glove. "In a way", he said, "Keith has been treating Thea and I as if we were his parents or older siblings".

Nick Gilman who was born in Brixton and Thea who lived at West Malling in a former RAF home close to the airfield first met at a meeting to discuss the phenomenon of Crop Circles. The date was August 25 — the anniversary of Keith Gillman's death. "Together with the five other people present at that meeting", said Nick, "we decided to form a spiritual group and very quickly began to experience similar happenings — extraordinary coincidences. We knew we had met before and were a soul group who were meant to be together again. All of us had connections with West Malling. None of us liked being under water. The name Guy Gibson kept cropping up. It occurred to us that perhaps we could be

A painting by Brian Petch of a Hurricane lying on the sea bed.

the reincarnated crew of a bomber that had crashed in the sea".

As time went on that feeling changed. "On one occasion I remember looking through the exhibits and memorials at Manston Museum", said Nick, "and was suddenly overcome with a feeling of sadness about the waste of young lives. I was crying and for a moment I lost it. Thea then said to me: 'Look at that photograph above your head'. It was a picture of Pilot Officer Keith Gillman".

Said Nick: "Now his name began to crop up all the time. I saw his inscription on the Runnymede Memorial. I caught the last few seconds of a war film on television and there was his name again. I saw his photograph on the front cover of the Battle of Britain book. I saw also a painting by Brian Petch of a Hurricane sitting on the seabed and I bought a copy.

"All my life I had been fascinated with RAF slang — the mannerisms, attitudes and the speak of Battle of Britain pilots. Now I began to make the connection. I could smell cigarette tobacco on my clothes and I have never smoked. Someone revived my old nickname, Jacko. Jacko, I discovered, was the code name for 32 Squadron".

Nick Gilman, confused and quite bewildered by this psychic onslaught of both the soul and mind decided to sell his flat and possessions. Thea gave up her business and the couple agreed to live each day as it came. They bought a camper van and went to Hawkinge, the airfield from where Keith made his last flight.

"We were devastated", said Nick. "Greedy farmers had sold that famous airfield for homes. That is where people like Keith Gillman gave up their lives to help win the Battle of Britain. That is where they posed for the famous Fox photographs of 1940 which you can find in all books about the Battle".

There were more curious links. The name Gibson again cropped up and so did those of Hugh Dowding and Keith Park whom Nick and Thea began to think of as spiritually the same person — brought together to win the Battle of Britain. They were drawn to Addington Park in Kent where RAF officers were billeted during the war. It is now the Seekers' Trust Centre, a place for prayer and healing. They discovered that Lord Dowding was a spirituralist. It was all tying up.

"I decided that Keith Gillman was not me but a younger friend and decided to find out more. I came across conflicting reports. Some say he was shot down 10 miles off Dover and others say three miles from St Margaret's Bay. I visited the South Foreland lighthouse at St Margaret's Bay, first buying the necessary visitor ticket. I looked at the number, 2508. Keith was killed on 25-08-40.

The couple then sought the help of a channeller (a medium) who said she saw visions of a Roman Road but little else. Thea bought a compass and drew circles on an Ordnance Survey map to find out exactly where Keith had crashed. First a circle that went 10 miles out to sea and then one of three miles out. The second took in an old Roman Road that the channeller had visualised. They crossed at a certain point and to Nick and Thea's surprise this was right over the Channel Tunnel workings where the tunnel veered off at right angles under the sea. This was almost certainly the spot where Keith Gillman had drowned.

Nick Gilman and Thea Keeler at Samphire Ho, below the White Cliffs of Dover, at the spot where they threw the wreath into the sea.

"Thea and I went back to Hawkinge", said Nick, "to recreate the Fox photographs taken on July 29, 1940. With a compass and by checking the positions of the chimney pots in the distance we found the exact position where the pilots of 32 Squadron lay on the ground on that beautiful summer morning exactly 60 years earlier. It was a magic moment....and then Keith Gillman spoke to me — not literally — but in my head I heard his voice saying that this was the pilot's land. I heard him telling me that they were still fighting a battle but this one was against jingoistic greed and avarice. We died, he said, not for authority, but so our loved ones could enjoy the future..."

On that 60th anniversary of Keith's death Nick Gilman and Thea decided to throw a wreath into the sea at the exact spot where the Hurricane pilot had died. The coastguard said the nearest they could get to it was a place called Samphire Ho, the land made up of chalk and marl excavated from under the sea to create the tunnel. "We made a biodegradable wreath", said Nick, "and threw it over the sea wall. It landed the right way up and floated out to sea towards the spot where we believed Keith had crashed. It seemed the right thing to do".

That is where this incredible story, for the time being, ends. Has Keith Gillman adopted Nick and Thea as his parents, or older brother and sister? Don't forget, in the spiritual world he is still only 19 years old. In his book *Many Mansions* Lord Dowding says that normal people pass into the hereafter exactly the same individuals as they were on earth and continue their lives without break or intermission in spiritual instead of earthly surroundings. This, he says, must affect the outlook and conduct of all who are not wilfully blind.

Nick and Thea are writing their own book, *Invisible Brother,* about their extraordinary spiritual relationship with the young fighter pilot. So far they have been careful who to tell. "There are too many cynics in this world" says Nick.

GOODBYE BIGGIN: Squadron Leader John Ellis sits astride the Spitfire shortly after 610 Squadron left Biggin Hill for Acklington. Back row (Left to right): Lecky, Clarke, Carter, Bacon, Draper, Brown, Baker, Corbin, Douglas, Horner. Front row: Davies, Lambe, Hamlyn, Pegge, Mileham, Hallam, Cooke, Norris, Smith, Murray, Ward-Smith and Wilson. Nine members had died during the 15 weeks at Biggin Hill.

SURVIVOR: Flight Lieutenant Norris (left) was the only 610 Squadron pilot in this group to survive the Battle of Britain. Squadron Leader Franks (second left) died in France, Squadron Leader Andrew Smith was killed on July 27 and Flying Officer William Warner was lost on August 16, 1940.

610 loses another nine pilots

SIX ONE 0 (County of Chester) Auxiliary Squadron, made its base at Biggin Hill on May 5, 1940 and remained in the front line until August 28 when the survivors were ordered to Acklington for a long overdue rest. In those hectic 15 weeks "when time seemed to stand still" No 610 lost a Squadron Leader, an acting Squadron Leader, a Flight Lieutenant, a Flying Officer, three Pilot Officers and seven Sergeant pilots.

Four of them died in the Battle of France and nine perished during the Battle of Britain. Many others qualified for membership of the Caterpillar Club by leaving their blazing aircraft and floating to earth above the brilliant kaleidoscope of Kentish fields. Some splashed in the Channel and a defiant few somehow made it back to England.

The Battle of Britain was only officially two days old on July 12 when Sergeant Sydney Ireland was killed on what had been a relatively peaceful day. The pilots of 610 Squadron conscious that, when the time suited the enemy, the onslaught would be fought on a much greater scale were required to put in a few hours of dog fight practice. Ireland, a 22-year-old Ulsterman from Newtownbreda, near Belfast successfully completed a few steep turns in the skies above Biggin Hill but tragically lost control in a dive through clouds and crashed his Spitfire in Titsey Park on the southern slopes of the North Downs. Years later the site was excavated by the London Air Museum who recovered much of the aircraft. They also discovered that Ireland's name was not on the panel in the chapel of St George's at Biggin Hill as he had not been killed in action.

Nor was that of Sergeant Peter Watson-Parker, a close friend of Syd Ireland who crashed and died in the grounds of Skid House, Tatsfield on July 13 during another dreary day of routine practice. Parker, also 22, was buried at St Peter and St Paul churchyard, Cudham.

Three more close friends died during those early days of the Battle of Britain in actions that were typical of hundreds fought out in the killing skies over Kent. On July 18, Pilot Officer Peter Litchfield, aged 25, was shot down in combat over the the Channel, north of Calais, by Hauptmann Tietzen of 11/JG 51. The aircraft was lost and Litchfield was reported 'missing'.

Flight Lieutenant Andrew 'Big Bill' Smith, a likeable, highly-respected Liverpudlian, who had taken command of 610 Squadron when the CO 'Bonzo' Franks died, had already diced with death when his Spitfire crashed heavily on landing at Hawkinge on July 10. Somehow the big fellow scrambled unhurt from the wreckage to lead his Squadron in combat again. Fifteen days later, in the early afternoon of July 25, Smith stalled as he attempted another difficult landing at Hawkinge after action with Bf 109s over the Channel. The Spitfire crashed again but this time there was no escape as it burned out in a disused engine testing shed. 610 Squadron had lost two COs in as many months. The next day Flight Lieutenant John Ellis, a 23-year-old pilot from Deal, was promoted to acting Squadron Leader and given the honour of commanding this tragic squadron.

The worst day in the entire battle for casualties came on August 11 when 25 airmen lost their lives — more than double those who died in the 'slaughter of the innocents' on July 19 or the "hardest day" on August 18 when 10 died or September 15 (later known as Battle of Britain Day) when 16 pilots were killed. Two Sergeant pilots from 610 Squadron, Bill Neville and John Tanner failed to return from a patrol over the Channel.

On this clear August morning, with only high cirrus clouds, a furious dogfight took place over the Isle of Wight where Luftflotte 3 were bombing naval installations on the mainland. History now shows it to be a dress rehearsal for Adlerangriff or Attack of the Eagles — Goering's new strategy to wipe the RAF out of the skies in preparation for the invasion of England. 610 Squadron was scrambled on this famous morning and alongside the young pilots were some of the great figures of the Battle. Peter Townsend, Alan Deere, Denis David and Sailor Malan were among those on the scoresheet on this day of critical fighting. It was to endure for more than a month and bring Fighter Command almost to its knees.

Many more mornings of dawn readiness faced the pilots of 610. A shooting brake took them to the dispersal hut, which was blacked out until the sun rose. There they waited for that moment of "pure terror" when the telephone rang and brought the men instantly to their feet. Sometimes it was to tell them that breakfast was on its way over and there were to be a few more hours of excruciating boredom. On other occasions it meant the plotters in the Ops Room had seen the build-up of enemy aircraft over the Channel.

Such a morning was Friday August 16. Three times the Squadron was scrambled. In fact the biggest battle that day took place above Sevenoaks and before the last dog fight was over Group Captain Grice was telephoned by an irate urban councillor complaining that the town had received so many jettisoned bombs that he thought it only fair that the station commander should arrange to intercept the Germans elsewhere.

By the evening the fields of Kent were littered with the burning wrecks of enemy aircraft and 610 Squadron had lost Flying Officer William Warner, who failed to return from combat with Bf 109s over Dungeness in the last action of the day. Warner, 21, a fighter pilot for less than a year, was due to be promoted to Flight Lieutenant.

On this day there were two German-speaking guests at Biggin Hill. One was taken to 32 Squadron's dispersal to see the Nazi trophies and the other, a cheerful little gunner, was entertained by some of 610 Squadron who plied him with drinks in the Mess. After several glasses of Westerham Ale he inquired after the names and ranks of his hosts. "I am most anxious", he said, "to see that you all receive equally courteous treatment after the Führer's forthcoming victorious invasion of your England". He was unceremoniously marched to the Guard Room and quickly locked up.

By now 610 were due for a rest but the great formations of Dorniers, Junkers, Heinkels and their escorts kept coming and Biggin Hill was definitely on the menu. Now came the most chaotic, frenzied fighting of the entire battle as 610 Squadron attempted to protect its base with several new pilots who were so inexperienced as to be non-operational. The Luftwaffe had reserves to call upon, both of men and machines but the RAF was finding it harder and harder to replace losses of both.

And the losses continued to mount. On August 26 Pilot Officer Frank Webster returned to Hawkinge in trouble, crashed in flames as he attempted to land and died in his aircraft. A pre-war member of the RAFVR, Webster was buried near his home at Sandown Cemetery on the Isle of Wight. He was, at 26, a veteran pilot.

There were to be two more fatalities before 610 left Biggin Hill and they both occurred on

Members of 610 Squadron who served at Biggin Hill during the Battle. The youngest in this group was Bill Gaskell, aged 17, the youngest airman to serve on the station.

the afternoon of August 28 when hundreds of enemy aircraft penetrated inland in seven separate attacks on the Kentish airfields and the Thames Estuary. Goering was attempting to wear down the British fighter force by sending over vast formations of Me 109s on provocative sweeps hoping to catch those moments when the Spitfires and Hurricanes were rearming and refuelling. Some 28 enemy aircraft were destroyed on this day and the pilots of 610 Squadron were adding to their impressive score at a great rate.

At 4.30 pm Sergeant Edward Manton was shot down and killed over Mayfield. The 25-year old from Bebington, Cheshire, who had joined 610 Squadron before the war, had been delighted to be selected for pilot training. Having completed his course on Hurricanes he rejoined 610 Squadron on July 27, 1940 and was immediately sent to 7OTU Hawarden for a three-week conversion course on Spitfires. He had less than 12 days combat experience when his aircraft was hit and he crashed at Great Wigsell Estate, Hurst Green. He was buried in Hawkhurst Cemetery.

Less than an hour later 610 Squadron lost Birmingham-born Pilot Officer Kenneth Cox, aged 24 whose Spitfire crashed on a house at Stelling Minnis.

The Squadron diarist had this to say on receiving the order to take a brief rest at Acklington: "We had mixed feelings about it. While we felt that it would be pleasant to be a bit further from Jerry for a while, we were secretly proud to be in the thick of it".

Not all members of 610 Squadron shared these sentiments. Soon after the Spitfires left for Acklington on this last day of August 1940 the equipment, loaded on to a "Queen Mary", followed by road and now only the ground crews remained. As they waited at the North Camp for the buses to take them to Bromley station they heard an Ack-Ack gun open up followed by a deafening roar as the others followed and a formation of Dornier 215s came threateningly into sight. The men left their haversacks and kit packs in the road and ran, full pelt, into the nearby woods, dodging a hail of machine-gun pellets. Some two hours later they were on their way to the north-east, happy to leave the battle-zone to 72 Squadron who were due to replace them.

EGG HEAD: Pilots outside 79 squadron dispersal in July 1940 are (left to right): Sgt Cartwright DFM, Pilot Officer Parker, (camouflaged as a poached egg to deceive the Luftwaffe!), Squadron Leader Joslin, Pilot Officer Stones DFC, Pilot Officer Murray, Flying Officer Edwards (Intelligence Officer).

79 Squadron pilots plan a patrol

79 Squadron

SURVIVORS from the battle-scarred 79 Hurricane Squadron could never really make much sense of the formal dates given for the start and completion of the Battle of Britain. In three tragic days before the battle officially began the Squadron lost its Commanding Officer and two experienced pilots. None qualified for posthumous membership of the Battle of Britain Fighter Association. They were among the forgotten men.

The supporting argument, of course, comes from those who say the battle had to begin and end formally at some time for the sake of history books — so July 10 and October 31 remain the key dates.

Pilots of 79 Squadron were at Hawkinge from the beginning of July with a new CO Squadron Leader John Joslin from Buckden in Huntingdonshire. "He was tough, enthusiastic and every inch a leader" said Donald Stones. "He inspired us with the hope that we would no longer be a rudderless ship and morale rose as he led us into the new battles with increasing numbers of Me 109s escorting their bombers over our convoys". In fact the fighting was just as tough as the official first day of The Battle of Britain.

On July 7 Joslin led his flight on another convoy patrol when they were jumped by fighters from astern, out of nowhere. Stones and Pilot Officer John Parker turned to face them and saw, to their horror, that the 'enemy' were Spitfires and John Joslin, their quite exceptional leader, was going down in flames.

Back in the Mess at Hawkinge, Flying Officer David Haysom took temporary command again and then had the painful duty to tell Louisa Joslin that her husband had been killed by Spitfire pilots from another Squadron. Imagine how she felt when a national newspaper, believing Joslin to be a German pilot, described his demise thus: "...They were quite low, and we realised unpleasantly, this was the Kill. There was a burst of machine gun fire and a sugar-like glow appeared in the body of the Messerschmitt. The glow spread to a flame and the machine rocketed to earth in a shroud of smoke and flame. The whole terrible drama lasted less than a minute".

The following day, Monday July 8, was an even blacker one. Scrambled at dawn on convoy patrol 79 Squadron spent an hour trying to peer out of a solid layer of cloud before they were told to return to Hawkinge and refuel. As they did so, a brace of 109s picked off Pilot Officer John Wood and Flying Officer Edward Mitchell who were at the rear of the formation.

Tubby Mitchell should have used his parachute but was unable to open the cockpit canopy on his burning Hurricane. Somehow he managed to

---

In Memory of
JOHN DAVIES CLEMENT JOSLIN
Squadron Leader
34158
Pilot
79 Sqdn., Royal Air Force
who died on
Sunday, 7th July 1940. Age 24
Son of Davies Clement Joslin and Elizabeth Joslin;
husband of Louisa Margot Joslin, of Buckden

Commemorative Information
Buckden Cemetery, Huntingdonshire, United Kingdom

Sergeants Whitby (right) and Cartwright who each won the DFM. Cartwright was killed on July 4, a few days before The Battle of Britain officially started.

Flying Officer 'Tubby' Mitchell, trapped inside his burning Hurricane on July 8, 1940.

force-land in a field near Dover and frantically tore at the hood but there was no escape. He was trapped inside and died.

It was time for a rest. 79 Squadron flew to Acklington and were given new pilots, new aircraft and a new Commanding Officer. Squadron Leader Harvey Heyworth, a Rolls-Royce test pilot, was able to put his young aces through their paces and introduce new dog-fight tactics in time for the return to Biggin Hill on August 27, 1940.

On their way south from Acklington they were vectored to intercept seaplanes which were harassing the British ships in mid-Channel. Unaware that the Mayor of Dover was standing on the castle ramparts with a special guest the Hurricanes put on a special show of strength, destroyed two He 59s and shot up two E-boats. That special guest, following the action through his binoculars, was the Prime Minister, Winston Churchill.

79 Squadron's return to The Bump coincided with the enemy's greatest blitz on Biggin Hill and the pilots were hard pressed to defend the station from the Luftwaffe's continuous strafing. On August 30, the day of the heaviest raid, Flying Officer E.J. 'Teddy' Morris claimed a Heinkel III by 'collision'. He was obliged to bale out of his Hurricane which crashed on Lodge Farm, South Holmwood and the HeIII less than a mile to the south. The young South African pilot, shaken by the experience but no less determined, was ready to fly the following day and was in his dispersal hut on 'readiness' when duty controllers,

79 Squadron pilots and ground crew. One pilot was Flight Lieutenant Rupert Clerke, a Flight Commander, who went on to make history by undertaking the first operational sortie in a Mosquito on September 17, 1941. Others included Pilot Officers George Nelson-Edwards and Bill Millington, who were both injured on August 31, 1940.

Squadron Leader Roger Frankland and 'Baron' Worrall, noticed a small formation of enemy bombers being plotted up the line of the Ashford-Redhill railway. The target was Biggin Hill or Kenley or possibly both. Most of the station's fighters were scrapping over the Channel but four Hurricanes of 79 Squadron managed to get airborne. One of the pilots was Morris who once again met the enemy, now Dornier 17s, head on. His 'borrowed' Hurricane was damaged but this time he managed to crash-land heavily at base and pull himself clear of the wreckage, badly injured. In hospital he learned that Sergeant Henry Bolton from West Hartlepool, shot down over Kenley, had attempted a forced landing at Haliloo Farm, Warlingham but succumbed from his wounds in his burning aircraft.

Four days later, with the Luftwaffe still keeping to its rigid schedule by timing each day's second blitz to coincide with the six-o-clock news, Sergeant John Wright, 24, was also shot down. After crashing at Surbiton he was taken to hospital where he died the next day.

In those hectic 13 days of non-stop action the remaining pilots of 79 Squadron somehow managed to avoid further fatalities and it was a great relief on September 9 to take a breather among the Welsh hills of Pembrey where the action switched to routine patrols in the skies above the Irish Sea. On September 29, Flying Officer George Peters failed to return from intercepting He111s and three weeks later Pilot Officer Stanislaw Piatkowski crashed and died near Carew Cheriton and was buried in St Peter's Churchyard, Pembrey.

ON THE 'PHONE: Pilot Officer Johnny Bryson, who switched from the Mounties in Canada to the RAF in England in 1939, rings home. Bryson, almost too big for a Spitfire, made a tempting target. He became a target all too soon.

Stage and screen stars who popped into Biggin Hill to entertain the boys included Laurence Olivier, Vivien Leigh, Bea Lillie, Carroll Gibbons, Jack Warner, Noel Coward and Clark Gable, who is pictured here with Pilot Officer Tony Bartley (left) and Flight Lieutenant C.D. Stephenson. Bartley, of 92 Squadron, was the archetypal playboy and a brilliant pilot, who married the gorgeous and talented film actress Deborah Kerr after the war and went with her to Hollywood. Stevenson, or 'Stevie' as he was always known, was an American who flew with the Royal Flying Corps in the 1914-18 war and was in charge of the Watch Office at Biggin Hill in 1940/41. He formed and organised the exclusive PYFO (Pull Your Finger Out) Club at Biggin Hill. His wife was Jeanne de Casalis — Mrs Feather of Radio fame.

92 Squadron

IN terms of casualties 92 (East India) Squadron were the highest scorers of all units based at Biggin Hill during the war. Fourteen pilots died during the Battle of Britain and, in all, 33 pilots died while flying from the Wing between September 8, 1940 and September 25, 1941 when they said goodbye to the station, to the White Hart and to the glamorous models they "befriended". During those 17 months of fighting and socialising they took their incredible score to 130 enemy aircraft destroyed with 60 probables. They also lost a huge number of Spitfires but the final balance showed a credit in their favour and they happily moved to Gravesend and the Elizabethan comforts of Cobham Hall, the home of the Darnley family.

Of the 33 to die, 20 were young Sergeant pilots aged between 19 and 24. Nine Pilot Officers, two Flying Officers and two Flight Lieutenants completed the tragic picture. On its arrival at Biggin Hill 92 was commanded by Squadron Leader Philip Sanders who was soon in hospital with severe burns having lit a cigarette while wearing a petrol-soaked uniform. His successor, Squadron Leader Alan McLachlan severed the tendons in one hand while forcing his way out of a jammed canopy. Neither returned to enjoy the company of the high-spirited, racing car mad, cravated, silk shirted "playboys" who went on to build for their squadron the most renowned reputation in Fighter Command.

The arrival of 92 Squadron at Biggin Hill coincided with the Battle of London and the Luftwaffe's desire to inflict the final, decisive blows in readiness for *Operation Sealion.* Day after day, night after night the ceaseless drone of the Dorniers, Heinkels and Junkers could be heard by personnel from the station as the swarming insect-like mass of machinery made its way to the London docks. The "playboys" were scrambled daily to intercept this great gaggle of bombers with their escorts below.

The first to die were Pilot Officers Frederick Hargreaves and Harry Edwards who were in combat with Bf 109s just three days after settling in at Biggin Hill. Edwards, from Winnipeg crashed into a field at Smeeth and his wreck was driven seven feet under ploughed land by the impact. Hargreaves, 21, is believed to have gone into the sea. At the time 92 Squadron were flying alone from Biggin Hill while the clearing up continued from the five raids in 48 hours at the end of August. On September 12, 72 returned home and the station settled down to life as a two-Squadron operational unit once again.

There was one big difference. In view of the likelihood that the Luftwaffe would return in even greater numbers Station Commander Group Captain Grice decided his two squadrons should be billeted as far apart as possible. 92 Squadron moved into Southwood, a large, imposing manor house at Westerham Hill. Here, between raids and funerals, they turned their new home into a sophisticated night club with Flying Officers Brian Kingcome, Tony Bartley, Wimpey Wade and Allan Wright as the pace setters behind the establishment of a terrific dance band. On the piano was Bob Holland, a talented swing pianist. In the audience were other members of the Squadron and scores of glamorous young ladies. The partying often went on to dawn. Then they were ready to fly again.

The boys of 92 Squadron came through Sunday September 15 — later to be celebrated as Battle of Britain Day — with just three damaged Spitfires (one lost) and two pilots hurt. It ended overwhelmingly in the RAF's favour and a decision, two days later by Hitler and his

Twenty-year-old Pilot Officer Howard Hill from New Zealand who died in the tree tops at West Hougham, Kent.

commanders, to postpone *Operation Sealion* indefinitely.

The weather was ideal for fighters so the patrols, the interceptions, the reckless head-on charges continued. The boys of 92 Squadron were always to the fore, tearing into the bomber packs, the sky filled with curling tracers, smoking aircraft and the crackle of ammunition. Down below, the people of Kent watched the whirling dog fights often unable to distinguish friend from foe.

After six weeks at Biggin Hill the Squadron Roll of Honour was depressingly large. Pilot Officer Howard Hill, from New Zealand, died in the tree tops at West Hougham on September 20. They found his body a month later, strapped in the cockpit of his Spitfire with the top of his head sliced off by cannon shell...Pilot Officer Johnny Bryson, the Canadian, who exchanged his job with the Mounties to join the RAF, crashed and died in Essex on September 24....Sergeant Trevor Oldfield came down at Fuller's House, Hesketh Park, Dartford and died from his injuries on September 27....Charles Sydney from St Mary Cray, who had joined the RAF at 15 as an apprentice fitter and volunteered for pilot training, died on the same day. His Spitfire is believed to have crashed in the grounds of the *Bird's Eye* factory in Station Avenue, Walton.

Flight Lieutenant James Paterson was also killed on September 27. A trooper in the Otago Mounted Rifles before the war, Paterson had been badly burned in the face when his Spitfire crashed at Ashford on September 11. Bravely, he insisted he should fly again before he could see properly and now he had no chance, shot down in a dog fight over Sevenoaks. His fellow pilots saw him struggling to escape from his blazing cockpit just seconds before he hit the earth at Sparepenny Lane, Farnborough.

In early October two other 92 Squadron pilots — Flight Lieutenant John Lund and Sergeant Kenneth Parker — came down in the sea. Parker's body was washed up in the Netherlands but Lund was rescued by *HMS Nyson*. Lund, who was at Oriel College, Oxford before the war where he read Mediaeval History and flew with the University Air Squadron, survived the Battle of Britain. He died on October 2 1941.

Of all the Squadrons who used the White Hart, Brasted as the local during these desperate days, 92 Squadron was the most regular and Kath Preston the landlady remembers them well. "We became familiar", she said, "with Bob Stanford Tuck, always immaculate in his uniform with his long cigarette holder. Then there was Brian Kingcome who used to arrive with his bull terrier, Zeke, and Tony Bartley who later married the actress Deborah Kerr. Bob Holland was a wizard on the piano, Wimpy Wade became a post-war test pilot.

By October 10 1940, 92 Squadron was still with the Biggin Wing but now at Cobham Hall — a perfect venue for a birthday party (92 Squadron had been formed at Tangmere just a year earlier). The boys had the occasion planned in detail but, first, Group Captain Grice had another, more pressing engagement — a dead-simple dawn scramble to intercept a lone Dornier 17 over the South Coast. Six Spitfires took off, led by Wimpey Wade, who said this

FOOT AND MOUTH was the nickname for 92 Squadron which arrived at Biggin Hill on September 8: Top row: Sgts Lloyd, Ellis, Bowen-Morris and Allison. Bottom: Pilot Officers Tommy Lund, Maitland Thompson, Bob Holland, Wimpey Wade, Bill Watling, Thomas Sherrington, Sgts 'Titch' Havercroft and Xavier de Cherade de Montbron.

routine destruction job should take about half an hour. Some 60 minutes later just four returned. Pilot Officer Desmond Williams and Flying Officer John Drummond had collided in mid air. Williams crashed near a church on Romney Marsh and a priest was able to administer the last sacrament before the young pilot died in his arms. Drummond baled out too low and was killed. His Spitfire finally crashed at Portslade.

Although Drummond, from Blundellsland near Liverpool, was only 21, he had won the DFC for destroying four Heinkel IIIs in a week off Norway, while serving with 46 Squadron. He did not fly off onto the *'Glorious'* when the Squadron was withdrawn from Norway and escaped the fate of most of 46's pilots who were lost when the Carrier was sunk.

To rub salt into 92 Squadron's considerable wounds, Lord Haw Haw on *Germany Calling* broadcast that night that a single reconnaissance aircraft returning from photographing the holocaust of London had fought off an attack by six Spitfires and killed two pilots.

Cobham Hall, with its splendid oak furniture, a library of leather-bound classics, spacious yew-trees and lawns and floral lavatory basins, should have been the venue for that night's birthday party. But there were no celebrations that night. The pilots were in a state of shock and it was to be several days before they recovered their old composure, panache and confidence.

TRAGIC: 92 Squadron pilots at Biggin Hill are (left to right): Pilot Officers Roy Mottram (died August 31, 1941 with 54 squadron), Cecil Saunders, Squadron Leader Phillip Sanders, Pilot Officers Frederick Hargreaves (died September 11, 1940), Harry Edwards, who died on the same day and Howard Hill (died September 20, 1940).

Flying Officer Maurice 'Tiny' Kinder of 92 Squadron was shot down and wounded on October 13, 1940. Weak from loss of blood, he sat in his Spitfire alongside the Ramsgate to Canterbury Road where he was discovered by Australian soldiers. Thinking he was dead they took his helmet, gloves and buttons as souvenirs and were surprised when Kinder came to and swore at them. Eventually an ambulance took him to Chartham Military Hospital where he recovered.

Harry Edwards of Winnipeg joined 92 Squadron in October 1939 and destroyed a Bf110 over Dunkirk on June 2 and shared in shooting down two others. He was killed on September 11, 1940 when his Spitfire crashed into a wood at Evegate Manor Farm, Smeeth. He was 24.

Flt Lt William Rhodes-Moorhouse

WILLIAM Rhodes-Moorhouse was 17 when he obtained his pilot's licence at Heston and joined 601 Squadron. He was not old enough to buy a drink in White's Club, where the Auxiliary flying club had earlier been born, but he could handle a Hawker Hart with the expertise of a veteran and was greatly admired by the older members of the 'gang', especially by those who remembered his father — one of the bravest aviators ever known.

Lieutenant William Rhodes-Moorhouse, senior, flew with No 2 Squadron of the Royal Flying Corps during the 1914-18 war. On April 25, 1915 he left Merville airfield in France, alone in a biplane, to drop a heavy bomb on the railway junction of Courtrai. Arriving at his destination he volplaned down to a height of 300 feet and dropped the bomb on his objective. Immediately, a tornado of fire from the ground opened up. Hundreds of rifles, machine-guns and shell fire ripped into the aircraft and Rhodes-Moorhouse was badly wounded in the thigh.

He could have descended into the German lines and surrendered where his life would have been saved but the aviator did not want his machine to fall into the hands of the Germans so he turned and made for the British lines. To increase the speed he dropped to 100 feet, crossed the enemy lines at this height and was again severely wounded by a bullet which ripped open his abdomen. Losing blood, falling in and out of consciousness, he made it back to Merville, effected a perfect landing and made his report.

Twenty four hours later William Rhodes-Moorhouse succumbed to his wounds. He had been the first man to do the "tail slide" and also the only man who had flown across the English Channel with two passengers. He was described as one of the most heroic aviators in world history.

His wife, Linda, who lived at Parnham, the impressive family home near Beaminster, Dorset, received this letter from her husband's acting Flight Commander, Maurice Blake: "It is with very great sorrow that I have to tell you that your husband died at 2.25 this afternoon. During the night he asked for your photo case with that of his little boy which was brought to him and he then fell asleep...The photos of you and his baby were on the pillow by him till the end...Before he slept he said to me: 'Oh boy, I'm going and can't last many hours. Isn't it pathetic to die when at one's prime with a wife and family to whom one is absolutely devoted? I brought my son into the world because there was no doctor there, and I think it has made me love him more than most fathers love their children".

That boy, also William, was 18 months old at the time. He grew up at Parnham remembering little about his father except that he had performed daring feats in the air and had, posthumously, won the first Victoria Cross ever given for supreme valour in air operations.

William could not wait to fly. After he had gained his licence, while still at school in Eton, and then joined 601 Squadron, he turned his attention to that other sport so favoured by those born into great wealth — skiing in the Alps. His ability on the piste matched his skills in the air and Rhodes-Moorhouse was invited to represent Britain in the Winter Games of 1937-38.

Going into full-time service with the RAF in August 1939, William was delighted to be

Second Lieutenant William Rhodes-Moorhouse of the Royal Flying Corps who died in 1915.

Flight Lieutenant William Rhodes-Moorhouse of the Royal Air Force who died in 1940.

based at Biggin Hill and even more so to be chosen to fly one of the six 601 Blenheims which attacked the German seaplane base at Borkham on November 27, 1939. As he left the station for the Friesian Islands and a 250-mile flight across the North Sea he must have thought of his father's last flight over similarly hostile territory 25 years earlier. William, junior, carried neither dinghy nor life-preserver jacket. Such safety requirements had not been introduced.

The Borkham mission was a dangerous one. Four sections of three Blenheims, two led by Flying Officers Michael Peacock and Max Aitken dived out of the clouds and strafed the slipways, hangars, ships and machine gun posts with bullets. They wrecked five seaplanes and sank several patrol boats. The Blenheims flown by Aitken, Peacock, Rhodes Moorhouse, Tom Hubbard, Sir Archibald Hope and Carl Davis returned to Biggin Hill without a scratch.

William's mother would have known little about that mission until it was all over because it was highly secret. She would not have known that her son flew at just 100 feet above the seaplane base in an action that replicated his father's feat. The feeling of déja vu, however, had not yet ended. On May 16, 1940 during the Battle of France, William was sent to Merville in France with A Flight of 601 Squadron. From there he shot down a Heinkel III east of Brussels on the 18th and destroyed a Me 109 on the 22nd.

William Rhodes-Moorhouse was now a senior fighter pilot and, at 26, one of the older members of the RAF and also one of the most experienced. By September 1940 and now stationed at Tangmere with the Hurricanes of 601, he had destroyed or shared in the destruction of 10 enemy aircraft — three Dornier 17s, one Junkers 88, one Heinkel III and five Messerschmitt 109s. He also had the DFC presented to him by the King on July 30.

On September 6, 601 Squadron was scrambled a few hours after dawn to intercept a bomber attack on southern aerodromes, including Biggin Hill. Escorting the bombers was a massive swarm of 109s. By now the Squadron were down to a handful of aircraft. Five had been destroyed in one day on August 31. The losses were grievous.

It was to be the last action in the life of Flight Lieutenant William Rhodes-Moorhouse. At 9.30 am he was shot down in combat over Tunbridge Wells and his Hurricane crashed near

Southwood, the large house in Buckhurst Road two miles to the south of Biggin Hill, was owned by Captain and the Hon Mrs McNair Scott who carefully put their valuable paintings and furniture in store and handed it over to 92 Squadron, whose pilots arrived complete with jazz band.
609 Squadron was also billeted there and like their predecessors had the run of the house. Mary Wells' parents were the caretakers at the time and she remembers how her family — there were two other sisters, Jean and Dorothy — lived in the large kitchen and slept in the cellar.
"On many occasions" she said, "the piano was played all night and the pilots partied until dawn. It was jolly but also terrible. We'd see them preparing for their ops in the morning and sometimes only three or four of them would return in the evening. They were very brave young men. I remember one day cleaning the boots of Flying Officer Ogilvie. He gave me a 3d silver piece and some Canadian chewing gum".

the High Brooms Viaduct at Southborough. The cheerful and mercurial son of the first airman to win a VC died in his aircraft. In the same action, at the same time, Flight Lieutenant Carl Davis was also shot down. The Hurricane of theAmerican, brother-in-law of Archibald Hope, crashed inverted and burned out in the back garden of a cottage at Matfield.

Friday September 6 was the day that headquarters and staffs on the German air bases were putting the finishing touches to their plans to carry out the Führer's order to switch the attack from the air bases to London. Dowding and his colleagues would not have known this at the time. In their view the collapse of Fighter Command was inevitable and in a measure to avoid more crippling losses exhausted squadrons were withdrawn from the front line and classified as training units. The Battle of Britain was over for the remnants of 601 Squadron.

William Rhodes-Moorhouse was buried alongside his father's grave in the private cemetery in the grounds of Parnham House, Dorset. He was 26. In 1976 members of the Kent Battle of Britain Museum recovered Rhodes-Moorhouse's Rolls Royce Merlin engine from its long-time burial site at Southborough. It was beautifully intact and so was a propeller boss and super-charger, radiator, tail wheel and cockpit components. They also discovered the pilot's wrist watch and put all on display.

*SCRAMBLED: Sergeant 'Tiny' Faulkner of 72 Squadron dons his Mae West and parachute ready for action.
Below the ground crews of 72 Squadron at Biggin Hill. Sgt Graeme Gillard is standing third from left and
Corporal Jack Lancaster standing eighth from left. The Squadron exchanged places with 610 Squadron and
found, on their arrival, that Jerry had just paid another visit to Biggin Hill. They were in action immediately.*

72 Squadron

HOW the Spitfires of 72 (Basutoland) Squadron were able to land at their new base is something of a miracle but in the late afternoon of August 31 the pilots flew down to Biggin Hill from the comparative peace of Acklington to find just one runway in use and that was pockmarked with craters. They would not have known about the frenzied activity that had preceded their arrival — for Group Captain Grice had set every available man and woman to work on repairing the runway.

Graeme Gillard, a member of the ground crew, remembers the astonishing sight which greeted them when they arrived at The Bump. "We knew Biggin had been having a rough time and we flew down in an Imperial Airways Hannibal complete with tool boxes and home-made spanners. The moment we arrived all haste was made to arm and refuel the Spitfires. We worked like demons to complete the servicing of all but one aircraft. Just as we finished RDF warned of enemy aircraft approaching and, as 72 Squadron was scrambled, we made a dive for the air-raid shelter.

"The Krumps came in. It was unbelievable. Frightening down there in the shelter but the spirits were good and the banter exceptional. The raid was soon over but it seemed like an eternity. We looked out and saw the damage. Our grounded Spit was just curling up in flames. One of our young electricians, a brave but foolish lad, picked up an unexploded bomb and ran towards the woods. It exploded before he got to the perimeter and he was badly injured".

A few hours earlier the pilots of 72 Squadron, led by Flying Officer Robert Deacon-Elliott, had been peering down at the rugged Northumberland coastline. Now they were above the shingle of Dungeness, scrapping furiously with Dorniers and their escorts. Only eight of the 10 Spitfires returned to Biggin Hill. They found the runway so badly cratered that they were diverted to Croydon leaving their possessions at Biggin Hill. The ground crew were bussed there almost immediately. "I'll never forget the courage of home-wrecked Croydonians as they cheered our maintenance men", recalled Flight Lieutenant Ted Graham.

The two Spitfires which failed to return were piloted by Flying Officers Edward Wilcox and Forgrave Marshal Smith. Wilcox, a Croydon lad, crashed in Hungerford Field, Checkenden Farm, Staplehurst and was killed. He was 23. Smith, a Canadian, baled out wounded and badly burned over New Romney. He spent the next three months in hospital.

Their troubles did not end there. Twice scrambled the next day "to search for bandits over Tunbridge Wells" they lost two more aircraft. Flight Lieutenant Ronald Thomson, from New Zealand, was wounded in the stomach, hands, chest, lungs and one leg by shell splinters. With a dead engine he glided down for a bell-landing near Leeds Castle. He found an ideal field but on his final approach saw anti-invasion steel hawsers stretched across it. With no choice he flew under the hawsers at 120 mph, lost speed by lowering the Spitfire's nose into the ground and skidded into trees at the end of the field. His aircraft lost a fin and rudder but Thomson climbed out and made his way to Leeds Castle military hospital.

There was no escape for the second pilot, Flying Officer Oswald St John Pigg, the son of a Northumberland vicar. His Spitfire crashed and burned out at Elvey Farm, Pluckley. He was 22.

For the next few weeks 72 Squadron were scrambled every day until October 13 when the surviving pilots were sent to Leconfield for recuperation. By that time the Roll of Honour was depressingly large and the absent faces at breakfast time in both officers' and sergeants' messes were most conspicuous.

One of the worst days was Thursday September 5 when Pilot Officer Douglas Winter, Sergeant Thomas Malcolm Gray and Flying Officer Des Sheen all crashed near Elham. Winter, shot down by a Bf109, was killed when he baled out far too low. His Spitfire crashed into Covert Wood. Gray went headlong into Elham Park Wood and died. Sheen baled out wounded but his aircraft was a write-off.

Eric Hymer, flight mechanic with 72 Squadron, remembers Tom Gray. "He was a York lad only a year older than me. He came to us as a replacement pilot and I saw his aircraft off on his first op. I remember saying 'Good luck Sgt Tom' and I seemed to know he wasn't coming back. Tom, I thought, was too gentle a chap for this type of thing".

On September 20, eight Spitfires left Biggin Hill in company with 66 Squadron to intercept Me 109s and 110s over Canterbury. Only seven returned. Pilot Officer Dennis Holland, who began his career as the youngest Civil Air Guard Instructor in Britain, baled out severely wounded and died in hospital. A week later Pilot Officer Ernest Males was shot down and killed in combat over Sevenoaks. His Spitfire crashed at Shadwell Dock, Stepney. He was just 20 years old. In the same hectic, whirling mêlée Flying Officer Paul Davies-Cooke, 23, was also shot down. He baled out but fell dead near Hayes Station and his Spitfire crashed into two houses at Queensway, West Wickham. .

On October 12, the day before the move to Leconfield, Pilot Officer Robert Case was killed when he dropped out of formation and crashed at Capel-le-Ferne, near Folkestone. He was 24.

In just six weeks at Biggin Hill, 72 Squadron had lost eight pilots and was down to just seven pilots of experience. Little wonder that some of the officers were unhappy with the lack of communication from Fighter Command. Pilot Officer Norman Norfolk, who had baled out of a burning aircraft on September 2, recalled that he never saw nor heard from the hierarchy and was never told the general strategy or day-to-day tactical principles. "As far as I know", he said, "the squadron commander was in the same position".

No such accusations could be levelled at Station Commander Dick Grice, whose calm presence during Biggin Hill's crisis weeks was admired by everyone.

Pilots of 72 Squadron outside their dispersal hut at Biggin Hill include Squadron Leader Desmond Sheen in doorway with Flight Lieutenant Newton, 'B' Flight Commander, on his right. The 'A' Flight commander, Flight Lieutenant Ken Campbell, is top right. Sergeant 'Tiny' Faulkner is holding the dog and PO Stone is behind Faulkner.

For 72 Squadron it was au revoir but not goodbye to Biggin Hill. In July 1941, after nine months absence, they returned to find the station patched up, the initial blitz over and the Wing involved in routine Circus operations over France. They were in action immediately, escorting Blenheims over to Gosnay power station. During the raid a long yellow wooden box was dropped by parachute over St Omer airfield. Its label read: *"Dieser Kasten enhält Beinprothese für Wing Commander Douglas Bader, RAF. Kriegsgefangener"*

'Tinlegs' Bader, shot down over Le Touquet and now a prisoner of war had lost his right artificial leg which sheared off as he struggled out of the cockpit of his burning Spitfire. It was Oberleutnant Adolf Galland, commanding the Fighter Geschwader who arranged for 72 Squadron to fly to France with a spare set of limbs.

For the next 12 months 72 Squadron flew on numerous sweeps with the Biggin Wing and suffered many more casualties. By July 1942 the Roll of Honour contained the names of another 24 pilots including Squadron Leader Herbert Tidd and Flight Lieutenant Dudley Stewart-Clark.

Sergeant Jack Lancaster, a fitter with 72 Squadron, remembers moving from Acklington to Gravesend in May 1941 and then on to Biggin Hill. "The North Camp was no longer like a battlefield but more a building site", he said. "We were billeted in huts on the South Camp while the pilots lived in country houses and rooms in the Officers' Mess. We stayed at

Biggin Hill for a couple of months and then it was back to Gravesend, returning to The Bump in 1942 for a longer stay".

He said: "My overriding memory is the wonderful welcome we received from the villagers who lived near the airfield. In those days there was a small fence running alongside Jail Lane and many of the aircraft were dispersed on the other side. It was not unusual on a hot summer's evening to find the locals coming along with a trayful of beer for the lads. We used to eat cakes baked by the women and they chatted amiably about our efforts to keep the Spitfires airborne. No-one, he said, was more generous than Ma, who ran the cafe just 100 yards south of the Black Horse. She made the most wonderful breakfasts and always seemed to have an endless supply of bacon, then of course heavily rationed. We later learned she was in prison. Her offence 'Bacon on the Black Market'!

Ben Hitt was another member of 72 Squadron ground crew. He remembers the sparsely-furnished crew room with a few pieces of shot-down German aircraft adorning the walls and a battered wind-up gramophone with just one record to play — Louis Armstrong's *'Stomping at St Barbecue'*. "Life at Biggin Hill was hectic", he said. "There was double summertime and we were out of bed around 4.30 am to warm up and test the engines for dawn readiness. Stand down came at 11 pm so it was a long day. I remember the bells ringing in the crew room, the scrambles, strapping in the pilots, the multiple take-offs and, from time to time, the returning planes performing the victory roll. We were really privileged".

STEPPING OUT: Squadron Leader Roger Frankland, a controller at Biggin Hill, with Sheila Shute in the entrance of a dispersal shelter in 1940. Sheila, one of a pair of identical female twins, lived at the Red House, Brasted and was the widow of Squadron Leader Freddie Shute, who had died in tragic circumstances in February of that year. Sheila and sister Moira, with their good looks and alluring personalities became friendly with the pilots and frequently invited the officers for drinks at their imposing home in Brasted Among those who became close to the twins was Brian Kingcome of 92 Squadron. After the war he married Sheila's daughter Lesley.

74 Squadron

SQUADRON Leader 'Sailor' Malan DFC, the redoubtable Commanding Officer of 74 Squadron and then the outstanding fighter pilot of the war flew in to Biggin Hill with his Tigers on October 13, 1940 promising that his tough, disciplined bunch of pilots — the very antithesis of the playboys of 92 Squadron — would soon be shooting down Huns for breakfast. He was as good as his word.

Alongside Malan were H.M.Stephen, a Scot who had been a copy boy in a newspaper office and his fellow Flight Commander J.C.Mungo-Park, a proud Liverpudlian. Between them the two men had already accounted for 20 of the enemy; now they announced a private sweepstake on who would kill the most.

Like all Battle of Britain Squadrons the Tigers had suffered their share of tragedy — in fact they were among six front-line fighter squadrons who had endured the most casualties. In the months before their arrival in Biggin Hill they had lost Pilot Officers Donald Cobden, a New Zealander, Harold Gunn from Oxley, Herts and Denis Smith. All were recovered by the Germans after being shot down in the sea. None were flying the Biggin Wing at the time but their names are engraved on the reredos in St George's Chapel nonetheless.

Two Pilot Officers, Douglas Hastings and Frank Buckland had also died just two days before their arrival, when they collided during practice attacks over the Thames on October 8 and their Spitfires crashed near Gillingham. Hastings' name is engraved on the reredos but Buckland is missing. Fighter Command could ill afford such losses as it became apparent that the fighter force was slowly wasting away through lack of pilots. Sailor Malan said: "The Luftwaffe has suffered even more severely than we have and the move to Biggin will allow us to get into our stride again".

The ground crews arrived by road to find that the centre of each 'H' Block of airmen's accommodation had been knocked out and the hangars were laid flat. They were billeted in The Warren, a bungalow-type construction on the South Camp, vacated by the Army. It had one long centre passageway leading in from the airfield with living rooms, bathrooms, kitchen, dining room, Naafi and Post Office. For the major servicing of aircraft a small blister hangar was erected in the Leaves Green corner of the airfield. As a Spitfire could only be wheeled in with difficulty most servicing was carried out in the

WELCOME to Biggin Hill. Pilot Officer Johnny Freeborn (in cockpit), Sergeant Pilot Hakins, Flying Officer Meadows, Flight Lieutenant Sailor Malan, Sergeant 'Polly' Flinders, Flying Officer Temple-Harris and Sergeant Tony Mould (sitting). The Tigers have arrived.

dispersal bays.

74 Squadron were in action over the Thames before most of the crews had unpacked their bags but alongside the satisfaction of three destroyed and two probables came the grim news that Flying Officer Alan Ricalton had become another kind of statistic. The 26-year-old was shot down over Maidstone on October 17 and he died as his Spitfire crashed at Hollingbourne.

The tragedies continued. A Yorkshireman, Sergeant Thomas Kirk was also shot down over Maidstone and admitted to Preston Hall Hospital with the most terrible injuries. He never recovered but lived a further nine months. Flying Officer Peter St John crashed and died at South Nutfield, Surrey. Sergeant John Scott, a newcomer who had been at Biggin Hill for less than a week, died when his Spitfire crashed and exploded at Dundas Farm, Elsted and Paddy Treacy, the tall, gangling Irishman who had joined 74 along with Malan in 1937 was missing, believed killed.

The cloud of despondency which hung over the Squadron was not helped by those who estimated that every pilot kept in action for more than six months would be shot down because he was exhausted or stale and in terms of flying hours the

Pilots of 74 Squadron are (left to right): Roger Boulding and Sam the dog, Henryk Szczesny, Johnny Freeborn and H.M. Stephen. Freeborn, a Yorkshireman and a fearless pilot, had been involved in a misdirected interception over the Thames Estuary soon after the outbreak of war in 1939. In the 'Battle of Barking Creek', as it was known, 74 Squadron attacked the Hurricanes of 56 Squadron thinking they were hostile escorts to a formation of bombers. Flying Officers Freeborn and Paddy Byrne shot two of them down. Tragically one of the pilots was killed but the other, Tommy Rose hitch-hiked back to North Weald still wearing his pyjamas. A Court Martial aquitted Freeborn of any liability or blame.

Szczesny, or 'Sneezy', or Henry the Pole, was an ebullient, headstrong, pilot anxious for revenge after the fall of Poland. "I could not care about R/T", he said. "When airborne I just searched the skies for Hitler's swastikas".

fighter pilot's life expectancy could be measured at 87 hours.

As the Battle of Britain officially ended the gloom was quickly lifted by the appearance in Sailor Malan's office of Paddy Treacy. Shot down in France, he had reached Marseilles via the escape line and flown back to England. A few weeks later there was more good news to celebrate as Flying Officers Mungo Park and H.M.Stephen shot down Biggin Hill's 600th enemy aircraft.

Awards and recognitions were showered upon members of 74 Squadron for their work during October and November. Sailor Malan won the DSO for commanding his squadron with outstanding success over an extensive period of air operations. H.M. Stephen became the first recipient of the DSO awarded in the field in Great Britain. Mungo Park and Pilot Officer Brian Draper won the DFC and there was a DFM for Sergeant Wilfred Skinner.

74 Squadron were to remain at Biggin Hill until February 1941 when fighter sweeps were flown in force enticing the Luftwaffe into the air. The casualties, however, were severe and more experienced pilots were lost including Sergeants Neil Morrison, 26 and John Glendenning, 28 who was shot down while patrolling Dungeness. Pilot Officer Edward Churches, 19, one of the youngest Battle of Britain pilots also died in battle but that was not the case with Pilot Officer Peter Chesters, 22, from Thorpe Bay.

On November 27, in combat over Chatham, Chesters was badly wounded in the leg from canon shell fire but heroically remained at the controls of his crippled Spitfire, steering it away from the built-up area, until he saw open countryside below. He baled out and the aircraft crashed on the mud at Blacketts Marshes.

Chesters also parachuted down in the mud of Conyer Creek and as he began to sink weighed down by his Mae West and flying gear he was rescued by 32-year-old Bob Hodges who had seen the parachute open high over Blacketts Marshes. Bob said: "He was sinking fast. I put my arm around his neck and pulled, all the while making sure I was moving my feet around. He was badly injured but still conscious so we struggled together off the mud to a house in Conyer. We called the Orpington Military Hospital who came to get him."

A few days later, as Chesters lay in bed in hospital, a letter reached Group Captain Dick Grice at Biggin Hill. "I and the people of Conyer would very much like to thank the pilot of a fighter plane for staying at his controls and steering the damaged plane away from the village and a factory before baling out".

Bob Hodges also received a letter which read: "Forgive me for not writing sooner but I had to have an operation and

RAF Biggin Hill — Ops Room pass

things weren't good for a few days....If any of the other pilots could have seen the welcome which you and the people of Conyer gave me I am sure they would agree with me when I say that alone is worth dying for".

Pilot Officer Chesters later showed his gratitude by sending Bob Hodges a new watch inscribed with the date of the rescue. "Please believe me", he said, "when I tell you that I shall remember you all my life".

Chesters recovered from his injuries and celebrated in the best way he knew — by shooting down a Messerschmitt 109 on April 9, 1941. By that time 74 Squadron was at Manston and Chesters, delighted by his success, executed a victory roll over the station. He was too low. His Spitfire crashed onto the parade ground and he was killed instantly.

Flying Officer Peter Chesters, having survived one terrifying brush with death, then killed himself in a moment of sheer jubilation. His desire to live was so strong that he may well be the Spitfire pilot who infrequently returns. His may be a good case for students of ghost lore or psychic researchers to consider carefully.

RESCUER: Bob Hodges in 1997 with a photograph of 74 Squadron and the inscribed watch from Peter Chesters.

5

Forty nine days of terror

For some people at Biggin Hill the seven weeks between August 18 and October 6 were fraught with excitement, as if a vast aerial circus had been staged exclusively for their benefit. For others — and for the vast majority — it was sheer terror. During that period the Luftwaffe appeared on 16 occasions, dropped thousands of tons of high explosives and incendiaries, killed 43 people and wounded many more. By the time the Battle of Britain was entering its final stage the destruction of Biggin Hill was virtually complete. The married quarters were uninhabitable, the road and runways had been cratered and the Ops Room switched to an empty shop in Biggin Hill village. Somehow, miraculously, it remained "operational".

In this section, with the help of eye witness accounts, the bombing of Biggin is told in detail. It includes the drama in the village itself where many died because they defied the enemy and refused to leave. The ordeal suffered by non-RAF personnel was intolerable.

Death had he seen by sudden blow,
By wasting plague, by tortures slow,
By mine or breach, by steel or ball,
Knew all his shapes and scorned them all.

Walter Scott: Rokeby, 1, 1813

June 25 - October 31, 1940

June 25-28: All Biggin Hill's Hurricanes and Spitfires are converted to constant speed propellers, therefore matching the Messerschmitt in climbing, ceiling and power diving.

July 10: 141 Squadron returns to Biggin Hill after an absence of 21 years. They fly in Boulton and Paul Defiants, a slim Merlin-powered monoplane.

July 19: Five pilots and five gunners killed in 141 Squadron's first action of the war. Remainder of Squadron returns to Scotland for conversion to night fighter duties.

July 20: Hitler nominates August 10 as *Adler Tag,* the *Eagle Day*, the start of the annihilation of the RAF as a preliminary to the invasion of Britain; this was later postponed due to bad weather.

August 16: Lord Haw Haw, on *Germany Calling,* warns Biggin Hill that the Luftwaffe will soon attack Biggin Hill.

August 18: Station attacked. Crew member of a Bofors gun site and several civilians killed. Wounded taken to the decontamination centre for medical attention. 32 Squadron lose six Hurricanes.

August 21: DSO for Squadron Leader Mike Crossley, DFCs for Flying Officers, Gardiner, Humpherson and Smythe and MM for Sergeant Elizabeth Mortimer.

August 24: Group Captain Grice, flying an unarmed Miles Magister from Hawkinge to Biggin Hill, is attacked by two 109s. He flies home at rooftop height knowing the Huns dare not fly so low.

August 25: 32 Squadron to change places with their peacetime brothers, 79 squadron. Mike Crossley in the Squadron diary writes: "You brought us fear, depression, happiness, tragedy, laughs, new associations and thrills".

August 30: Noon raid on Biggin. Flying Officer Edward Morris claims a Messerschmitt "destroyed" in collision. He is in hospital recovering from the experience. Evening raid devastates station. Many killed and injured. Biggin Hill virtually out of action.

August 31: Signals section, post office engineers and civilian workers work for more than 24 hours to restore vital nerve centre. Station attacked again. Ops Room destroyed. Main road badly cratered. Pam Beecroft and Felicity Hanbury tour Biggin Hill village looking for billets for homeless WAAFs.

September 1: Funeral of those killed in bombing raids briefly abandoned as Luftwaffe attack again — Biggin Hill's fifth raid in 48 hours. Ordeal set to continue.

September 2: New Operations Room set up in an empty shop in the village of Biggin Hill. Controllers and plotters continue with chalk and a blackboard.

September 3: Group Captain Grice makes the decision to blow up the only remaining hangar to fool the Luftwaffe into believing that Biggin Hill is totally destroyed. He later appears before a Court of Inquiry and is heavily censured by Fighter Command.

September 4: German pilot parachutes down in field between Westerham and Sevenoaks. He is attacked and then arrested by driver and conductor of a passing bus.

September 7: Respite for Biggin Hill. Hitler calls off his offensive against sector airfields and launches the full might of his air force against London. The Blitz has begun.

September 8: 92 Squadron, commanded by Squadron Leader P.J.Sanders, takes the place of 79. They are billeted at Southwood, a mansion two miles south of the airfield. WAAFs now billeted in the Cedars in Keston village.

September 15: More squadrons are scrambled before dawn than at any other time in the battle. Most hectic day of all for Fighter Command and for Biggin Hill. Later to be celebrated as Battle of Britain Day.

September 16: 141 Squadron, almost wiped out in July, return to Biggin Hill as night fighters. This time they are able to celebrate after destroying a Heinkel.

October 13: 72 Squadron, down to just seven pilots of experience, ordered to leave Biggin Hill. They are replaced by 74 Squadron, commanded by 'Sailor' Malan.

October 31: Biggin Hill officially designated as the most bombed station in Fighter Command. Total score stands at just under 600 "kills". Group Captain Grice proud to announce that "we never closed". Day to be designated later as the end of the Battle of Britain.

Sunday August 18, 1940

EVERY man and woman at Biggin Hill knew that Biggin Hill was now on Goering's schedule, especially the vigilant staff in Operations Block and those who had heard, on the wireless, the upper-class nasal bragging of Lord Haw Haw. "This is Germany Calling, Germany Calling", he crowed. "Yesterday our mighty Luftwaffe bombed Croydon from the map. Soon, it will be your turn Kenley and Biggin Hill".

Sure enough, as Sunday lunchtime approached, the air-raid sirens warned the people of Kent of approaching aircraft. There were several formations and all were heading across south-east England towards London.

Kenley was first to suffer. Six Hurricanes on the ground were destroyed and every hangar but one was systematically bombed. The runways were cratered and communications so badly mauled that the Operations Room had to be later transferred to a butcher's shop in Caterham.

Ten minutes later Croydon was bombed again while another formation concentrated on a medium dive bombing attack on West Malling, damaging hangars and three Lysanders.

By now the final formation of 50 plus was over Tunbridge Wells and Biggin Hill's fighters, which had remained on hold, were climbing high in a bid to protect the base.

Group Captain Grice reckoned there were about five or six minutes left before the bombers arrived and ordered all personnel except those engaged on essential services to take cover immediately.

The first bombs fell to the east of the airfield, away from the station's buildings. Stick after stick rained down, one hitting the MT sheds and another falling close to where the army gunners had their Bofors trained to the sky.

Section Officer Felicity Hanbury, in one of the airwoman's trenches with her assistant, Hope Embry, listened to the explosions and recalled some of the flights of imagination among the airwomen during the period they called the "phoney war". All letters home were censored and one airwoman had written a vivid account of a heavy bombing raid on Biggin Hill to her mother. This, before a single raid of any importance had taken place in the British Isles.

Section Officer Hanbury knew the girls had volunteered in the spirit of St George and when the dragon did not appear they invented one. Now they faced the real thing and, in letters to their mothers, would probably minimise the danger.

The raid lasted barely ten minutes but, as the airmen and WAAFs emerged from the shelters and surveyed the shrapnel that carpeted the ground, stories of heroism began to emerge that were to take a place in RAF folklore. First, was the rumour that a company of Local Defence Volunteers had brought down a Dornier 17 on the far side of Leaves Green, arrested the crew and brought them to the airfield under guard. The second story concerned the heroism of Sergeant Elizabeth Mortimer who had carried on with her job in the Station Armoury when the alarm sounded, maintaining contact between the different defence posts. Before the Squadrons returned to re-arm she had rushed out on the airfield to mark all the unexploded bombs with red flags.

Sergeant Mortimer's bravery was recognised with the first Military Medal to be awarded to a WAAF in Great Britain. The achievement of the Local Defence Force — reported in full in the next day's newspapers — was not so sound. Information gathered after the incident gave equal credit to Kenley's ground defences and attacks by Sergeants Dymond and Brown of 111 Squadron.

BOMB DAMAGE: The King's Arms pub after the raid on August 18, 1940. Pub landlord Fred Horwood said he could see the rear gunner firing his gun as the Dornier flew low over the building. The holes in the boot of the car give credence to that alarming observation.

Several bombs fell short of the airfield and five people living in Leaves Green Crescent, opposite the King's Arms pub died. They were Annie Hallsworth, aged 40 and her daughter Marjorie, 10 of No 2 and Ethel, 57, and Rupert Lomas, 56, of No 3. A visitor, William Dean of Chislehurst, who was injured in this attack later died in the County Hospital, Farnborough.

Over at the King's Arms a few customers had chosen, as an act of defiance more than courage, to remain in the pub when they heard the bombers arrive. Bill Blundell from Grubground Farm was among them. So was his mate, Lou Deane, owner of a china shop in Chislehurst and Fred Horwood, the jovial landlord. For a while they crouched under the bar listening to the explosions and the crackle of machine gun fire but curiosity overcame them and they went outside. They chose the wrong moment. Machine gun bullets raked into the body of Bill, Lou and Fred sending them sprawling on the ground. As they picked themselves up a high explosive burst by the side of the road and smashed against the side of Bill Blundell's leg exposing a raw gaping wound. Somehow they crawled back into the pub, which was now on fire and waited for help. It was 1.30 pm.

Bill lost part of his leg but recovered to carry on farming. Fred Holwood also had a leg amputated a few years later but gangrene affected the wound and he died. Lou Deane also died from his injuries.

Hundreds of craters now pock-marked the airfield and while officers and men of the Air Force and Army and scores of willing volunteers from the village set to work filling them in, a bomb disposal squad discovered that many of the unexploded bombs were British, presumably captured during the Battle of France. They estimated that about 500 bombs had been released on Biggin Hill during those terrifying 10 minutes and the casualties were two killed and three wounded.

The schoolboy's story

PETER Halliday of High Wycombe, Bucks was a nine-year-old schoolboy living at Biggin Hill with his parents when war broke out in 1939. For a while they lived in the married quarters but Peter and his mother were quickly evacuated to Somerset to escape the expected blitz on the airfield. When that failed to materialise they came back to Biggin Hill — first to a small wooden bungalow called *'Grandee'* in Moselle Road and then to a larger bungalow *'Lingmulla'* on the Main Road which was a converted railway carriage. During the 1920s it had been used by Londoners as a weekend retreat in the country.

Peter attended Biggin Hill school on the main road behind Abbot's Bakery. He remembers that it did not have any air raid shelters so a temporary shelter was constructed in Class One using blackboards from other rooms. They were propped between desks and window sills and then covered with sandbags and gave protection for about 30 children.

For several weeks Peter played happily with the other kids who lived in that area of Biggin Hill. He remembers the severe winter of 1940, the arrival of the Anderson shelters, the blast wall built in front of the doorway, the wailing of the air-raid sirens, the false alarms and, in July, the increased activity on the airfield as the Battle of Britain began in earnest.

The month of August, 1940 was perhaps the most memorable of his life. This is his story.

"During the first two weeks of August we had an air raid warning nearly every day — mostly in the afternoon — but nothing happened. The Spitfires would take off and return an hour or so later. Dad would come home about 8.30 in the evening for the night and return to camp about 7.30 in the morning. Because of security the bus service to Bromley had been a bit of a hazard to the RAF and buses were only allowed through the camp after all identity cards had been checked at the Black Horse. They would proceed with an armed guard on the top deck watching the passengers. From the beginning of August, however, the bus was diverted via Downe and Dad had to walk both ways, morning and night.

"On Wednesday August 14 the siren sounded about three o'clock in the afternoon. Mum and I sat in the shelter awaiting the all-clear but all was quiet until we suddenly heard three or four loud explosions. We later heard that bombs had fallen on Westerham a few miles away. Dad told us that the Germans were fitting whistles to the tails of their bombs to make more noise and frighten their intended victims.

"Our first taste of battle happened four days later (August 18) at lunch time on Sunday. We had passed a quiet morning without incident. Mum was sitting in the sun by the back door reading the Pictorial and I was playing with my meccano when suddenly our peace was shattered by planes taking off from the airfield.

"As we stood by the back door watching them climb single file into the sky our next door neighbour said: 'Look at those

BOY AT BIGGIN: Peter Halliday in 1940.

Jerries, Mrs Halliday. Bloody hundreds of them'. As he was speaking there came a long drawn out whine and I spotted a small plane, glinting silver in the sunlight, coming straight down towards the aerodrome.

"Protesting that the siren had not sounded I was bundled into the shelter. Then the siren started to wail and the guns opened fire. The noise from the big guns and the bofors was unbearable — just like one big roar. They stopped when our fighters went in and the noise changed to straining engines and the rat-tat-tat of the German gunners trying to defend themselves.

"Then came a different sound — the most frightening of all — the whistling of falling bombs. Mum laid partly over me on the shelter floor, the ground jumped and swayed and loose dirt fell from the cracks above. I began to feel ill. After ten minutes the bombing stopped and the guns started again. Mum said: 'Let's put a record on' and reached for the gramophone. The familiar strains of *'Who's Afraid of the Big Bad Wolf'* seemed to fit the situation perfectly.

"From the shelter door we could see the Hurricanes and Spitfires returning to base to re-arm and re-fuel. One or two looked a bit battered and one had a large hole through the wing. Still the fury of the battle raged overhead but slowly the noise faded and the silence returned. We could hear the birds singing and then they were drowned by the sounding of the all clear.

"We emerged from the Anderson dusty and shaken to see the sun shining brightly. I picked up an empty bullet case, British made and still warm. The date on the bottom read 1939. An hour later Dad came through the gate covered in dust chalk carrying a small parcel. 'A souvenir', he said. It was half the tail of a small German bomb, badly bent, painted green. Stamped on one fin was a German eagle with a swastika. My second souvenir in one day.

"Dad said most of the bombs fell on the golf course on the far side of the airfield. A few had landed on the North Camp. A German plane had been shot down near Keston Church and some of the crew were in the guard room. A gun site had been hit killing and injuring two men.

"During the next two weeks we had more raids. I was now 10, not 'streetwise' but certainly 'skywise'. Nearly all the boys of my age could identify instantly most of the aeroplanes and, in many cases, by the sound alone. Even the Hurricane and Spitfire, which used the same Rolls Royce Merlin engines, sounded different. We knew that to watch gun fire was dangerous because a minute or two later jagged pieces of shrapnel would rain down, bouncing off concrete and roofs.

"German bullet cases recovered from crash sites became schoolboy currency — far more valuable than marbles or cigarette cards. To add to our trading problems the school did not reopen after the summer holiday as they still did not have the shelter dug.

"Mid-day on Friday August 30 there was a much heavier raid and, in the shelter, mum played the gramophone again in defiance of the racket. *'Who's Afraid of the Big Bad Wolf'* and *'The Laughing Policeman'* were played over and over again.

Left: Peter Halliday on top of the bunker with his eyes trained towards the east. "I was 10 and skywise", he said. "All boys of my age could identify most of the aircraft". The drawing below, also by Peter, illustrates the moment at 6.30 pm when a formation of Junkers arrived without warning. "Christ", said Dad, "they're Jerries not Blenheims. He pushed me in a shelter and ran to get Mum".

"Dad was still on the airfield. He came home at half past four that afternoon and said that the men had been told to move their families away. Most of the bombs had dropped in and around Jail Lane. Many of them were D.As (delayed action) and could go off at any time. 'For the brave men of the Bomb Disposal Unit', Dad said, 'it was like playing a game of Russian Roulette'.

"About six o'clock Mum asked Dad to go round to *La Daceda* and buy a packet of tea and some sweets. 'Take Peter with you', she said 'and I'll get something to eat'. Dad was just about to open the gate when I looked over to the right. Flying very low in what appeared to be a line abreast formation were a number of twin-engined aeroplanes coming straight towards us. Dad said: 'I expect they are Blenheims coming back from Manston, then changed his tune. 'Christ', he said, 'they're Jerries'. He pushed me towards the shelter door and ran into the bungalow to get Mum.

"I watched from the shelter door. What had appeared to be a line turned out to be three 'vics of three planes flying side by side. Their formation was as precise and as steady as a pre-war air display. The noise was deafening as I took in their detail — the pale blue of the underside, the black crosses and the sun glinting on the perspex noses. I stood as if in a trance and Dad gave me a push into the shelter. Mum followed. Then I noticed he was shaking like a leaf.

"Little did I know that most of the Biggin Hill personnel were beginning to suffer from 'nerves' and Dad's reaction was typical of the effect the heavier bombing was having. He sat down in the shelter heavily and right on top of the gramophone record *'Who's Afraid of the Big Bad Wolf'* smashing it to smithereens.

"For half an hour I crouched in the shelter with my hands over my ears as the guns and the bombs battled it out. The noise was terrific and, as a little girl in the village used to say, my eyes began to sweat!"

"When the all-clear sounded we came out of the shelter and saw a large light-grey cloud of dust and smoke hanging over the airfield. Something terrible had happened. The silence seemed unnatural and that was broken only by the occasional fire bell ringing down the main road as it made its way to the foreboding cloud of dust.

"The next door neighbour was in a state of shock. All he could say was 'There was no siren...no warning...poor devils'. People stood around in little groups. No-one spoke. They just watched the cloud disperse. About seven o'clock Dad went back to camp, his cigarette shaking more than usual. About the same time a white chalk-like dust began to settle and within half an hour the window ledges, roofs, leaves on the trees and clothes had taken a shade of white. As night fell the sky was clear of any trace of the raid. Only a small flickering glow could be seen in the direction of the airfield.

"People who lived in the village now shared a concern for each other's welfare. Nobody would admit to being frightened as that would seem to let the side down. After each raid the station's Commanding Officer would make sure that victims in Biggin Hill were looked after. He sent vehicles to move people out of bombed bungalows and maintenance men to patch up any damage. Now it was our turn to look after them. Our mums made sandwiches and endless cups of tea for the ground crews who were trying to keep the planes flying. Our Dads got old cars out of 'mothballs' and used their precious petrol to rescue Biggin Hill pilots 'downed' somewhere in deepest Kent.

"Neighbours helped to clear the main road, knock down unsafe buildings and make sure the access to the airfield was clear. Villagers were united by a common danger — in some wonderful way it brought us all together.

"At mid-day on August 31 the sirens started again. We now went into next door's shelter. It had a carpet, a table and a little bedside cabinet with a bowl of fruit and even a curtain over the door. The bombs soon came whislting down but the whistle lasted much longer, indicating they were being dropped from much higher up. The ground started jumping and heaving again and the fruit bowl started moving across the cabinet top. This time the bombing seemed heavier and it was almost an hour before the all-clear sounded.

"Dad came home at three o'clock. He looked all in — very rough with his uniform ragged. His face was dirty and unshaven and his boots were covered in chalk. He didn't say a word and nor did we. He tried to light a cigarette but could not keep it still long enough for the match to light it. Mum lit it for him. Dad went to wash and shave and when he returned his chin was covered in blood, caused by his shaking hand.

"He then told us that the camp had nearly been knocked out in the previous night's raid and many had been killed. Apparently men were just going into the cookhouse for tea when the planes struck. They were caught in the open and machine-gunned to death. A WAAF shelter had received a direct hit burying many inside. He had spent the night digging and they had even used floodlights despite the blackout.

"He told us that the milkman arrived just after dawn, saw what was happening, uttered the words 'sod the milk' and began to dig. Four hours later he was still there, digging for the trapped victims. Dad told us that by mid-morning the roads were clear but then the raiders returned. This time No 5, Married Quarters had received a direct hit, flattening it to the ground. A huge bomb fell in the road outside the main gate, and demolished the cafe opposite together with a Lyons Swiss Roll lorry which was making a delivery. All that was left of the lorry were the wheels and engine. The bodywork and the timber from the cafe was hanging around trees and the ground was covered with fruit pies, Swiss rolls and jam tarts. Chocolate and cigarettes littered the floor of the demolished cafe. Airmen were told to take what they wanted. Dad had three one pound blocks of Cadbury's Fruit and Nut and 40 Players'

"At five o'clock the sirens started again. This time we suffered about three quarters of an hour of intermittent gun fire and falling bombs. The following day the airfield received three attacks. The dust which hung over the airfield was now a regular feature. Our shelter was also damaged and mum spent a morning carrying out essential repairs.

"So it went on, night after night. The airfield was now covered with little flags which taxiing aircraft had to weave in and out of on their way to take-off. I and my friends made model aeroplanes and ran around the garden simulating aircraft noises. The retired couple who lived opposite complained that my impression of an air-raid siren was so like the real thing that they had taken to the shelter on three occasions.

WAAFS AT WORK: *The plotters in the Operations Room at Biggin Hill before it was put out of action in the raid of August 31, 1940.*

Friday August 30

THANKS to the brilliance and bravery of 79 and 610 Squadrons who had torn straight into a formation of bombers and fighters, sent to wipe Biggin Hill off the map, the lunchtime raid of Friday August 30 was like a damp squib. Those that did get through dropped their bombs wide of the airfield, causing damage only in Biggin Hill village and Keston.

The evening raid, however, was a different story. As a group of airmen came pouring out of the Mess they saw nine Junkers 88s appear menacingly from the east. There had been no warning from the station sirens. As machine gun fire strafed the aerodrome and bombs began to fall the men ran full pelt for the nearest shelter and dived for safety. There was not room for all the airmen and many were left in the open exposed, like sitting ducks, to the machine gun fire. They were the lucky ones. The air raid shelter received a direct hit from a 1,000 lb high explosive, leaving a vast crater and dozens of mangled bodies, some hardly recognisable.

Over in the Officers' Mess, 30 pilots were taking lunch when the tannoy blared out — "B Flight 79 Squadron to readiness immediately". Within minutes a Humber shooting brake, driven by WAAF driver Lonsdale, drew up to take a few of the pilots from Mess to dispersal. They had reached the hangar area when Rupert Clerke suddenly yelled to his colleagues — "Junkers 88s. To the shelter quickly".

Flying Officer Teddy Morris recalled this moment: "We piled down the steps into the nearest shelter a few yards away and just made it as the ground shook from a near miss. Bombs then went off all around and eventually the all-clear sounded and we crawled out into a world of smoke, dust and damage.

Our Humber, parked by a tree, was missing, just a huge hole in the ground where it had been. A little later there was a shout from inside the hangar and there were the remains of the shooting brake. It had been lifted up some 60 feet by the blast and deposited through the roof of the triple bay hangar landing on its back, a flattened wreck. It was less than 100 yards from the bomb shelter which had received a direct hit.

Section Officer Felicity Hanbury was talking to Flight Sergeant Gartside by the WAAF guardroom when the civilian air-raid warning sounded. At first they decided to go into one of the airwomen's trenches but as nothing happened and there was no warning from the station sirens SO Hanbury decided to walk alone to the HQ building 300 yards away and go into the officers' trench. The Padre was already there. So was a WAAF cypher officer, Pam Beecroft and also Michael Crossley of 32 Squadron who had flown down for the day from Acklington and had been 'caught' on the ground.

SO Hanbury remembered that moment: "The trench filled rapidly", she said, "and we sat packed like sardines, with tin hats on, waiting. I could heard the aircraft taking off, first one, then another and another

HEROINE: Felicity Hanbury, later awarded the MBE.

THUMBS UP. A bomb crater in the garden of a house near the airfield. — a photograph taken early September 1940.

until all our Squadrons were airborne. Things then happened quickly. Bombs fell on the far side of the aerodrome, each one seeming to come nearer until one fell just outside out trench. The vibration and blast were such that I thought my limbs would come apart. Bombs fell continuously, the noise was undescribable until, finally, there was a lull and I could hear our aircraft returning to refuel and re-arm". When a messenger arrived to tell the Padre that an airman's trench had received a direct hit — and would he go at once — the other officers also decided to leave, even though the all-clear had not sounded. The sight that greeted them was appalling. Sixteen high explosive bombs, estimated at 1,000 llbs each, had fallen among the buildings. The workshop, transport yard, stores, barrack stores, armoury, guardroom, meteorological office and the station institute were all wrecked. The cookhouses and the Naafi were damaged and the airmen's barracks uninhabitable. One aircraft had received a direct hit, two aircraft were burnt out and all electricity, water and gas mains cut. One bomb has fallen near the Airmen's Married Quarters which were being used as accommodation for WAAFs. Worse still was the sight of the gaping crater, mangled flesh and bits of uniform. Nearby, close to what was left of the Guardroom, the concrete walls of another shelter had caved in, trapping inside scores of terrified WAAFs.

"When I arrived there were many airmen digging to reach the trapped women", said SO Hanbury. "The dry summer had made the ground unusually hard and the task was no light one. Ambulances and stretcher parties were standing by and, one by one, the airwomen were brought out. One was dead, several were badly injured including Flight Sergeant Gartside who had a broken back. Miraculously, the majority had escaped unhurt".

The dead WAAF was Aircraftswoman (1st class) Edna Lena Button. The daughter of Bertha Button of Scottsdale, Tasmania, Deaconess of the Methodist Church of New Zealand and her husband Edmund. Lena was Biggin Hill's only nursing orderly. She was 39.

As darkness fell on the airmens' crater the digging continued by the light of an emergency generator, torches and motor car headlamps. The dead were taken out, stored in a separate room and an orderly detailed to take particulars from their identity discs. The badly injured were given a dose of morphia by doctors from Downe and Orpington who had arrived on the scene. In many cases injections had to be made in the face as this was the only part of the body visible. A few were freed only after having their limbs amputated.

All night long the digging continued. The airmen were now assisted by ARP teams from Orpington, many villagers from Biggin Hill and Cudham and a gang of Welsh miners. Meanwhile Flight Lieutenant Osmond and his Signals Section toiled vainly to restore the telephone links with No 11 Group headquarters, the Observer Corps and the R/T transmitter and receiver. By morning the Operations Room was back on the air.

Felicity Hanbury found that her own Mess was uninhabitable as there was a delayed action bomb in the garden and the only other intact Mess for the WAAFs was that belonging to Other Ranks on the edge of the

VIP TOUR. A few weeks before the bombing, Secretary of State for Air, Sir Kingsley Wood and the Chancellor of the Exchequer, Sir John Simon toured Biggin Hill station to meet the personnel at Britain's premier fighter station. Here they chat to Corporals Dobell and Bishop, Sergeant Mitchell, FS Cripps and SO Petrice outside their block in the Airmens' Married Quarters. This house was severely damaged on August 30.

aerodrome. There, she found the girls cooking sausage and mash virtually in the dark, by the light of a few hurricane lamps. Outside was an endless stream of airmen, soldiers and rescue teams filing slowly past a serving hatch.

Group Captain Dick Grice sat up well into the night sending telegrams to the parents of those known to be killed. It was important to get the funerals over as soon as possible, so he and the Padre had chosen the following Sunday. He then slept for a few hours on the terrace of the Officers' Mess, having relinquished his own house to the bombed out WAAF officers.

Section Officer Hanbury also had the duty to inform the next of kin. She sent a letter to Corporal Button's parents, saw the wounded airwomen in sick quarters and hospital and then found billets in the village for the WAAFs whose quarters had been completely demolished. "The attitude of some householders", she said, "came as a shock. Some rudely slammed their doors while others made us stand on the doorsteps and listen to their views of the RAF in general and Biggin Hill in particular. They said that had it not been for Biggin Hill the lives of innocent civilians would not have been in danger. Eventually other villagers rallied round and my faith in human nature was restored".

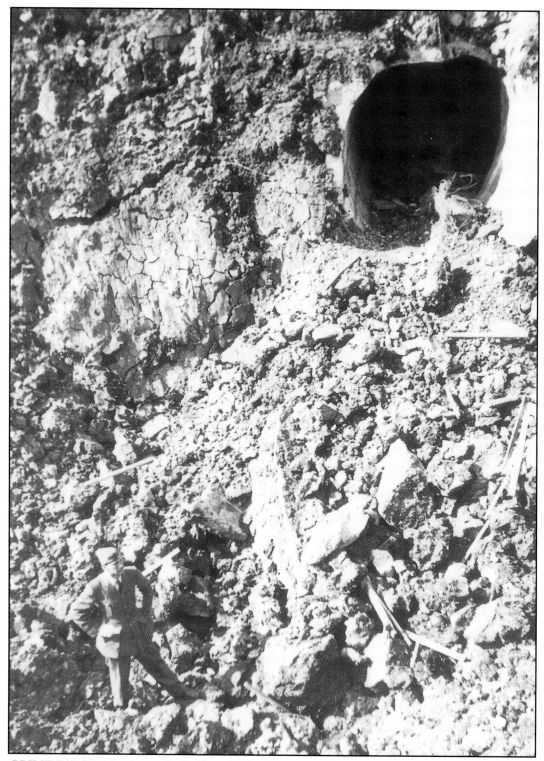

PRIME TARGET: Senior medical officer, Flight Lieutenant Curwen, stands some 15 feet below what is left of the trench shelter, bombed on the evening of August 30, 1940 killing 39. In all 16 high explosives fell and Section Officer Felicity Hanbury later wrote that it was the smallness of the target that Biggin Hill presented and the sight of aircraft actually diving down to destroy the station which made all the raids so terrifying. "In the London Blitz", she said, "I felt almost safe by comparison".

An aerial photograph taken during a raid on Biggin Hill airfield, with German markings indicating bomb bursts and presumed installations

1. Bomb explosions
2. Hangars
3. Assembly shops
4. Store houses
5. Repair shops & store houses
6. Workshop
7. Briefing hall
8. Barrack huts
9. Power station
10. Administration block
11. Dispersed aircraft

2965

This is a German photograph of Biggin Hill under attack on August 30, 1940 when 16 high explosives estimated 1,000 lbs weight each fell among the buildings. The bottom right hand key gives the details.

BRAVERY: This picture of the girls of 'D' Watch was taken outside the Ops Room by Elaine Lewis just a few days before the Ops Room was bombed with many of the girls inside. Elspeth Henderson who won the Military Medal is centre in the middle row. The other girls remembered only by their Christian names are Pam, Sylvia, Yvonne, Joyce, Elaine, Rachel, Josephine, Paddy, Dulcie and Vivienne Lee.

GOODBYE BIGGIN: Airmen await transport from the South Camp for the peace of Acklington, Northumberland.

The 39 victims in the trench shelter

THE high explosive which scored a direct hit on the trench shelter killed every occupant inside except for one airman. The first to take cover, he was crouched right at the back protected by the unlucky 39 around him.

It is almost impossible to imagine the scene on that Friday evening of August 30 — the worst day ever known in the history of Biggin Hill — but one who has a clear recollection of the horrors that unfolded before him is Gordon Clark, 81 in 2001 and living in Sevenoaks.

Gordon was among the 1,000 airmen who worked on the station. Newly promoted from Leading Aircraftsman to Corporal he was 20 years old and had more than a year's experience as an engine and airframe fitter with 32 Squadron. In fact his skills were so appreciated that when members of 32 Squadron took a well-deserved sabbatical in Acklington, Gordon didn't join them. Instead he found himself seconded to the workshops which were situated behind the Guardroom and slightly to the right of the Equipment Store.

This area was the nerve centre of RAF Biggin Hill. Beyond the workshops and slightly to the right was the transport yard, while the canteen, Naafi and cookhouse were over to the left. With more than 1,200 airmen working at the station alongside 250 WAAFs, and now scores of civilian workers, the area buzzed with activity.

With the Battle of Britain at its zenith, life in the workshops was far from dull. Here the airmen worked overtime meeting the station's many engineering requirements. Gordon found himself working in the machine room, or plug bay or on the vertical drill; sometimes he was in the tractor yard. He was also a key member of the technical crash and rescue party and it was in this capacity that he was required to help in the likely event of another raid on the airfield..

Gordon remembered how, on this perfect late summer's evening, the whole of Biggin Hill was braced for the day's second attack. The nerves of everyone from the Station Commander to the youngest apprentice were frayed and that was caused, not only by the constant bombing, but also by the possibility that Biggin Hill was harbouring fifth-columnists. There were many would-be suspects but these lurked more in the imagination than in reality.

As six o'clock approached on this fateful evening some off-duty airmen were enjoying tea time in the Welcome and Ace cafes. A few were on their way to the Black Horse Inn just down the road but the majority were still in the area where the main road (then closed to civilian traffic) weaved between the busy cluster of buildings. At the back of the transport yard towards the tarmac road that led to the hangar were two Chevron-shaped slit trenches which had been quickly dug in 1938 after the Munich scare — one for men and one for the women. These were of "lance corporal" shape with an entrance at both ends and covered

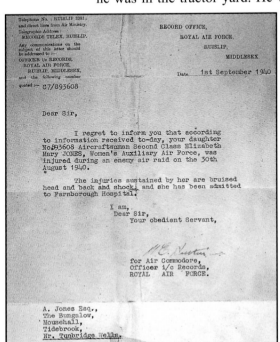

An official letter to the family of Mary Jones, who was injured in the raid of August 30 1940.

GRISLY SCENE: This gaping crater was the airmens' trench. Rescuers worked all night carrying out the dead and giving morphia to the injured. Of the 40 personnel in the shelter it is believed that only one survived.

by a protective concrete roof. They were a larger and cruder version of the later Anderson version and provided shelter for about 40 people.

Some airmen were in the Naafi. They included corporals, leading aircraftsmen, a mixture of reservists (1st and 2nd class) and a few officers. Members of the Squadron ground staff, the ARP workers, the GPO (war group) team responsible for operational landlines and scores of civilian workers were at their posts. The tension was unbearable.

Many were still in the Mess and in the yard when the expected warning sounded — too late. Pouring out into the sunshine they saw the Junkers bearing down on them from the east and they heard the crackle of machine gun fire from the perimeter posts. They piled into the shelter. There was not room for all, but 39 airmen and civilian workers managed to squeeze into the narrow confines of the darkness. A terrified Naafi girl, who had been serving drinks just seconds earlier also threw herself into the airman's shelter. Another Naafi girl chose to sprint to the next airwomen's shelter.

By now the bombs were falling and the 40 people sat tight together with their arms folded listening to the vibrant roar. Some would have silently prayed as the head-splitting inferno grew in its ferocity. They may not have spoken and they would not have had time to experience that moment of horror that precedes death as a bomb weighing a thousand pounds ripped into their trench and erupted with a detonation that echoed round the valley . A monstrous gaping crater and scores of mangled bodies were left in its wake.

Corporal Gordon Clark's shift had ended at 4pm on that Friday evening. Planning to go out he had returned to his billet, washed and shaved and was pushing his bike towards the main road when the bombs started falling. He quickly sought refuge in the underground shelter behind the workshops and waited for the all-clear.

POPULAR: Naafi girl Trixie who was shot and killed by an attacking aircraft a few days after this photograph was taken.

The scene outside was chaotic. As a member of the rescue party Gordon needed to join his colleagues in the lorry which was equipped with cutting gear and everything necessary for such an emergency. The shelter was uncovered and one by one the bodies were brought out including that of Mary Cremin, a 24-year-old Irish Naafi girl. Her friend Trixie was also dead — gunned down in the open and found by the side of a hedge. She had never made it to the second trench. Ten civilian workers and 23 airmen were also dead but, miraculously, six were taken out alive and given morphia. Only one survived.

As the mutilated bodies were taken from the crater to a surviving building nearby an orderly was given the horrific task of identifying the dead from their identity discs. Doctors from Orpington and Downe, the station's own medical staff and rescuers worked all night. The gruesome task continued in the light of the following day while a temporary morgue was established at Redbrick Farm , Jail Lane. Following the mass funeral at Biggin Hill many familes removed their loved ones for burial elsewhere. Elizabeth Burton, for example, wife of AC2 Archibald Burton buried her husband at Eastbrook Cemetery, Dagenham while William and Rose Crane removed the body of their son Herbert Crane to Islington. Many others were taken to the Star Lane Cemetery at St Mary Cray which was used regularly by RAF Biggin Hill. After the war the remains of some were exhumed for repatriation elsewhere.

Amid the chaos and the tragedy of this day came many stories of lucky escapes. Robert Burkin of Biggin Hill remembered his father telling him that he was driving back to the station on that day with two fellow workmates, Joby Lambert and Fred Skinner. Approaching Keston Church they were flagged down and told that the station was being bombed. Uncertain whether they should carry on or wait until things quietened down they tossed a coin — and it told them to wait. "Fate or possibly premonition took a hand", said Robert. "Had my father managed to get back to the yard he would almost certainly have gone straight into the trench shelter which took the direct hit".

There was one incident to smile about. One of the contractors helping to repair the runway was a firm called Sherfield and they employed a rather exceptionally fat man to operate the steam roller. He was actually on the runway when the raiders appeared and, with nowhere to hide, used great initiative to crawl into the vacant wheel space of his roller. There he crouched, well protected but uncomfortable, while the explosions echoed around him. When the raid ended he found he was stuck in the roller and it took more than two hours to free him.

FRIDAY AUGUST 30 — THE CASUALTIES

The RAF personnel killed in the trench shelter on August 30 were:

LAC Richard Cross, aged 42, son of Henry and Ann Cross and husband of Winifred Cross of Aldershot. Buried at Aldershot Civil Cemetery.

AC2 Archibald Burton, aged 26, son of Archibald and Rose Burton and husband of Elizabeth Burton of Dagenham. Buried at Eastbrook Cemetery, Dagenham.

LAC George Riggs, husband of Lilian Riggs of Luton. Buried at Luton General Cemetery.

AC2 Leonard Moors, aged 25, son of Walter and Annie Moors of Mow Cop. Buried at St Thomas Churchyard, Mow Cop.

AC2 John Whitford, son of John and Jessie Whitford and husband of Anne Louise Whitford of Ilford. Buried at Chingford Mount Cemetery.

AC1 William Wright, aged 22, son of William and Margaret Wright of New Ferry, Birkenhead. Buried at Bebington Cemetery.

LAC Deric Carter, aged 31, husband of Grace Carter of Barking. Buried at Rippleside Cemetery, Barking.

AC1 Herbert Crane, aged 23, son of William and Elizabeth Crane of Shoreditch, London. Buried at Islington Cemetery.

AC2 Arthur Hudson, aged 20, son of Elizabeth Hudson of Warrington. Buried at Warrington Cemetery.

AC2 Dennis Murton, aged 28, son of Charles and Ellen Murton of Tostock. Buried at St Andrew's Churchyard, Tostock.

The following are buried at Star Lane Cemetery, St Mary Cray, Orpington:

AC2 Douglas Emery, aged 21, son of Frank and Mary Emery of Pimlico, London.

LAC Thomas Brunning, aged 30, son of Thomas and Catherine Brunning and husband of Lena Brunning of Stamford Brook, London.

Cpl Percy Clark, aged 39, son of George and Minnie Clark and husband of Daisy Clark of Ware, Hertfordshire.

LAC James Dyning, aged 21, son of James and Emma Dyning of Lewisham, London.

The following died of their injuries on August 31 1940.

Cpl Bertram Imeson, aged 27, son of Bertram and Rosette Imeson of Acock's Green, Birmingham.

AC1 John Jackson, aged 23, husband of Hilda Jackson of Wellington, Shropshire.

Cpl Walter Mumford, aged 40, son of Walter and Elizabeth Mumford and husband of Dorothy Mumford of Southville, Bristol. Vorporal Mumford.

Corporal Richard White, aged 50, son of Richard and Lilian White and husband of Lottie White of Guildford, Surrey.

AC2 Joseph Musgrove, aged 21, son of Joseph and Caroline Musgrove of Chadwell Heath, Romford, Essex.

AC2 Eric Stopher, aged 26, son of Edwin and Fanny Stopher, husband of Beatrice Stopher of Ipswich, Suffolk.

There are no details of **Flying Officer Peter Desmond, AC1 Albert Wren, AC2 Edward Veae, LAC Edwin Butterfield, Cpl Alfred Baker, AC1 Jim George, AC2 James Barnett** who were all killed in the airmen's trench.

WO Edna Lena Button, aged 39, daughter of Edmund and Bertha Button of Scottsdale, Tasmania died in the airwomen's trench.

The civilian casualties were as follows:

Mary Cremin, aged 24 (Naafi).

Thomas Curtis, aged 63 of High Beeches, Sunningvale Avenue, Biggin Hill.

Albert Davis, aged 49 of 7 Plantation Cottages, Crofton Road, Farnborough.

George Dunn, aged 40 of 3 Pawley Cottages, Napier Road, Bromley.

Thomas Evans, aged 35 of Crown Ash Cottage, Saltbox Hill, Biggin Hill.

Robert Gibson, aged 51 of 3 Cramworth Cottages, Leaves Green, Biggin Hill.

George Hollingsworth, aged 58 of 9 Gravel Pit Cottages, Bromley.

William Kingston, aged 58 of 14 Crescent Road, Bromley.

Frank Longman, aged 56 of Lyndhurst, Westerham Hill.

Herbert Lowe, aged 58 of Park View Bungalow, Main Road, Biggin Hill.

Norman Roberts, aged 39 of Maytrees, Main Road, Biggin Hill.

These were all registered in the Orpington (Bromley) Register Office and the entries state — "due to war operations".

The mortuary at Biggin Hill (left) was not large enough to accommodate all the bodies from the tragedy of August 30 so many were taken to a temporary mortuary at Redbrick Farm, Jail Lane.

CEDARS: The house in Keston village requisitioned as a billet for Biggin Hill WAAFs. For many evenings during the raids the girls slept in the entrance hall of the mansion and on one occasion heard the ominous and familiar whistle of a falling bomb. The ensuing explosion was strangely muffled — it had penetrated harmlessly deep into the trunk of the wonderful cedar tree which stood outside. The house was demolished after the war.

***THAT SUMMER:** A feature of life at Biggin Hill were the many parties, usually organised by Squadron officers. Here the WAAFs prove that they too could enjoy the long summer evenings of 1940 and the message from 'A' Watch is "to hell with Hitler". Within a few weeks these girls were homeless.*

The man who died intestate

THOMAS Curtis, painter, decorator and odd-job man, was one of those many civilians who responded to the call for help after the bombing of Biggin Hill on August 18. His skills were required to help get the station in some state of order despite the threat of more attacks.

Tom was 63 and lived in Sunningvale Avenue, Biggin Hill with his mistress or common-law wife, Louisa Webb. Although he was still married, the much-younger Louisa called herself Mrs Curtis, kept an immaculate house and looked after her and Tom's five children (four boys and a girl). Living within a few yards of a Battle of Britain senior sector station with five children made everyday life rather stressful but the couple had many friends and were in love. There was work at Biggin Hill for the previously-unemployed Tom and he, along with all those at The Bump, was determined that the Luftwaffe would not break that spirit of defiance for which the station was becoming famous.

Tom was working at Biggin Hill on August 30 when the sirens wailed again and the Junkers appeared. Along with other civilian workers and airmen he made his way to the concrete covered trench shelter at the back of the transport yard. The shelter took a direct hit. Tom Curtis was one of 39 killed outright. He died intestate, leaving a complex domestic plight — a wife, Amelia (living near Biggin Hill), a mistress Louisa and their five children at High Beeches, Sunningvale Avenue.

His wife, Amelia immediately claimed the house was hers. Louisa challenged that claim, explaining that Amelia had left Tom and the children some years earlier. For two years she fought with the authorities for the right to continue to live in Tom's home and for the custody of her own children. She had not been married. She lost both battles. In 1942 Amelia Curtis moved into High Beeches and Louisa moved out.

The boys were sent to an orphanage at Tiptree in Essex but the youngest child, Margaret — then aged three — was recommended for adoption by Ernest and Doris Fowler who were billeted at Biggin Hill and had been friendly with Tom and Louisa. In fact it was Doris' sister, Elsie Palfrey who became Margaret's new mother and the little girl moved to Bristol where Frank Palfrey worked for the Gloucester Aircraft Company.

Margaret grew up knowing nothing of her tragic background or the whereabouts of her real mother. When Margaret was 14 Louisa was taken into St Mary Cray Hospital. She had contracted gangrene and both of her legs were amputated. That was in 1953. She never recovered from the shock of that operation.

Many years later the adopted Margaret Palfrey was able to trace the tragic story of her father's demise, track down her brothers and discover how her mother had died. Her married name today is Margaret Marfell. She has a son, daughter and four grandchildren and she lives at Longlevens, Gloucestershire.

ADOPTED: Margaret Curtis, who knew nothing of her tragic background.

OPS ROOM: Flight Lieutenant Curwen, senior medical officer, examines the mangled remains of the Ops Centre. This picture was taken to the north with the main entrance to the right of Flt Lt Curwen. The four steps behind him are those which lead up to the remains of the Operations Room.

Saturday August 31

THE Luftwaffe had not finished with Biggin Hill. Punctually, they returned at noon on Saturday August 31 and again the sirens were unable to give sufficient warning in time for all the station personnel to take cover.

This time a small formation of Dornier 215s appeared but, wary of the fighters below, they dropped their bombs from the safety of 12,000 feet. There was further damage to buildings and services. The runways were so badly cratered that the Spitfires of 72 Squadron, on their way down from Acklington, were ordered not to land at their new base.

There were no casualties but there was a mighty scare for the ground crews attached to 610 Squadron. They were waiting patiently by the entrance to the North Camp for the buses to take them to Bromley station and then on to London and Acklington, to be reunited with their pilots who had flown north in their Spitfires a few hours earlier. As bombs rained indiscriminately from the sky the men dropped their haversacks and kit bags in the road and scattered in all directions. Most fled for the woods where they crouched in terror listening to the explosions all around them.

As soon as the all-clear sounded every available man and woman set to work again filling in the craters, reconnecting the services and making life as comfortable as possible in the badly mauled, terribly scarred environment that surrounded them. In the village of Biggin Hill, Felicity Hanbury and Pam Beecroft, the Cypher Officer continued their quest to find billets for the "homeless" airwomen.

There had been enemy activity over the south east for most of the day and by six o'clock the Biggin Hill squadrons were still scrapping many miles away and in no position to defend the station. For Controllers, Squadron Leaders Roger Frankland and John Worrall the signs were ominous. They knew the Luftwaffe was keeping to a tight schedule and wondered if the small formation of bombers following the Ashford-Redhill railway were on course for Kenley or Biggin Hill. They soon found the answer. Ten Junkers suddenly swung north-east and headed for the station. The sirens wailed again.

WAAF officers Hanbury and Beecroft were returning from Biggin Hill village when all the preliminary noises of the day before began again. "We jammed on our steel helmets and ran for cover", Felicity Hanbury said. "As we did so a policeman's bell-shelter at the crossroads opened up and a voice said: 'You'd better come in here'. It was a tight squeeze and became tighter when a bus driver banged on the door and was also admitted. We waited in that bell-shelter for what seemed an eternity, listening to the thunderous noises outside".

Five minutes of intense bombing followed and there was further extensive damage to the domestic and technical areas. Telephone and power cables were again severed, eight Spitfires on the ground destroyed and the station armoury set on fire. The runways were plastered and the road through the camp made impassable. The most calamitous scene of all was the sight of the Operations Block with gaping holes in the roof where several high explosives had fallen.

Most of the Ops staff had taken cover and were clambering through the broken window. Miraculously no-one inside was killed but Group Captain Grice and several plotters had been injured by flying glass when the plotting screen shattered.

Two WAAFs who miraculously escaped injury were Sergeant Helen Turner, a veteran of the

CRUNCH SCENE: It was in this room that the 500lb bomb exploded. Flight Lieutenant Curwen walks among the rubble.

1914-18 war and Corporal Elspeth Henderson. Turner, a telephone operator, disobeyed an order to take cover by staying at her switchboard in a small cubicle outside the Operations Room. She moved only when a warrant officer dragged her under a desk as a 500 pounder crashed through the roof and exploded in the Defence Teleprinter Network room. Henderson, who was in charge of her watch of plotters, maintained communication with Headquarters at Uxbridge until that line was severed by the same bomb. Bowled over by the blast she was picked up by the Station Commander and coolly said that she had joined the WAAFs because because she had wanted to see a bit of life!

What must have been their feelings during that raid? The girls had already lost friends in the previous bombing raids yet here they were at their posts as low-flying enemy bombers enjoyed a clear run over what remained of RAF Biggin Hill. It was a super-human show of bravery, deservedly rewarded by the presentation of the first Military Medals to be won by WAAFs.

In the village of Biggin Hill a small crowd of bewildered onlookers surveyed the scene before them with abhorrence. The road ahead and through the camp was impassable with craters and there was no way round. Small fires flickered everywhere; a larger fire indicated that the armoury was still blazing. Ambulances and fire engines, with their bells ringing furiously, were on their way from Sevenoaks, Westerham and Bromley and the wounded were being stretchered across mountains of rubble towards those ambulances which had already arrived.

By now many of the airwomen had no clothes apart from those they were wearing. Most of their belongings had disappeared in the debris of their quarters, there was no water for washing and the laundry had been completely flattened. As the Equipment Office had also been bombed SO Hanbury with the help of some airmen with wheelbarrows took all the clothing they could find from the clothes store and then issued it to the airwomen in need. "I had the time of my life", said SO Hanbury. There was no paperwork, no tally cards, no signatures, nothing. In the next raid that clothing store was razed to the ground but some months later I was severely reprimanded for taking clothes illegally from the stores!"

There was just one fatality after that raid of August 31. A young bugler, borrowed from the local boys brigade for emergency signal duties, died from blast injuries to his lungs.

Sunday Sept 1 — Thursday Sept 5

THE familiar pattern of twice-daily German raids on the station continued unabated. By lunchtime on September 5, after five more attacks and more loss of life, the destruction of Biggin Hill was virtually complete. Only a few hardy souls lived in what remained of the Married Quarters, all the main services and communications were destroyed, the runway was badly cratered despite the constant patching up, the road through the camp was hardly passable and all the buildings were smouldering wrecks, apart from one hangar which was just about serviceable.

On that afternoon Group Captain Grice, in the station's Miles Magister, took an inspection flight to see what Biggin Hill looked like from 10,000 feet and decided that the attacks would continue while the old hangar was still standing. With the encouragement of Engineer Officer, Flight Lieutenant Jackson and Royal Engineers' officers, the CO laid charges of gun cotton, wired it up and waited for the six o'clock raid. It didn't materialise so Grice ordered all personnel in the vicinity of the triple bay hangar to take cover immediately.

The resulting volatile eruption confused the residents of Biggin Hill and Keston villages. A mushroom cloud of dust and flying debris was seen rising into the sky but there had been no civilian or airfield air-raid warning and the last bombers had passed over many hours earlier. It was some time before they learned that the explosion which destroyed the hangar — the last of any note to be seen and heard at Biggin Hill — was caused by a satisfied CO rather than by enemy bombers.

Apart from the odd hit and run raider, the Luftwaffe did not return to Biggin Hill in any force again. But this had little to do with the actions of the obsessive CO. Unknown to Grice, Hitler was becoming more and more incensed by the bombing raids on Berlin and was about to issue the order switching his point of attack to London. As Biggin breathed again the Blitz began.

The funeral of those who had been killed in the raids had taken place on Sunday September 1 at noon in a little purpose-built cemetery beyond the boundary of the airfield. Beside the rows of newly-dug graves were more than 50 coffins and representing the station was Group Captain Grice and Section Officer Hanbury. Relatives and other mourners stood silently as the Padre, the Reverend Cecil King, commenced the service.

He had just begun to speak when the station's klaxons warned of an impending raid. Everyone took cover until the danger passed and the Padre was able to continue calmly with his words of comfort. As he did so the enemy aircraft returned but this time no-one moved even though shrapnel was heard pinging off the gravestones.

Then, in the distance, was the sound that everyone dreaded — the screech of an aircraft diving with gathering speed. The Padre faltered slightly as the sickening noise of a faraway crunch was clearly heard, then continued with the service. Hours later it was reported that a Messerschmitt 110 had been shot down by Pilot Officer Paul Mayhew of 79 Squadron during another raid on Biggin Hill. It crashed into the Toys Hill woodlands, Brasted Chart, a few miles south of the station, and exploded. Fw M Jäckel and Flgr H. Rösler were missing, believed killed.

The severity of this crash prevented any proper identification of the crew. The remains were recovered by the authorities and buried in the nearby churchyard at St Martin's, Brasted.

Two civilians severely injured at Biggin Hill in this raid were John Wilcock, aged 64 of Addiscombe and Reginald Child, aged 43 of Montbretia, Hawthorn Avenue. Both were taken to

Defiants returned to Biggin Hill on September 15, 1940 as night fighters — and with them came 141 Squadron which had lost six aircraft and nine crew killed in the infamous 'Slaughter of the Innocents' two months earlier. Flying Officer Dennis Williams and Air Gunner Pilot Officer Geoffrey Pledger survived that terrible day on July 19 but died together on April 4, 1941. Here they are at Biggin Hill.

the County Hospital, Farnborough where they died.

By now the Ops Room Staff had moved to an Emergency Operations Room in one of the smallest shops in the main street of Biggin Hill village. The plotting table was a blackboard and the plotters were equipped with pieces of chalk and dusters while the search took place for a house which could be turned into a new Operations Room. Eventually, Towerfields at Keston Mark was located and successfully requisitioned.

One story of this period, told repeatedly in the Officers' Mess, concerned the army units based on the South Camp, who were detailed to site more ack-ack guns on the edge of the aerodrome. The men spent some hours digging the foundations of the new gun emplacements and after a strenuous day retired to their Mess for a well-earned drink. Imagine how they felt the next morning when they found that airmen, whose job it was to fill in bomb craters as fast as possible, had also filled in the foundations. The "brown jobs" were not happy.

Also unhappy was Group Captain Dick Grice who had to appear before a Court of Enquiry over his unorthodox action in destroying one of His Majesty's hangars. He was severely censured.

Many of the WAAFs, now billeted in Keston village, were suffering badly from the stresses caused by the five raids in 48 hours on the aerodrome. Some were unable to sleep, others went absent without leave and many were late on duty. They were duly disciplined by Section Officer Hanbury who "fairly let them have it".

In a famous tirade to the airwomen she said she was ashamed of them and their behaviour. "The eyes of the world", she said, " have been on us and the excitement has carried us through but now we are becoming slack and careless. The worst is over for us but it is not over for the pilots and aircrew. It is up to us now to prove ourselves as worthy members of His Majesty's Royal Air Force".

Felicity Hanbury later said: "I was being cruel to be kind. All the time I was terribly proud of them with every sympathy for their feelings and failings. I wished that I had got half the character and pluck that many of the girls had". The Section Officer later learned she had been recommended for a Military MBE for "setting a magnificent example of courage and devotion to duty during the heavy bombing attacks on Biggin Hill".

The Padre's story

THE Chaplain, or Padre, at Biggin Hill during the last few weeks of the Battle of Britain and for two years thereafter was the Reverend Douglas O'Hanlon, a "flying churchman" who won his wings at Old Sarum Aerodrome in 1931 and was ordained at Salisbury Cathedral in 1937. In a spiritual sense he was closer to the pilots than any other officer. Douglas O'Hanlon took services at dispersal points, visited the sick and injured and lent an ear to the distressed. When a pilot was killed he often had the task of giving comfort to their best friends and listing and sending off to relatives the sad little possessions left beside a bed - the watch, the wallet, the framed photo and the diary.

O'Hanlon arrived at the station just a few weeks after Hitler had called off the offensive against the sector airfields and instead launched the full might of his Luftwaffe against London. After the battering Biggin Hill had received during August and early September the new Padre was amazed to discover that not only was it operational and morale exceptionally high but there was a huge determination among all those who worked there to carry on as cheerfully and normally as possible. There were also two new squadrons — 92 and 72 — and they were well established.

The new Chaplain had been married for just six months. His wife was Katherine, one of the first of a few women to qualify as a pilot in the short-lived Civil Air Guard and a member of the original company who performed T.S.Eliott's *Murder in the Cathedral* at Canterbury and London. When Douglas arrived at Biggin he stayed for some months in the Officers' Mess and then found a house in Westerham where Katherine joined him. This is his story

FLYING PADRE: Reverend O'Hanlon in 1941. "It was a humbling thing to live very close to the brave".

"92 Squadron arrived at Biggin Hill from Pembrey on September 8, 1940 and I was posted there soon afterwards, so it is natural that members of that squadron should remain most vividly in mind. The north of the airfield — the main RAF buildings — had been bombed out of action so the army camp on the south west corner of the airfield was taken over.

"The Chapel was a little building now under the widened road. It was possible to send out notices, concerning services or welfare, on the tannoy system. The Chaplain's office was nearby in the Admin block. A corporal who helped me with typing was later promoted sergeant when it was discovered that he was the author of '*No Orchids for Miss Blandish*'.

"The chapel pianist, when available, was AC2 John Russell, 92 Squadron (later for 30 years professor of music at the Royal College). There was a cinema projector, plenty of evening activity and means of refreshment provided by the WAAFs.

"I had an accordion and found that short services at dispersal points were well attended. If 72 Squadron had a good turn out then 92 Squadron must do better. The army chaplain is aided by loyalty to the Regiment, the Navy Chaplain by loyalty to the ship and the RAF Chaplain found loyalty strong in the squadrons and grieved to see them so quickly decimated or so soon posted away.

"One of the first important visitors to Biggin Hill was the Duke of Kent, later killed on his way to Iceland. As Padre/Welfare Officer it was my duty to show him round. He was shocked at the conditions and kept saying "disgusting", but he was impressed by the splendid improvisation and was obviously caring and concerned. He went on to visit the satellite station at Gravesend, commanded by my cousin George Harvey, later Air Vice Marshal. He learned how to fly 10 years before in the Cambridge University Air Squadron.

"It was natural among pilots billeted — as they were — away from the station that discipline, except in the air, should be somewhat relaxed. While at Pembrey, 92 Squadron pilots had achieved a fair success hunting enemy aircraft far and wide. This type of sortie had fostered a brand of individualism among the pilots who included such figures as Stanford Tuck, Wimpey Wade, Brian Kingcome and Don Kingaby.

"Pilot Officer Maitland Thompson, when reproved at station HQ for the state of his uniform, torn in a crash (Battle dress had not yet arrived), with the words - 'You would not dress like this at home' replied - 'You ought to see the home I come from, Sir'.

"I officiated at his marriage in London to a young woman known as the Merry Widow. Maitland Thompson was her third military husband. It was not long before she was a widow again.

"Quite apart from the blue cloth, they all wore the same uniform of "illogical light heartedness". At that time fighting all alone against advancing Germany, the idea that the war might be lost never seemed to cross, let alone, enter their minds. Those killed in action were referred to as "gone for a Burton". A greeting overheard sometimes at the bar was "Cheers, old boy, I thought you were dead".

"I remember sending off to relatives the little possessions left beside a bed and, on occasions, dead pilots' parents came to the station. I recall one couple whose son had earned a DFC but they had to be told it could not be posthumously awarded,

"This almost-tangible atmosphere of fellowship, common purpose and complete mutual trust is recalled after all these years with a sense of wonder. Nothing like it had ever been encountered before, nothing like it has been experienced since.

"It seems fitting, therefore, that in the Memorial Chapel at Biggin Hill the names of some of the 92 Squadron dead are inscribed low down on the Reredos so that one has to kneel to read them. For this reason it was a little time before I discovered the name Flight Lieutenant John Lund. I recall that Lund had a scholar's place waiting for him at Oriel, Oxford. He and Maitland Thompson were philosophic types who, in the fog-bound times, talked long into the night.

"They came to supper in our temporary home, Tudor Cottage, on the western edge of Westerham which was rented — together with a gardener — for 2½ guineas a week from a Mr Bonham Carter, a friend of the Prime Minister. It overlooked the little valley of the infant Darent towards Squerryes Court. We were able to let the newly-married 'Wimpey'

WINNER TAKES ALL: Two pilots of 92 Squadron in another kind of battle. The background board lists the operational pilots — Holland, Lewis, Monty, Mottram, Lund, Watling, Havercroft and Sherrington. See page 87.

Wade have it for 10 days with his Josephine (nee Gibbins).

"A product of Tonbridge, Wade was inwardly deeply thoughtful. Outwardly he was, perhaps purposely, outrageous. He was fond of pungent remarks, not as offensive when he spoke them as they seemed to be when written down. Describing his home he said: 'My parents are typical middle-age stooges'. To his new Commanding Officer, Johnny Kent: 'Stick around and we'll show you the form'. Later when he was officially 'grounded' for persistent inverted flying over 92s dispersal he took me on leave to Bedford in a Tiger Moth. The front cockpit controlled the automatic stall flaps which I was asked to close from time to time to enable him to perform aerobatics.

"By early October 92 Squadron had achieved its 100th victim and Brian Kingcome, Flight Commander since May 1940, had won his first DFC. I remember being taken by Group Captain Grice to the hospital in Orpington to visit Kingcome recovering from a canon shell wound in the leg. Between us we carried in several bottles of beer which we left under the bed. I doubt whether the patient was later allowed much of that medicine.

"Brian Kingcome himself became a Group Captain at the age of 25. 'Mac' McGowan, 92's much-loved adjutant, named his own son Brian after Kingcome. Years later at a 92 Squadron reunion dinner ar RAF Benson I met this Pilot Officer McGowan. On this occasion 'Tich' Havercroft, the famous 92 Squadron sergeant pilot, saved me from being the only man present with grey hair. I last saw Brian at the 40th anniversary of the Battle of Britain at Biggin Hill. At the service Archbishop Runcie preached the sermon and I had the honour of speaking Churchill's words about The Few.

"My duties included regular visits to Gravesend. I remember standing beside my cousin, the station commander. High above us 92 Squadron, patrolling the Estuary, had been

SPECIAL FRIENDS: Pilot Officers Gaskell, Lund and Folkes of 92 Squadron Below (right) Maitland Thompson, who along with John Lund, was the philosophical type. Below (left) 'Wimpey' Wade, who the Padre considered thoughtful but outrageous.

"bounced" by some 109s. Tony Bartley, just shot down, described the sudden appearance of tracers which he attributed at first to the spots one sees after liver trouble. Sergeant Walter Ellis came in with a dead engine and a canon shell in each wing roof. Skidding on the Gravesend mud he ended up within yards of the control tower. Geoff Wellum was the next to arrive. He was able to fly back to Biggin but Ellis returned in my van.

"Officially, Chaplains were not allowed to fly. This applied even to my friend Canon Guy Bowden who spent the first half of the war as a flying instructor and the second as a Chaplain. However, no-one seemed to notice if, when a pilot went on leave, the Squadron Magister flew itself back. Flight Lieutenant Gordon Brettell famously used this facility with a blonde on his lap. Some years later he sent us a postcard from Stalag Luft III. A few weeks later we heard that he was one of the escapees shot on Hitler's personal order.

"In this and other ways I flew many hours in the two years at Biggin with the pilots and sergeant pilots. It was sad that these latter men had a separate mess. They must have missed out on many lessons learned late at night in conversation. I often visited the sergeants' mess and one night played snooker with a young pilot just arrived. He was killed the next day".

The pilot's story

WHAT is it like to die in a fighter plane, defending your country from the scourge of a foe determined to kill you before you kill him? Only the ghosts know the answer to that one and they are in no position to tell us, yet. But, the flimsy green combat reports, now lodged with the Public Record Office, give an idea of what it was like to face death. And they show the punishment that both pilots and planes routinely took.

Flight Lieutenant Brian Kingcome of 92 Squadron had several brushes with death but the most harrowing occurred on October 15, 1940 when he was returning to his station after an encounter with raiders over Maidstone. The sky — just a few minutes earlier full of swooping aircraft, tracer bullets, smoke and flying debris — was now miraculously empty. Biggin Hill was in the distance and Kingcome was admiring the view and the sensation of speed as he pushed his nose down for the familiar landing. In his excitement of nearing safety he had forgotten the fighter pilot's golden rule — to watch his tail, always.

Kingcome later remembered how his reveries were rudely shattered by an almighty thump to the back of the right leg. "It came as bit of a shock" he said, "to one who believed himself alone with 20,000 clear feet between himself and other human company".

With blood welling out of the top of his flying boot and more bullets striking in and around his cockpit Kingcome looked around for the enemy. All he saw was three Spitfires who drew briefly alongside then peeled away. "I was panic-stricken", he said, "gripped in a blind, paralysing terror...I sat rigid and disbelieving, my stomach churning. Here was the real thing. This is what it felt like....

"The effect was devastating; one minute relaxed and carefree in total control with nothing more dramatic in mind than a simulated forced landing and the day's lunch menu; the next inhabiting a doomed aircraft at 20,000 feet. losing blood at a rate that suggested consciousness might slip away at any moment with death following within minutes......Death now became a terrifying reality so close I could smell him. Or was this simply the smell of my own fear..."

Brian Kingcome explained how sanity finally returned, how he became curiously calm and rational and almost detached giving him the opportunity to assess his chances of living. The thought of launching himself into a hostile, freezing, airless void caused his stomach to churn again but his Spitfire was badly damaged and his ailerons were sluggish. He decided to get rid of the canopy, undo the straps and give the stick an

Flight Lieutenant Brian Kingcome — "I could see the workers armed with pitchforks heading across the field towards which I was drifting".

***SQUADRON TRANSPORT:** A few of the old cars in the centre of 92 Squadron's dispersal at Biggin Hill. This picture was taken on February 21, 1941 by Flying Officer Allan Wright.*

almighty shove forward. He would, he hoped, be catapulted out by centrifugal force.

"I never got as far as testing it", he said. "No sooner had I undone the straps than I was plucked violently out of the cockpit and hurled into the furious maelstrom of wind and storm and raging elements that whirled me head over heels, arms and legs windmilling uncontrollably, helpless as a rag doll in a clamouring hurricane.

"The brutal blast of air assaulted me with all the solid physical force of a jackhammer, blacking my eyes and bruising my face with a ferocity of which I had never dreamed air to be capable.....But air resistance put on the brakes surprisingly quickly and slowed me down...the gale abated and so did my mood....a deep, dreamlike lethargy enveloped me...I found myself cocooned in a silent world, all tension departed, comfortable and relaxed, occupying the centre of the universe and sky and earth slowly revolved about me. A combined lack of oxygen and blood was insulating me from all fear and all emotion.

"I knew I could safely free-fall 15,000 feet before I hit the clouds and then would have time to open my parachute...I broke through into the sunlight and saw the glorious patchwork quilt of the Kent countryside spread out before me. I reached for the ripcord and pulled...and with a satisfying crack, it snapped open and braked my downward rush with a bone-bending jerk.

"As I floated over open farmland I could see below me a small group of agricultural workers armed with pitchforks and other businesslike farm implements heading across the field towards which I was drifting...I was wearing the German Mae West I had commandeered from the body of a crew member of a Ju88...and as the ground rushed up to meet me I could see the group were gripping even tighter the formidable tools of their trade".

Brian Kingcome survived. He was not one of the many Allied airmen beaten up by incensed locals who worked on the patriotic assumption that those who had been shot down must be the enemy. He was wearing British uniform and his Spitfire crashed close by at High Halstow. He was admitted to the Royal Naval Hospital at Chatham and later transferred to Orpington Hospital not far from Biggin Hill.

A vivid description of death comes from the pen of Wilf Nichol in *The Battle of Britain*

Then and Now which has become the "bible" for most aviation historians. He writes: "Death when it came was not always clean and swift. Many died trapped in the confines of the cockpit while the fighter plunged thousands of feet before burying itself in the earth; conscious every second of the fall, struggling to release a trapped limb or jammed hood, coolly and clinically at first until realisation came that there was no release and that time and height had slipped away; then, before the final impact with the earth, the final indignity of befouling themselves.

"Others watched the sea close over them or suffered the agonies of being cremated alive. Men died burnt or wounded, helpless and alone, drifting down on the end of a parachute at the whim of the wind.....The lucky ones were killed outright in combat by enemy gunfire; of the injured who survived, many were to linger in hospital perhaps for weeks or months before succumbing to their wounds. Others pulled through only to live out their lives mentally and physically broken".

Pilot Officer Bill Millington, a 23-year-old Australian of 79 Squadron, pulled through. Chasing one of the Dorniers which had bombed Biggin Hill on August 30 the young pilot suddenly found himself alone with two Messerschmitt 109s. He sent one spinning to earth near Romney Marsh and made the fatal error of watching the pilot crawl out of the wreckage. In those split seconds the second 109 pumped cannon fire into his Hurricane. A flicker of flame suddenly burst into life. Blinded by scalding oil Millington forced the hood back and prepared to bale out. Below was a small town (Tenterden) and there were villages all around. Somehow he fought back the urge to save his own life, righted the aircraft and crashed in an open field at Conghurst Farm, Hawkhurst, Badly burned, he dragged himself clear as the Hurricane exploded.

Some days later Millington found himself in hospital at Hawkhurst alongside Flying Officer Peter Townsend. Peter read the letter that Bill sent to his parents: "I go forth into battle light of heart...I regard it as a privilege to fight for all those things that make life worth living — freedom, honour and fair play...Flying has meant the companionship of men...the intoxication of speed, the rush of air and the pulsating beat of the motor awakens some answering chord deep down which is indescribable..."

Bill Millington did go forth into the Battle once more on his discharge from hospital. Transferred from the Biggin Hill squadron to 249 Squadron at North Weald he was engaged in sporadic fighting on Wednesday October 30. This time he failed to return, possibly drowning in the Channel. He was the last airman to die in Kent during the Battle of Britain.

The last civilians to be killed in Biggin Hill village during the Battle were Special Constable Reginald John, aged 40, and Daisy Alexandra Rogers, aged 39, who died at Journey's End, Lebanon Gardens. The last fatality of the war in the village was that of Marjorie Maude Dryden, 39 at Cotehele, St Winifred's Road, Biggin Hill on Tuesday 21st December 1943.

November 1940 - September 1943

November 2 1940: Section Officer Felicity Hanbury receives her MBE from the King. Sergeant Elizabeth Mortimer, Corporal Elspeth Henderson and Sergeant Helen Turner also receive their Military Medals on this day. A civilian, Dr A.M.Cole is awarded the OBE for assisting in the rescue of a 32 Squadron pilot who force-landed at Biggin Hill on August 6, 1940.

November 7 1940: Pilots of 74 and 92 Squadrons are joined by 66 Squadron from West Malling. South Camp now vacated by Army and more than 1,000 airmen living in the huts there. Pilots still billeted in country houses.

November 8: Squadron Leader John Kent, the new CO of 92 Squadron, writes a letter to his senior officers saying their behaviour is blatantly arrogant and they are the most insubordinate lot he has ever known. He says they have turned the living quarters into a night club and invite various lady friends whenever they please.

November 9: As reconstruction of North Camp continues Station Headquarters is the first building to be opened. Daily PT drill for WAAFs, abandoned after bombing, starts again much to their distress.

November 25: Air Marshal Sir Sholto Douglas succeeds Hugh Dowding as head of Fighter Command. Air Vice Marshal Trafford Leigh-Mallory takes over command of No 11 Group.

November: Nos 124 and the Canadians of 401 Squadron now billeted at Biggin Hill. The Canadians destined to lose 17 pilots during the sweeps over France in the next few months.

December 1: Flight Lieutenant 'Pancho' Villa of 92 Squadron destroys an enemy aircraft by cannon fire, much to the pleasure of Stanford Tuck and 'Sailor' Malan who had advocated the adoption of cannon fire to replace the .303 Browning machine guns.

December: Group Captain Grice leaves Biggin Hill with a farewell party at the White Hart, Brasted. He is replaced by Group Captain F.O.Soden, nicknamed 'Mongoose'.

December 19: Group Captain Soden writes to the Secretary of State for Air: "I have just taken over Biggin Hill and the chaps are living under conditions of unnecessary filth and squalor. In fact, seldom, if ever, has so little been done for those few who have done so much for so many!".

February 1941: 66 Squadron is replaced by 609 (West Riding of Yorkshire) Squadron, commanded by Squadron Leader Michael Robinson with Spitfire IIs. B Flight is made up entirely of Belgium pilots. They become joint tenants at Southwood. The next day they are scrambled for a sweep over France.

February: 'Sailor' Malan leaves his beloved Tiger Squadron in order to command the Biggin Wing. His friend Douglas Bader commands the Tangmere Wing. Jamie Rankin, rugger player and golfer replaces Johnny Kent as CO of 92 Squadron.

March: Pilot Officer Gordon Brettell flies to Tangmere to collect girl friend for a party at Biggin Hill. He returns with her on his lap and is charged with endangering one of His Majesty's aircraft. The charge is quashed after Tony Bartley admits that he too has flown a Spitfire with a female passenger.

March: Fighter sweeps over France continue in earnest. Briefing conferences are held by the station Intelligence Officer, Squadron Leader de la Torre.

May: Pilots of 92 and 609 Squadron forge a new relationship with the London cabbies who offer to drive them home free of charge from their "nocturnal excursions" to the heavily blitzed capital city.

June: Group Captain Philip Barwell replaces 'Mongoose' Soden as station CO.

July 1: Station CO Philip Barwell is shot down and killed by Spitfire pilots flying from Tangmere. They did not recognise his new Spitfire VI.

July 26: 72 Squadron returns to The Bump. During one of its first operations the pilots drop a wooden box over St Omer airfield. It contains new tin legs for Wing Commander Douglas Bader, now a PoW in Germany.

February 12, 1942: Six Swordfish of the Fleet Air Arm shot down in the Channel while attempting to torpedo three German battle cruisers which had slipped cover. Biggin Hill squadrons provide cover.

April: Army finally quits Biggin Hill having been there in some capacity since 1918.

May 3: No 133 American Eagle Squadron replaces 124 and joins 72 and 401 Squadrons at Biggin Hill. They adopt the Queen's Head at Downe as their pub.

August 19: Five Biggin Hill squadrons help maintain a fighting umbrella over Dieppe to help protect 6,000 troops on the ground.

September 23: No 340 Squadron becomes the first Free French unit to be based at Biggin Hill, flying Spitfire IXs. They replace the American Eagles who are transferred to the US Army Air Force.

January 1943: 'Sailor' Malan, now Station CO, publishes his 'Ten Rules for Air Fighting'.

6

The fighter sweeps

In four years of front line fighting 453 aircrew, flying from the Biggin Wing, lost their lives. Many died during the Battle of France and the Battle of Britain but the vast majority were killed in the years that followed. The strain of long hours over enemy territory, with taut nerves and eyes unceasingly alert for 'snappers' and flak, became unbearable. This phase of the war was known as 'Lean forward into France'. It began in 1941 and lasted until the autumn of 1943 when Biggin Hill became part of the 17th Fighter Wing of the Royal Canadian Air Force, flying Spitfire XIs. During that period fighter sweeps were flown whenever the weather allowed, with a variety of squadrons escorting bombers or enticing the German Air Force into the air. 'Circus' was the code name for the sweeps. 'Roadsteads' were anti-shipping strikes and 'Rhubarbs' were attacks against opportunity targets on the ground. In this section it is possible only to give a flavour of the fighter sweeps with special features about a few of those who paid the ultimate sacrifice. We believe some of these warriors, whose lives were so dramatically foreshortened, return from time to time to the scene of their last earthly happiness.

"I have just returned to Biggin Hill after a day at headquarters. Night was falling. The familiar scene of the narrow road reacted with the hour to tell over a whole chaplet of memories set to the monstrous rhythm of flight and combats. War, like a subtle poison, penetrating us through every living fibre, has numbed both body and spirit. Death and fire have lost their constant effect on us, being only associated now with our flying"

Commandant Bernard Dupérier, of 341 Free French Squadron, writing about the death of Commandant René Mouchotte — one of Biggin's greatest pilots.

***BORN AT BIGGIN:** The Belgian Flight of 609 Squadron — joint tenants of Southwood Manor with 92 Squadron.*

***ON THE TERRACE:** Pilots of 609 Squadron outside the Officers' Mess at Biggin Hill. Left to right: Flying Officer Jean Offenberg, (not known), Flying Officers Ogilvie, Bisdee, McKenzie (not known), Sqd Ldr Sailor Malan, Sqd Ldr Michael Robinson, (not known).*

The Belgium Wing of 609

SOON after the pilots of 609 (West Riding of Yorkshire) Squadron, led by Squadron Leader Michael Robinson, had arrived at Biggin Hill in February 1941 they were joined by a colourful batch of young Belgians anxious to bring a little bit of Continental flair to this most cosmopolitan of squadrons. They included Pilot Officer le Comte du Monceau de Bergendael — better known as the Duke — Comte Rudolphe Ghislain Charles de Hemricourt de Grunne (the Count), W. Van Lierde, Roger Malengreau and Francois de Spirlet. All of them hated the Nazis and were keen to avenge the occupation of their country.

They had joined 609 by the invitation of Michael Robinson who remembered how a Belgian air force detachment had helped him to escape to England after he had been injured in a flying accident in France in May 1940. Michael had evacuated himself from hospital to hospital, just ahead of the German advance, until he reached the Pyrenees. Here, the Belgians equipped him with air force blue and put him on a plane for England.

When Michael took command of 609 he repaid his debt by applying to the Air Ministry for Belgian pilots. So Belgian Flight of 609 was born at Biggin Hill — all of them having made the perilous pilgrimage from France, via North Africa and Gibraltar, to join the RAF.

One of them, Flight Lieutenant Jean Offenberg described that journey in his diary. When France surrendered, all Belgian forces were ordered to lay down their arms and return to Belgium. But Offenberg and his best friend and fellow pilot, Alexis Jottard disobeyed.

Flight Lieutenant Jean Offenberg — stole an aircraft and flew to North Africa where the Belgians had a flying school.

They stole two small single engined Caudron Simouns, took off from Montpellier and flew to Oujda, North Africa where the Belgians had set up a flying school. From there the men, disguised as Polish soldiers, boarded a ship to Gibraltar, sailed to Liverpool and joined the RAF.

Intelligence Officer of 609, Frank Ziegler, remembered how they wanted to be known by their christian names only. "There was Bob (Wilmet), Strop (Segers) and Van (Lierde). Another was Francois (de Spirlet), an entertaining individualist who did not give a damn for anyone, yet who evinced a curiously English sense of humour. Wildest, dashing and most irresponsible was Vicki Ortmans, already credited with three Battle of Britain victories with 229 squadron. Bob could play the piano. Vicki could tap dance on top of it and the West Riding Squadron became indoctrinated with foreign songs".

609 became joint tenants of Southwood Manor with No 92 who were entertainers themselves and much enjoyed the company of these good-looking young men with an above-average social sense. And, of course, when they were not dancing and singing they were involved in the whirling mêlée over much of North Kent and London, because this was also the height of the Blitz.

The first pilot of 609 to be lost while at Biggin Hill was Pilot Officer Rudolphe de Grunne, the Belgian count who had flown with 32 Squadron from The Bump in the summer of 1940, accepted a secret mission to Portugal and then joined 609 at Biggin Hill.

On the warm, humid day of May 21, 1941 609 were ordered to escort 18 Blenheims on a raid on an oil refinery at Bethune and 'Sailor' Malan was leading the Biggin Wing, covering the raiders withdrawal. As bandits were spotted the instructions came over the R/T "Bounce the bastards good and hard. 'Sailor' speaking". In the battle that followed five Messerschmitts were claimed destroyed but two Spitfires were missing and one of them had been flown by de Grunne. Two of his fellow Belgians saw him jump and they circled his parachute as he descended. They saw the distinctive yellow dye as he hit the water and alerted a rescue Lysander. A long search ensued but the Count was never found.

Two weeks later Flight Lieutenant John Curchin, 'B' Flight Commander, was also dead. Curchin, accompanied by his great friend Sydney Hill and nine other pilots, had been involved in a dog fight with just three 109s but 609 came out of it so badly that only six out of 11 Spitfires made it back to Biggin Hill. Calls eventually came from West Malling where four had landed and another was reported to be at Manston. Curchin had been shot down and killed. Paul Richey remembered the tragedy: "Sydney Hill was so upset that he never really got over it. They were good scratch golfers and John drank a lot. Sydney drank too but not so much. He would wake up in the morning and his eyes would clear and he would fly".

On June 11 'Sailor' Malan led a roadstead sortie with 609 acting as top cover to five Blenheims. They were bounced again by Me 109s and the Spitfires of the second pair of Blue Section, Pilot Officer A.K.Ogilvie and Sergeant Guy Cheshunt, both Canadians, were damaged. Michael Robinson saw glycol streaming from Cheshunt's damaged fighter as he glided over the sea a mile from the Ramsgate cliffs. He signalled Cheshunt to bale out but the NCO tried to get over the cliffs and struck them a few feet from the top. The wing was ripped off and the aircraft slithered down.

Six days later, on June 17, Pilot Officer Boudouin de Hemptinne joined 609 Squadron and was in action the next day acting, alongside Sydney Hill, as rear support to a returning Circus. They became separated by 109s and Hill's machine was hit. Flight Lieutenant Paul Richey tells the story: "We advised him to bale out but he wanted to get back home. Like Cheshunt, he too failed to get over the cliffs, the Spitfire falling in flames to the beach below. The pilot was incinerated. His family asked for the ring on his finger but it had melted in the heat".

Hill's funeral was memorable. As the mourners were moving towards the cemetery it had been arranged for two Spitfires to fly low in salute. Two aircraft duly arrived — 109s! The

PRESENTATION DAY: The Officers of 609 (West Riding) Squadron on the day they were presented with the Squad-ron crest. Left to right: Flight Lieutenant John Bisdee DFC, Squadron Leader Paul Richey DFC, Group Captain Philip 'Dickie' Barwell DFC, (station commander Biggin Hill), Wing Commander Michael Robinson DSO, DFC.

party scattered leaving the coffin with Hill inside in the middle of the road.

In July 1941 during another Circus, Flying Officer Keith Ogilvie and Sergeant Kenneth Bramble were attacked by a pair of 109s. Ogilvie, hit twice in the arm and shoulder, later wrote in his diary: "There was blood all over and I felt sick, so I blew my hood off and turned the oxygen full on to keep awake...Eventually I figured 'this is where I leave'....Sometime later I came to in a field surrounded by sympathetic Frenchies who tried to get me up and away but I could not make it. I had lost too much blood. A little while later a German 'sanitar' informed me: 'For you the war is over' ". Sergeant Bramble was unable to leave his aircraft. He crashed in France and was killed.

Three more pilots, Sergeant 'Goldy' Palmer, Pilot Officer Douglas Cropper and Sergeant Ernest Pollard were killed before 609 said goodbye to the Biggin Wing. The squadron also 'lost' Flying Officer Vicki Ortmans for the third time — and on this occasion he was reported as "missing believed killed". Intelligence Officer, Frank Ziegler takes up the story: "Vicky survived an Me109 attack but had then been assailed by five FW190s one of which he shot down before having to bale out himself badly wounded. He had spent no less than two days and nights in his dinghy, longing to die, before being picked up unconscious by the Germans after falling out of it. Later, remembering the rule that to protect their families at home captured Belgians should give false names, Vicki had given the name of Ogilvie — only to find the real Ogilvie (Keith) in the camp to which he was eventually sent".

609 Squadron left Biggin Hill on November 21, 1941 and returned for two months the following year with Typhoons. But the tragedies continued. Bob Boyd was killed in action in 1943, Eugene Seghers rose to Flight Lieutenant and died in July 1944 while attacking a VI flying bomb, Jean Offenberg, then Flight Commander, was killed in collision in 1942,

124 Squadron, which spent six months at Biggin Hill under the command of Squadron Leader Raymond Duke Woolley and then Tommy Balmforth, was even more cosmopolitan than 609 with pilots from Belgium, Czechoslavakia, France, Norway, Australia and Canada. When, in February 1942, Germany's powerful pocket battleships, Scharnhorst, Gneisenau and Prince Eugen made a dash for shelter in Brest Harbour and were attacked by six torpedo-carrying Swordfish of the Fleet Air Arm, 124 was one of the squadrons assigned to give cover. It was one of the most tragic and depressing battles of the war. 124 claimed at least four German fighters but the RAF lost 42 aircraft and every one of the Swordfish were shot down. 124 Squadron left Biggin Hill in May, 10 pilots lighter. Duke Woolley is pictured above centre (with scarf). Tommy Balmforth is on his right and 'Slim' Kilburn on his left (each with a cap). Second from left (standing) is 'Timber' Wood.

Francois de Spirlet died in a take-off accident with 609 in 1942, Stan Meares was killed in November 1943 in a collision with an American pilot, Michael Robinson was lost over the English channel in 1942, Vicki Ortmans survived the war but killed himself soon afterwards by trying one too many air stunts.

If there are any ghostly representatives of this squadron around the old airfield today then it is likely you will find them down the lane on their way to or from the pub they call the Old Jail. In 1941 it was run by a Belgian lady called Biddie and much patronised by the Belgian pilots, particularly Vicki Ortmans. Ziegler writes: "He so endeared himself to her by his self-accusative smile that she kept her best bedroom and wine cellar constantly at his disposal. One morning when pilots came to dawn readiness they found Vicki asleep at dispersal with a small brown kid on his chest, a gift of the pub. It was promptly given the rank of Flying Officer William de Goat, became the Squadron's mascot and accompanied 609 all over the world".

William de Goat was last seen in Germany with Air Commodore's stripes painted on his horns when only two men in the Squadron knew of his origin.

Flying Officer John Mungo Park DFC

FLYING Officer John Mungo Park came to Biggin Hill with the Tigers of 74 Squadron in October 1940. A handsome, carefree almost flamboyant character he was quite the opposite to Flying Officer H.M. Stephen, his imperturbable, unruffled fellow Flight Commander and great friend. As a team, the two men were awe inspiring. They led their Flights to the high standard demanded by 'Sailor' Malan and by November 30, 1941 had shot down more than 30 enemy aircraft. More important to the four squadrons billeted at Biggin Hill was the impressive overall total on the station scoreboard. It stood at 599.

The pilots ands ground staff of all squadrons on the aerodrome had subscribed for a handsome present for the pilot who could bag the 600th Nazi and everyone was keen to make the winning hit. But John Mungo Park was the most determined of all. On that damp and muggy morning of November 30 he quietly encouraged Flying Officer Stephen to join him in stealing a march on their colleagues. Having obtained 'Sailor' Malan's permission they climbed into their Spitfires and taxied from their dispersal point to the nearest runway. Biggin Hill was awakened by the roar from the aircraft as they took off on their voluntary patrol.

Wing Commander 'Taffy' Jones, a former ace of the 1914-18 war and a founder member of the Tiger Squadron kept a diary: On this day he wrote: "Pilots inside the Mess rushed out onto the lawn and someone shouted: "Who the hell are they. They must be crackers". 'Sailor' Malan laughed but didn't speak. He climbed into his car and drove up to the Sector Ops room. "Has Mungo called up?", he asked. "Yes" said the controller. 'We've informed Group they are up. We are sending them to patrol a convoy off Deal".

Mungo Park takes up the story: "I was Blue leader", he wrote on his combat report. I was informed by Ops that many 'snappers' were in the close vicinity so I climbed to 29,000 feet and sighted eight plus raiders coming in from the south towards the convoy. We (Stephen and myself) climbed to 34,000 feet and engaged the 'weaver'. I opened fire with a two-second burst at 150 yards and the enemy aircraft immediately dived. I broke off and Stephen went into attack. The 109 then half rolled and I followed him down with another two-second burst. I broke away to avoid being hit by the hood which had become detached and Stephen attacked again. He was vertical when I last saw him going through a cloud".

The pilot, later identified as Uffz F Wägelein, had baled out but his parachute was holed and he died on December 3 of injuries received on landing. He came down at Ruckinge, near Ham Street and was buried with full military honours. It was Biggin Hill's 600th kill and Mungo Park and H.M.Stephen shared the £30 sweepstake prize.

Park was then 23 and a big hero at home in Bolton where his parents Colin and Marion Mungo Park had lived for many years. John, educated at Liverpool College, had joined the RAF on a short service commission in 1937. He was posted to 10FTS, went on to 2AACU and then to the Fleet Requirement Unit of *HMS Argus* in August 1938. He joined the Tiger Squadron on the day after war was declared and was naturally a good friend of 'Sailor' Malan, his famous CO.

"What I like about 'Sailor'", he once wrote, "is his quiet firm manner and his cold courage. He is a gifted pilot with uncanny eyesight and a natural fighter pilot. When he calls over the

HUNTING IN PAIRS: H.M.Stephen, the Scot and his fellow Flight Commander John Mungo-Park, a proud Liverpudlian who shared the destruction of the 600th Hun on November 30, 1940.

R/T 'let 'em have it' there's no messing. The bastards are for it, particularly the one that 'Sailor' has in his own reflector sight".

It was on August 31, 1940 that Mungo had taken command of 'B' Flight from Piers Kelly and just over three months later was awarded the DFC as an acting Flight Lieutenant. His portrait was painted by the great war artist Cuthbert Orde at Biggin Hill and his reputation was growing with every new scramble.

On November 14, when 'Sailor' was on leave, Mungo Park led the Squadron in one of the Tigers' most famous interceptions. They shot down 15 confirmed, two probables and several damaged and 'Sailor', green with envy, sent a telegram to Mungo Park which simply read: "Congratulations you rat". It was immediately stuck in the Squadron scrapbook.

When 'Sailor' was posted, as an acting Wing Commander in charge of the Biggin Hill Wing on March 10, 1941 it was compensated by the appointment, as CO of 74 Squadron, of Acting Squadron Leader J.C.Mungo Park. By that time the Squadron were flying almost every day on the wearisome sweeps over France. Raids on the airfield of Arques near St Omer and the industrial complexes around that town were a favourite target. Pilots were disappearing regularly and John Mungo Park badly needed a rest from operations.

On June 16 1941, on yet another sweep, Mungo Park was attacked by six Messerschmitt 109s over the French coast and shot down two in a hectic do-or-die scrap. On this occasion his Spitfire's glycol system was damaged and his engine seized. He was left with two choices — to ditch in the sea and bale out knowing he would almost certainly be arrested if he survived or to try and glide across the Channel on a dead engine. Mungo Park opted for the latter losing height all the time as the White Cliffs loomed nearer and nearer. He cleared the cliffs at Folkestone and crash landed heavily in a field near Hawkinge. It was the first time he had returned with a damaged Spitfire.

Two weeks later, on June 27, 1941, 74 Squadron's exhausted, pilots led by Mungo, took off on another mission to St Omer. Now billeted at Cobham Hall, they flew from Gravesend with the CO flying his faithful Mark V Spitfire X4668. No-one is certain what happened but the boy from Bolton didn't return and was posted as missing, believed killed. They found his body some weeks later and he was buried in Adinkerke Military Cemetery, De Panne, West Vlaaderen, Belgium — three kilometres from the coastal town of Koksijde.

John Mungo Park was 74 Squadron's first (and only) Commanding Officer to be lost. He had been a friend of the Malans and was to have been godfather at the delayed christening of their son, Jonathan. A few days after his death two more pilots were killed and the "indestructible" Flying Officer Bill Skinner was shot down and taken prisoner. It was time for 74 Squadron to leave the Biggin Wing. They never returned.

Michael Robinson

TOWARDS the end of July 1941 Squadron Leader Michael Lister Robinson succeeded 'Sailor' Malan as Wing Commander Flying of the Biggin Wing. At the same time he was awarded the DSO and the Croix-de-Guerre by the Belgian Government in exile. The son of Sir Roy, later Lord Robinson of Chelsea, this was the highlight of a brilliant aviation career.

One of his pilots Joe Atkinson described Robinson as totally committed to his job in the same way as was expected of a crack cavalry commander. He took a great pride in commanding 609 Squadron.

In July 1941 Robinson scored half of the Squadron's dozen or so victories for the month and had proved to be a master of tactics with an ability to communicate his own self-assurance to those around him.

Frank Zeigler, Intelligence Officer of 609 knew him well: "Once, while manoeuvring to intercept a formation of 34 enemy fighters, he suddenly changed course and height, enabling the Biggin Wing to take the fighters completely by surprise, 609 alone scoring four destroyed, two probables and five damaged without loss". Group Captain Philip 'Dickie' Barwell, then station commander and among the scorers that day, said it was "a proper bounce".

Michael Robinson's greatest friend was Paul Richey who also happened to be his brother-in-law. Paul was born into a military family and went to Downside School, Bath where Mickey was the head boy. When they left school Paul became known as the 'Deb's delight', a most suitable dancing partner and eligible prospective husband who liked to wear a white tie and tails. It was a dress code that certainly impressed the mothers of the Debs. They were not impressed, however, with the way he attempted a hand stand while drunk on the roof of a London cab as it went down the Strand.

LOST ON A SWEEP: Squadron Leader Michael Robinson.

Michael, more disciplined than Paul, who spoke with the staccato tones of Noel Coward, was first to join the RAF. He applied for a short commission and, by 1937, was a member of 111 Squadron's crack formation aerobatic team. Paul had other matters on his mind like wooing and then marrying Michael's beautiful sister Teresa but he, too, joined the RAF and was astonished by his brother-in-law's versatility in the air. In 1938 Robinson flew 200 miles from Middlesex to Lancashire in 35 minutes at an average speed of 380 mph. The man was destined to be an aviation hero.

Both were badly injured early in 1940. Paul was absent from flying for a year and spent most of the time convalescing and writing one of the first second world war aviation books, *Fighter Pilot*. Robinson was also injured in France but recovered, flew successfully in the Battle of Britain and was given command of 609 Squadron on October 4, 1940. One of his first moves was to invite Paul Richey to be Commander of his 'A' flight, "a posting", said Frank Ziegler, "which was sheer, if legitimate, nepotism". *See picture page 145.*

FOOLING ABOUT: Flying Officers Charles Neil Overton (left) and Alfred Keith Ogilvie of 609 Squadron. Ogilvie, a Canadian was shot down in July 1941 and was so weak from loss of blood he was unable to take up offers from French people to help him escape. He was sent to Stalag Luft III and took part in the Great Escape. See page 169. In December 1941 Overton went to the Middle East and took command of 145 Squadron.

May 8, 1941 was Michael Robinson's 24th birthday and and the pilots of 609 Squadron were looking forward to a few drinks in the Officers' Mess. In the evening, however, they were scrambled to go to the aid of a British air-sea rescue launch which was being harrassed by Me 109s. Robinson led the mission with Ritchie leading a second section. Having reached the scene Robinson dived down and shot down two aircraft while his section finished off another four. He then ran out of ammunition and was set upon by a whole *Staffel* of enemy fighters.

As Intelligence Officer Frank Ziegler wrote in the combat report: "This superb pilot, disarmed as he was showed the mastery in the air that brought ground staff and other pilots out to watch each time he indulged in aerobatics. But this time it was to save his own life. With split second judgement, again and again, he turned sharply towards each opponent at the very moment the latter opened fire, and, with some eventual help from 'Goldy' Palmer got home without a single scratch".

The engagement later became known as *'Battle of the Dinghy'* and inspired aviation artist, Frank Wootton to immortalise it in an oil painting which hung over the fire place in the Officers' Mess at Biggin Hill for many years.

It was during July 1941 that 609 Squadron pioneered a new type of tactical flying known as Three Snakes. In place of the traditional four sections of three aircraft in 'vic' as used during the Battle of Britain, there were three sections of four aircraft in line astern, staggered in altitude and all weaving. This contributed to many of Biggin's great successes during the fighter sweeps. It meant that the Squadron was continuously covered visually against attack from any angle. Michael Robinson introduced the tactics but attributed the credit for inventing it to his brother-in-law.

Michael Robinson led the Biggin Wing until September 1941 when he was rested from operations and given command of RAF Manston. An appointment as aide to the Inspector General of the RAF followed but in January 1942 he was back on operations leading the Tangmere Wing.

On April 10 this tall, fresh faced, handsome young man always immaculately dressed, led his Wing at the head of 340 Squadron on yet another sweep. No-one really knows what happened except that Squadron Leader Michael Lister Robinson, did not come back.

Group Captain Philip Barwell

THE Station Commander at Biggin Hill from June 1941 was Group Captain Philip Reginald Barwell but always known as 'Dickie'. He was shorter in stature than the average fighter pilot but a big man in every other respect. He knew the names of all the pilots under his command — and most of the ground crew as well. Following his appointment as CO he made it his duty to tour the station each night, chatting to his NCOs and airmen. "Are you well?" "Have you any complaints?" "Feel free to chat to me any time".

The evening he walked into the Mess for the first time he found the Belgian pilots 'reasonably well oiled' and introduced himself. "Have a drink on us", said Strop Seghers who was at the bar with Van Lierde. Barwell, not wishing to offend the polite allies, accepted but then said he must go and dine. "Ve vill dine vith you" said the Belgians. And, to the amazement of their colleagues, they did!

'Dickie' Barwell came from Peterborough, Northamptonshire and had been commissioned into the RAF in 1925 at the age of 18. After various staff appointments, engineering and instructor's courses he took command of 46 Squadron and, on the outbreak of war, became one of the first recipients of the DFC (November, 1939) for leading a flight of six aircraft in a hostile area over the North Sea to intercept enemy bombers.

On his arrival at Biggin Hill he made it clear that administrative duties were not at the top of his list of priorities. When he was able to extract himself from his office — and that was often — Barwell flew with the Wing, usually as number two to Michael Robinson. And he hugely enjoyed these opportunities to escape the tedious day-to-day routine of running the busiest fighter station in the country.

One day early in 1942 Barwell took off on a sweep but as he gained height his engine went dead, forcing him to crash land in the valley west of the station. The impact was violent and Barwell was dragged out of the wreckage with a broken vertebra but, as one of his senior officers later said: "Nothing so trivial as a broken back inhibited his zest for partaking in operations and for several months he flew on sorties with his body encased in plaster".

By now the more regular squadrons at Biggin Hill were 72, 124 commanded by Squadron Leader Raymond Duke-Woolley and the Americans of 133. Barwell, with his plaster strait-jacket adorned with autographs, flew whenever he could, completely ignoring doctor's orders. His favourite position was number two to Duke-Woolley and that enabled the pilots in the Wing to assess his progress because Barwell could not turn his head sideways and he relied greatly on instinct — and luck!

He also flew on occasions with 133 Squadron and they revered him. One evening after a particular busy day Barwell decided to have a game of squash with his American friends. Later, in the Mess, one pilot noisily described the result to the entire bar. "Jesus", he said, "I was beaten by a Groupie with a broken back".

On July 1, 1942, Barwell had an urgent appointment with Squadron Leader Bobby Oxspring CO of 91 Squadron, who was stationed at Hawkinge. Oxspring was concerned about the new Luftwaffe tactics of sneak raids on south coast towns and ports. Fighter bombers were coming in fast at such low level that radar was unable to pick them up until a very late stage as their approaches were below the horizon line of flight. 91 Squadron had little success in

CRASH VALLEY: The Spitfire flown by Station Commander, Group Captain 'Dickie' Barwell which crashed soon after take-off in the valley to the west of Biggin Hill. He suffered a broken vertebra.

intercepting the raids so Oxspring flew to Biggin Hill to pass on his worries to the Sector Commander, 'Dickie' Barwell.

Barwell was so concerned he decided there was only one way to assess the problems. "I will accompany you on a standing patrol this evening", he told Oxspring. "Bill Igoe (senior controller at Biggin Hill) will control us".

Oxspring takes up the story. "We took off from Biggin Hill an hour before sunset and patrolled just off the coast between Dungeness and Beachy Head. There was a thick haze up to 16,000 feet and we were stationed just above it. As we approached Beachy, Bill Igoe warned us of unidentified plots in our vicinity and we peered into the haze for signs of activity. Suddenly I sighted two fighters approaching us out of the glare of the setting sun and warned Dickie who was abreast of me and nearer to them. I identified the leading fighter as a Spitfire and called the fact to 'Dickie'. I watched as it faded to my rear and then turned back to see the second aircraft, another Spitfire, opening fire on Dickie Barwell.

"Calling an urgent break to 'Dickie' I flew on collision course at his attacker and succeeded in distracting him enough to force a break away. I turned back close over the top of Dickie, whose aircraft was flaming from the petrol tank and I could see him desperately trying to open the canopy to bale out. I glanced back to see the first Spit swinging in behind me and opening fire. I broke hard round and down into the haze to shake him off but search as I might I could see no sign of 'Dicki'e. My frantic calls bore no response and I circled through the murk of the Channel. All I could find was what I took to be an oil slick on the surface. There was no sign of either a parachute or a dinghy".

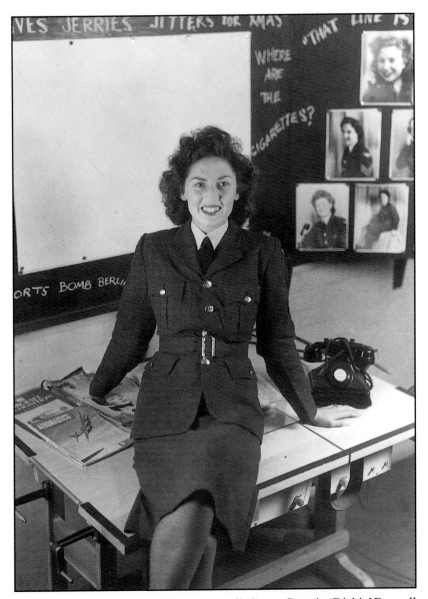

Leading Aircraftswoman Lorraine Tydeman (right) remembered 'Dickie' Barwell with great affection. Just before he died he gave her and Squadron Leader Tommy Balmforth permission to get married in yet another popular Biggin Hill love match. Tommy, who had replaced Duke-Woolley as CO of 124 Squadron, fell for the pretty young WAAF driver. Lorraine also remembered the frisky Free French pilots and was quite relieved when her skills as a driver were required by the WAAF officers and people like Padre O'Hanlon. When Lorraine first came to Biggin Hill in 1941 she was billeted in a house on the camp. She later lived with WAAF officers in more comfortable accommodation in Keston Park.

Extensive air-sea rescue searches were launched but to no avail. Group Captain 'Dickie' Barwell was dead. The popular Station Commander had perished in the most deplorable circumstances — shot down by two Spitfires from the Tangmere sector, one of which was on his first operational sortie and the other on his second.

The subsequent Court of Inquiry revealed that the Tangmere pilots could not tell the difference between a Messerschmitt and a Spifire. It also noted that Barwell's body was still strapped in plaster and he would have found it too severe an handicap either to abandon his aircraft or even to jettison his canopy.

'Dickie' Barwell had been at the helm for 11 months and was 35 when he died. His wife Mary was distraught and his death unsettled the whole station and particularly Bobby Oxspring at Hawkinge. Some months later Barwell's body was washed up on the French coast leading to speculation that his Spitfire broke up on impact with the sea. He was buried in a Canadian War Cemetery at Leubringhen, Pas de Calais, where more than 700 second world war casualties are commemorated. His spiritual home, however, remains at Biggin Hill.

BRIGHT ONES: The Intelligence staff well established at their new premises in Keston. Left to right: Flying Officer Hackforth-Jones, Flying Officer Sanker, Pilot Officer Bennett and WAAF officers Beecroft and McCall.

NIGHT FIGHTERS: 264 Squadron moved to Biggin Hill in January 1941 with Defiants to continue the night patrols which 141 Squadron had so bravely pioneered four months earlier. Two of their number, Roland Thorne (pilot) and Fred Barker (gunner) claimed 13 victims at night. Here they are relaxing outside their dispersal hut.

Where Eagles dare

THE youngest of the three American Eagle Squadrons, No 133, flew into Biggin Hill on May 3, 1942, unfurled the Old Glory outside their dispersal hut and then serenaded a watching group of admiring WAAFs with their battle song. Having met the Station Commander, Group Captain Dickie Barwell, they then toured the countryside looking for an English pub to call their own. The "Yanks" settled for the Queen's Head at Downe, a small village on the far side of the airfield.

The squadron had been formed at Eglington on December 7, 1941 a few days before Pearl Harbour. Its pilots came from 13 of the States and had been inspired to join the RAF by their knowledge that Britain desperately needed men who could fly, by their desire for adventure and by their impatience at the delay of their own country entering the conflict.

Four pilots — George Middleton, William Arends, D.E. Lambert and Grant Eichar — came from the area around the small town of Visilia in California and were known as the "Four Horsemen of the Apocalypse". Roy Beaty came from New York, Don Gentile from Piqua, Oklahoma, G.B.Sperry from Alhambra and Dick Gudmundsen from Burley, Idaho. There were about a dozen other men and most had flown light aircraft before volunteering.

Of the experienced pilots who had flown with British squadrons before joining the Eagles there was Spike Miley, Dusty Miller, Dickie Alexander and Don Blakeslee — a veteran of 401 Squadron who had insisted on a transfer when he knew his chums were coming to Biggin Hill. The Flight Commanders were 'Colby' King, a Hollywood stunt pilot and Red McColphin, from Buffalo, a poker-player of some repute. The Third Eagles had trained on Hurricanes and transferred to Spitfires before the move to Biggin Hill. "Give us the operations that are too tough for the Englishmen", they begged of Barwell.

By the end of September 1942 the three Eagle squadrons had transferred to the US Army Air Force and, of course, No 133 was among them. But it was a depressed, subdued group of pilots who listened to the AOC Fighter Command, Air Marshal Sholto Douglas say his farewell with a small address. There was no enthusiasm at the news that America had joined the war and they were to be part of No 4 Pursuit Group. There was no *espirit de corps*. 133 Squadron had been decimated.

Thirteen of the pilots who sang the battle song on May 3 and played shove half-penny at the Queen's Head were dead. The first was killed on May 31, 1942 and the last on September 26 — the day they left Biggin Hill to escort Flying Fortresses to Brest. Having achieved that, they were due to fly to Debden and take a breather.

First to die were Pilots Officers Moran Morris, aged 25, of Los Angeles and William Ford of Las Vegas who were shot down on Sunday May 31 while accompanying the mighty B-17 Flying Fortresses on their inaugural raids of Occupied Europe. On Friday June 5, 22-year-old Fletcher Hancock from Santa Cruz, California was killed near Abbeville followed by the first of the "four horsemen" Pilot Officer William Arends.

A month later, on July 26, Pilot Officer Gilbert Omens, 23, from Chicago died followed, two days later, by Ben Perry de Haven from Lexington, Kentucky and then the most senior of them all, Flight Lieutenant Coburn King, the stunt pilot from Hollywood who was shot down over Abbeville without ever having fired a shot in anger himself.

Although 133 Squadron had lost seven pilots in addition to the station Commanding Officer, Dickie Barwell they had little time to mourn. They were ordered to Lympne in readiness to cover Operation Jubilee — the assault by 6,000 troops on the port of Dieppe. Billeted in Sir Philip Sassoon's luxurious country house, Port Lympne, they enjoyed sumptuous accommodation before participating in 'the biggest show of all'. In the air they were partnered by Squadron Nos 222, 401 and 602, the latter led by Squadron Leader Peter Brothers who was returning briefly to the station where he had served for so many years with 32 Squadron. Also covering the Dieppe raid was the 307th Pursuit, the first of two regular American fighter units to go into action in Europe.

Furious air battles took place as the enemy attempted to break up the aerial umbrella over the land and sea forces. The Allies lost 85 planes including six of Biggin Hill's Spitfires. On land more than 1,500 prisoners including 60 Canadian officers were taken. The fighting on land and in the air was confused and very fierce. 133 squadron, now under Red McColphin, escorted the invasion fleet during the last stages of withdrawal. Inconclusively attacked by FW190s they were the last fighter unit to return and they did not lose a single pilot. For them the worst was yet to come.

In mid-September 1942 the Third Eagle Squadron heard they were to be disbanded and transferred to the US Army Air Force. They had been something of a headache for Fighter Command but the Americans were now in Britain in great numbers and it made sense to allow them to fight in the uniform of their own country.

Among the pilots who were filling the gaps of those lost was James Goodson who had actually joined the RAF after escaping from the torpedoed *Athenia* on the day that war was declared. "The Eagles had shot down 73 enemy aircraft", said Major James Goodson. "Now we had a split loyalty. We loved and respected its people, the RAF and its Royal Family. We made our demands and one of them was to wear our RAF wings on our US Air Force uniform. To our great surprise the top brass agreed providing they were miniature RAF wings worn over the right breast pocket".

The pilots of 133 Squadron had certainly earned their RAF wings and, led by an Englishman, Flight Lieutenant Gordon Brettell, took off on their final Eagle mission with mixed feelings. They were to accompany 24 Flying Fortresses on a daylight raid on Brest, first refuelling at Cornwall. The Met Office warned them that there was thick cloud cover over the target area and a wind of 100 mph from the south at 20,000 feet.

The wind, in fact, was from the north and both the bombers and fighters were carried well off course. Eventually, with the fuel running out, the Spitfires were forced to turn back. They dived down expecting to see the clear rocky outline of the Cornish coast but they were over Brest, a full 100 miles out in their navigation. The flak defences in this heavily-guarded port opened up. By now the Spitfires were out of fuel and completely vulnerable. Picked off one by one they were forced to crash-land in fields and a Luftwaffe aerodrome. Only one pilot, Pilot Officer Beaty, was able to make it back to England but he glided in with empty tanks and crash-landed at Kingsbridge, Devon. The Operations Record Book of 133 Squadron indicates that some landed on the island of Ouissant and others on the French mainland. It was

THE VICTIMS: Pilots of 133 Squadron on the Reredos at St George's Chapel, Biggin Hill.

The reredos text reads:

N⁰ 2 · SQUADRON
F/O · BERNARD · CYRIL · TASKER
F/LT · WILLIAM · ANDERSON · BLACK · A.F.C

N⁰ 133 (EAGLE) SQUADRON
P/O · WILLIAM · ALBERT · ARENDS
P/O · BEN · PERRY · DE · HAVEN
P/O · DICK · D · GUDMUNDSEN
P/O · WILLIAM · KENNETH · FORD
P/O · DAVID · RAY · FLORANCE
P/O · GRANT · EUGENE · EICHAR
P/O · FLETCHER · HANCOCK
P/O · CARTER · WOODRUFF · HARP
F/LT · COBURN · CLARK · KING
P/O · MORAN · SCOTT · MORRIS
P/O · GILBERT · INLAND · OMENS
P/O · ROBERT · LEWIS · PEWITT
P/O · SEYMOUR · MORTON · SCHATZBERG

N⁰ 316 (POLISH) SQUADRON
SGT · MARIAN · SZMIT

N⁰ 609 (WEST RIDING) SQUADRON
SGT · GUY · ALEXANDER · CHESTNUT
SGT · KENNETH · WALTER · BRAMBLE
F/SGT · GEOFFREY · CHARLES · BENNETT
F/O · JOSEPH · DAWSON
SGT · ALAN · RONALD · NEWNHAM · DAVI
F/LT · JOHN · CURCHIN · D · F · C
P/O · DOUGLAS · LINDSAY · CROPPER
P/O · SYDNEY · JENKYN · HILL
F/O · RAYMOND · DOPERE
P/O · RUDOLPHE · CHRISTIAN · CHARLES · DE · HEMRICOURT · DI

subsequently agreed, on good authority, that the majority were now prisoners of war.

Goodson, already at Debden waiting for his Squadron, remembers the moment that Don Gentile walked into the barracks reserved for officers at Debden. "Hi", he said, "I'm sure glad to see you. I'm all alone here".

"Where are the others?", he was asked. "None have come back from the mission", he said "They were escorting the first Fortress raid to Brest. There was a lot of wind and I guess the Forts kept going and our guys stayed with them. They were bounced by Jerries and couldn't get back across the Channel. I've heard that Beaty made it back to the South Coast, but he's the only one".

Don Blakeslee, not on that raid, was later appointed CO of the new Fourth Fighter Group. He nearly blew it by entertaining two female officers in his barrack room the night before General Hunter was due to tour Debden. His colleagues thought that feat alone deserved promotion.

So 133 Squadron lasted for less than a year and experienced less than four wonderfully hectic but tragic months at Biggin Hill. The Queen's Head was a popular destination but so was the American Club in Piccadilly, the Eagle Club in Charing Cross Road and the Regent Palace Hotel where they met — and later married — their English dates. They enjoyed the RAF tradition of hard drinking and high living but never permitted either of those to interfere with their readiness to fly.

In all the RAF Eagles shot down 73 enemy aircraft but the cost was high with 100 pilots killed or missing in action. By the end of the war the leading aces included two who had flown from what they described as "Biggin Bump, in the heart of the big flap country" — Colonel Don Gentile, christened Captain Courageous by President Roosevelt (21 victories) and Col Donald Blakeslee who became known to the Germans as "The Blakesleewaffe" (15 victories). On an equal score was Col James Goodson who was shot down over Germany and captured in July 1944. After the war Goodson made his home in Kent and was a regular visitor to Biggin Hill.

Americans make their pilgrimages to Biggin Hill in great numbers every year. They visit the Chapel but they know the reredos can tell them only a fraction of the true story behind the great sacrifice of their countrymen. The ghosts from 13 US States, and especially those from California, would know more! *See the panel above.*

THE GREATEST: Sailor Malan's most onerous duty was writing the many letters of condolence.

Sailor Malan — the tiger of the skies

'SAILOR' Malan DSO and Bar, DFC and Bar, Croix de Guerre and the top scoring ace in Fighter Command took control of Biggin Hill in January 1943 when morale was at its lowest ebb. Foul weather and lack of operations meant that the pilots were spending more time in the cinema in Bromley and Sevenoaks than in their Spitfires. Mike Robinson had been lost while leading the Tangmere Wing, Dickie Barwell was dead and many other once-cheerful faces were no longer in the Mess holding centre stage.

Albert Gysbert Malan, of course, knew Biggin well having led 74 (Tiger) Squadron in the latter stages of the Battle of Britain and then, from February 1941, taken command of the Biggin Hill Wing. Born in South Africa, Malan went to sea at 15 with the Union Castle line, first as a cadet and then an officer. He joined the RAF in 1936, quickly qualified as a pilot and proved to be so skilful that he was nominated to collect the first production Spitfire from Vickers Supermarine. By then he was known throughout Fighter Command as 'Sailor'

By January 1943 the two Squadrons based at Biggin were now 611 (County of Lancashire) Squadron led by Squadron Leader Hugo 'Sinker' Armstrong and 340 (Ille de France) commanded by Capitaine J. Schloesing. They had arrived together on September 23 1942 from Redhill and Hornchurch.

Malan's posting received tremendous coverage by the newspapers and on the wireless. Biggin Hill was the number one fighter station. 'Sailor' was the number one fighter pilot and the new improved Spitfire IX, which could match the mighty FW 190s in performance, was number one fighter aircraft. With a fourth ring on his sleeve and gold braiding around the peak of his cap Malan made it clear that he intended to practice what he preached and the pilots knew it. His first act was to draw up his own Ten Commandments and his second was to declare that he would join operations whenever he could.

Throughout the winter and summer of 1943 'Sailor' Malan guided the Biggin Hill squadrons through some of the most hectic and tiring days of the war. He flew on Rodeos, often as Red Three to Jack Charles of 611 Squadron. He led the Squadron on Circuses. At the same time he made his reports and attended various meetings throughout the country.

As the weather improved the losses mounted and 611 Squadron, which had long since lost all trace of its Auxiliary status, was suffering badly. Just a few weeks after arriving at Biggin Hill Sergeant George Kraus of Paddington, London and Flying Officer David Fulford of Dinnington, Yorkshire died on the same day. On January 27, 1943 two young Australian Sergeant pilots John Gilbert and Alton Mackay were shot down and killed. The two friends, aged 20 and 25 were buried at the St Mary Cray Cemetery, then used almost exclusively for Biggin Hill's casualties.

'Sailor' Malan was devasted by the frequency at which he had to write letters of condolence to the parents of the young airmen. On Friday February 5 he was at his desk again, this time telling Percival and Grace Armstrong in Travancore, Victoria, Australia that their son, Hugo 'Sinker' Armstrong, CO of 611 Squadron had been 'bounced' by eight Huns off Boulogne. Flying 1,000 feet under the clouds Armstrong found himself fighting for his life. The unmistakeable Aussie accent was then heard to say: "This is it, chaps. I'm baling out". He was never seen again.

The Australians toasted absent friends in the Mess and wondered who would be next. The answer came within four weeks. Flight Sergeant Allan Pearce from Malvern, South Australia, just 21 years old, died followed by his friend and colleague, Flight Sergeant Robert McLay. In less than 10 weeks five Aussie pilots had been lost while flying from Biggin Hill.

On March 14, 1943 Dickie Milne, Wing Commander Flying, led his Wing on a Rodeo and bumped into eight Focke Wulfs. Milne attacked and after a hectic skirmish found himself on his own and a sitting duck. He was shot down and taken prisoner. At the same time Wing Commander James Hogarth Slater of Hungerford, Berkshire and Commandant Reilhac, 340's CO were shot down over Le Touquet. Neither returned to base. Reilhac had been CO for just a few weeks. His predecessor, Capitaine Schloesing — having failed to return from an attack on an armed merchant ship in Boulogne harbour and posted as "missing" — was, in fact on his way back to Biggin Hill. He appeared in the Mess one day in August with a hair-raising story of his survival and escape to Switzerland.

On April 1, 1943 'Sailor' Malan invited all personnel to a special ceremony on the parade ground. It was the 25th anniversary of the RAF and he wanted to tell them that they were members of the foremost sector in Fighter Command. "Today, as you know" he said. "Biggin Hill is closely approaching its 1000th confirmed victory". He then spoke in recognition of the magnificent support the pilots had received from ground personnel.

Within a fortnight the score had moved to 1001 and two pilots — Canadian Jack Charles of 611 and Frenchman René Mouchotte of 341 (Alsace) Squadron — had shared the great landmark together with the £300 prize money, the sum collected in a sweepstake. Malan, as Station Commander, Al Deere, as Wing Leader, the Frenchman and the Canadian were besieged by journalists, newsreel cameramen and radio reporters. Biggin Hill celebrated by staging the "greatest party ever known" and certainly the most lavish of the war years in the Grosvenor Hotel for 1,000 cheering guests.

On June 25 'Sailor' flew as number three to Jack Charles on his last show as station commander of Biggin Hill. By now 611 Squadron had left and their place was taken by 485 New Zealand Squadron with Johnny Checketts in command. The Frenchmen of 341 Squadron were still actively involved on many missions, now against the newly-located V2 rocket launch sites.

'Sailor' was tired and needed a rest from operations, from running the busiest fighter station in Group 11 and from constant requests for interviews from the press. In September he performed his last big function by unveiling a memorial to the pilots from the Biggin Hill sector who had given their lives in four years of war. It was held in the little chapel of St George's on the North Camp and among those in attendance was the Marshal of the RAF, Viscount Hugh Trenchard. One month later, on October 16, Malan was taken ill at his home and Squadron Leader Marten took temporary command of Biggin Hill.

Malan never returned on active service to the station but he continued to fly and to command, first with No 19 Fighter Wing and then 145 Wing, consisting of three French units. On D Day he led yellow section of 340 Squadron on Ramrod 976. It was June 6, 1944 and Malan was not going to miss the biggest show of all. Escorting TAF Albermarles towing Horsa gliders into the assault area, he saw many gliders shot down but also saw the paratroopers

VIP's: Group Captain Malan with Squadron Leader 'Spy' de la Torre, the station Intelligence Officer (in the background) and visitors outside the Officers' Mess.

landing on either side of the Orne River.

A month later he was Commanding Officer of the Advanced Gunnery School at RAF Catfoss where fighters of all nationalities came to pool ideas and develop new techniques and tactics. Here, he met many old friends and made the decision to return to his native South Africa when the war was over. Through Sir Ernest Oppenheimer and his son Harry he was offered a senior post with the Anglo-American Diamond Trading Company and a home in Johannesburg for himself his wife, Lynda, and children Jonathan and Valerie.

Before leaving he was invited to the White Hart, Brasted, the Biggin Hill pilots most regular wartime haunt, to unveil the famous black-out screen containing signatures of the greatest fighter pilots to fly from Britain's senior sector station. "My feelings are mixed", he said. "This is a happy occasion and I am trying to smile. But it would be a strange man who didn't have sadder thoughts when he reads some of these names and remembers. We built up a 'fighter' tradition that will not easily die. I hope you will come here often to steep yourselves in a bit of tradition."

A few weeks later he was on his way home to South Africa — free passage by courtesy of the Union Government. Five years later he took out a mortgage on a farm at Benfontein, eight miles outside Kimberley. In that vicinity he remained a local hero and a national figurehead, often in demand to attend meetings and rallies and fly the flag for freedom. But he was not well. The years of strain at Biggin Hill, and all that preceded and followed, was taking its toll. He began to lose weight and to be unsteady on his feet.

In mid-1959, approaching his 50th birthday 'Sailor' Malan flew to England for the final time and was met by Al Deere and his wife Joan. There were many friends and old haunts to visit and one of them was the White Hart. He was astonished by the reception awaiting him. It was the greatest gathering of fighter pilots the old pub had ever known.

'Sailor' Malan chatted about the old days, about his great score of 34 "plus 11 probables" and drank a toast to absent friends in front of the blackout board. He then told his friends he had Parkinson's Disease and was in England to see specialists. He also penned a letter to Kath and Teddy Preston of the White Hart, Brasted. "They tell me this inflammation in the central nervous system might take over a year to burn itself out....so I'll be back to pay another visit.... Meanwhile we have a lot of pleasant memories to sustain us for a few years. Everybody was incredibly kind to us in England and you two were no exception.

'Sailor' Malan never returned. He died in 1963 aged 52. His memorial service was held in St George's Chapel. He was the greatest of them all.

THE ONE THOUSANDTH: *Left to right: Squadron Leader Jack Charles of 611 Squadron, Captain René Mouchotte of 341 Squadron, Group Captain 'Sailor' Malan, Station Commander and Flight Lieutenant 'Al' Deere, Wing Leader — May 15th, 1943.*

Mouchotte — legendary hero of Alsace

A FEW days after the great German rocket base at Peenemunde on the island of Usedom in North West Germany had been identified and attacked by the whole weight of Bomber Command, the vigilant staff of photographic reconnaissance at Medmenham in Berkshire spotted, on a set of aerial photographs over Pas de Calais, a new construction site hidden in a forest near the town of St Omer.

Nobody knew at the time that this was a bomb-proof launch pad for the V2 rocket and was scheduled to enter service in December 1943. The bunker was well hidden in the Forêt d'Éperlecques near the village of Watten. Only keen and well-trained eyes could identify it as being a suspicious object, but that is just what it was so orders were issued to bomb the site and the marshalling yards nearby. The job was given to the US Eighth Air Force and the Biggin Hill Wing formed part of the escort.

On August 27, 1943, 240 Flying Fortresses took off from East Anglia. Near the coast the leading wave of bombers were joined by the Alsace Squadron, the Free French of 341. Right in front, shepherding the massive formation behind, was Captain René Mouchotte, a hero in England and a legend in France. Holder of the Croix de la Legion d'Honneur and a Companion of the Conseil de l'Ordre de la Liberation. Mouchotte was already part of the Biggin Hill folklore. Three months earlier he had shared in the destruction of the station's 1,000th Hun — a feat which culminated in the most lavish celebration wartime England had ever known.

Mouchotte was then 29 years old. Born at Saint Mande in 1914 he joined l'Armée de l'Air before the war but soon after the outbreak became a flying instructor. When France fell Mouchotte took a Renault Goeland and flew to Gibraltar with five other Frenchmen. He sailed for England on July 3 and by August was at Sutton Bridge as a Sergeant Pilot. Mouchotte quickly went through the ranks. Adjutant, Flight Commander, Captain. He was posted successively to Aldergrove, Prestwick, Turnhouse and Hornchurch. He helped to form le Groupe Ile-de-France and in September 1942 had the honour of being posted to Britain's premier station, Biggin Hill.

Many French pilots had fought from Biggin Hill but this was the first French unit to be stationed there. Led by Commandant Bernard Dupérier the pilots looked forward to flying the new Spitfire IX's in place of their Mark Vs and their main task would be to accompany Flying Fortresses on daylight raids over France, Belgium and Holland. The pounding of the Luftwaffe's airfields continued almost daily and without respite and only the thought of the thousandth victory kept spirits high at the station.

When that was achieved in May 1943 Mouchotte — and Squadron Leader Jack Charles of 311 Squadron who shared the historic "kill" — had suddenly become the centre of attention. Requests for signed photographs came from all over England and France. Mouchotte answered them all. In his diary he wrote: "The sweeps go on at a terrible pace. I am at the record figure of 140 and I feel a pitless weariness from them. It is useless for me to go to bed at 9.30 each night. I feel my nerves wearing out, my temper deteriorating. The smallest effort gets me out of breath".

Biggin Hill Station Commander 'Sailor' Malan urged him to take leave, but he refused and he also stubbornly rejected any suggestion that his Alsace Squadron should transfer to a quieter station. By the end of August, René Mouchotte was in desperate need of a rest.

As the great raiding party crossed over the French coast an enormous swarm of Focke Wulf's dived out of the sun. Wing Leader Mouchotte quickly gave his orders: *"Turban aircraft stay together"*. Then, at the very last moment, *"break port, attack"*. Suddenly the sky was full of whirling patterns, depicting a maniacal dance of life and death. Cocooned in his Spitfire, subjected to colossal stresses and his senses battered by the sudden chaos around him, Mouchotte attempted to regroup his unit but found himself isolated from the fray. His last words over the R/T were: *"I am alone with the bombers"*.

One by one the broken formation flew back to Biggin Hill, landed on the flarepath and reported to Intelligence Officer de la Torre and Station Commander 'Sailor' Malan. Two pilots were missing Sergeant-Chef Magrot and Commandant René Mouchotte. Immediately calls were made to other airfields and to air-sea rescue but there was no news.

Had René Mouchotte died in the cockpit of his Spitfire in the great forest or was he a prisoner in his own beloved France? No-one knew...the waiting was agonising. Day after day the Alsace pilots stood by the radio hoping their friends of the Resistance would send good news from France, that René was safe and sound and already on his way to the Spanish frontier. Nothing came through. The Commandant had disappeared in the open sky.

Bernard Dupérier, was given the painful task of drawing up a report on the operation over France and later he wrote: "I have just returned to Biggin Hill after a day at headquarters. Night was falling. The familiar scene of the narrow road reacted with the hour to tell over a whole chaplet of memories set to the monotonous rhythm of flights and combats. War like a subtle poison penetrating us through every living fibre, has numbed both body and spirit. Death and fire have lost their constant effect on us, being only associated now with our flying...."

"Three years of operations had seen the end of nearly all those who had wanted to keep the French cockade high in battle in the sky in June 1940. There were still two of us at Biggin Hill; I had René Mouchotte there with me, one of the very first of the Free French, who had been my companion in 615 Squadron in 1941. Together, then we patrolled the grey immensity of the North Sea and daily faced the inferno let loose by the German guns. Later we trained our juniors to form Ile-de-France Squadron and led it together in its first battle. Together we went through Dieppe; a thousand details, a thousand memories. How could I not feel some presentiment of the terrible news awaiting me when I came back to Biggin Hill? Boudier, Martel and de Saxce were waiting for me and on their downcast faces I read the whole tragedy at once.

"Mouchotte was missing. Mouchotte the wise, great, skilful, calm pilot had not come back. Separated from the companions whom he had in vain sought to rally in the hostile, cold immensity of the twilight sky, he had met the soldier's death...His spirit remained behind and those he trained will make the Germans pay dearly for his victory. Few men have made themselves loved as he was by the pilots whose fate he held daily in his hands. His loss tonight made tears glisten in fighting men's eyes."

By the time that Dupérier had completed his report the Flying Fortresses of the US Eighth were safely back at base unaware at the time that the raid had been a complete success. Only the lower level of the rocket launch pad had been built and the 'Kraftwerk Nordwest' had been badly smashed up. It was later decided to abandon the idea of rebuilding the launch pad but to press ahead with the building of a bomb-proof factory alongside to manufacture liquid oxygen to fuel the rockets and move the rocket site to a quarry 10 miles away at Wizernes.

After the war, evidence proved that René Mouchotte's Spitfire came down in the sea and not in the Forêt d'Éperlecques. His body had been washed up at Middlekerke, Belgium and he was buried there. He did not remain there for long. In October 1949 his body was exhumed, returned to France and in a ceremony at Pére-Lachaise Cemetery he was re-interred in the family vault. General Valin, former chief of the Staff of the Free French Air Forces spoke movingly at the service.

"While the words were being measured out, 'legendary hero, lost in the open sky of glory', I thought of those who during the dark days nevertheless maintained the tradition. I visualised them on such a morning on the burning sand of the desert, in Libya or the Sahara, amid the luxuriant vegetation of the Equator or among the birches which alone break the vast monotony of the plain of White Russia.

"But above all I recalled a corner of traditional England, set on an old park where buildings to which the Virginia creeper had given an air of some ancient seigneurial domain, rising from an airfield so green that it looked like a golf course — Biggin Hill. There are Spitfires drawn up there. The Alsace Squadron is on parade and before these few fighting men their leader, as admired by them as he is loved, a tall, handsome, dark young man, is reading Guyemer's citation as the sun begins to pierce the morning mist. It is Mouchotte, one of the better fighters of the Free French Air Forces.

"René Mouchotte will remain one of the purest figures, if not the purest, among the sons of France who fell beside their heroic comrades of the Royal Air Force in those noble combats between 1940 and 1945".

BIG X: Squadron Leader Roger Bushell, formerly of 601 Squadron and CO of 92 Squadron at Stalag Luft III with Paddy Byrne, known among his PoW friends as the "little leprechaun".

Squadron Leader Roger Bushell

THE city of Poznan can be found in the west of Poland on the main E30/2 road. To the north of the city in the district of Winogrady is the old Garrison Cemetery containing the graves of more than 400 prisoners of war from the British Commonwealth who died in captivity or were murdered. Every year, thousands of pilgrims — including coach parties of young children, relatives and old comrades — arrive from all parts of the world to say a prayer and bring flowers. Most visitors stop to look at the headstone above Grave 9.A. It belongs to Roger Joyce Bushell, who was shot by the Gestapo for daring to escape from Stalag Luft III.

Squadron Leader Bushell flew with 601 Squadron from Biggin Hill in the early days of the war. He later became the first Squadron Leader with No 92 and was the inspiration behind the spirit of gaiety and verve with which that successful but tragic Squadron was blessed. Sadly, Bushell was no longer with 92 when it moved to Biggin Hill in September 1940. He would have rejoiced in a return to his old hunting ground but by then he was a prisoner in Germany, shot down over the beaches of Dunkirk.

On the night of March 24-25, 1944 80 Allied PoWs escaped from the most secure and the most notorious prison in Poland, Stalag Luft III. Four were captured in the mouth of the tunnel but 76 cleared the camp area and prepared to make their way home. Roger Bushell was among them. In fact he was 'Big X', the officer in charge of escaping and the man who masterminded the mass break out — for ever known as *The Great Escape.*

As Bushell, in civilian clothing and carrying a brilliantly forged pass, a compass and a map of this area of Poland, took his first tentative steps through this vigilant area of Nazi Germany — travelling by night, sleeping by day — he would have reflected on the quality of life back in "dear old Blighty" with the boys of 92 and, perhaps, at Lincoln's Inn where he could soon continue his successful career as a barrister-at-law.

Roger Bushell was born of very wealthy parents in South Africa, the son of Benjamin Daniel and Dorothy Bushell of Mossel River, Cape Province. At the age of 11 he was sent to Wellington School and then on to Oxford University where he read law and languages. He spoke French and German fluently, the latter with a Swiss accent. He won a blue at rugby, excelled at athletics and was a British ski champion.

When war broke out, Bushell was 29 and already a brilliant criminal barrister, whose weekend passion was flying from Hendon with the RAF Auxiliary and Reserve Volunteers Squadron, No 601. Along with his great chums, Michael Peacock, Whitney Straight, Sir Archibald Hope and Max Aitken, Bushell was summoned by telegram to report for duty. He was then told that RAF Biggin Hill would be the Squadron's wartime base.

This brilliant flyer with an equally brilliant mind was quickly promoted and by May 1940 was commanding the newly-formed 92 Squadron at Hornchurch. The situation in France at the time was critical; the war was moving towards the beaches and Bushell was in action soon after dawn on his first full day at the station, May 23. His orders were to take 12 Spitfires on their first combat mission to Bolougne, make a sweep left along the coast over Calais and Dunkirk and then return by the same route. Bushell briefed his pilots. He said they would encounter large formations of Me109s. "Keep a tight formation and look out for Stukas dive-bombing out of the sun".

Only 11 pilots returned from that mission. Pat Learmond was the first from 92 Squadron to die. Another pilot, the charismatic, popular Bob Stanford Tuck scored his first victory, enjoyed the adventure and craved for another. It wasn't long coming and just before 2 o'clock 92 Squadron rose again. Each Spitfire was camouflaged, carried a 1175hp Rolls Royce Merlin engine and was armed with eight lethal .303 machine guns set in the wings. As the 11 Spitfires wheeled back towards Boulogne they were aerial spectators of the dramatic panorama below where thick black smoke was accompanied by occasional yellow flashes of shell burst.

92 Squadron was quickly into its first dog fight and the odds were heavily stacked against the British pilots — 50 to 60 Me109s. Approaching each other at a closing speed of 70mph the aircraft broke and Bushell found that five 109s were on his tail. He turned inside, he slipped and dived and used every trick to dodge the foe knowing the Spitfire was far more manoeuverable. He sent one 109 into a long curving dive and then discovered that he, too, was rapidly losing height. The engine was on fire and he was spewing glycol. At about 5,000 feet the controls failed completely.

Bushell switched off his engine and glided above stalling speed at a rapid and dangerous angle. He hit the grass, bumped across a field, taxied to a halt and climbed out of the aircraft onto a bank and waited for the BEF boys to appear from west of Boulogne. A motorbike came in sight and Roger Bushell knew the game was up. The rider was not in khaki uniform but field grey and he was pointing a pistol in his direction. This squadron leader and worldly barrister was now a PoW and the war was less than 12 months old. He vowed to escape.

Meanwhile, back at Hornchurch, the 92 Squadron diarist had this to say about May 23, 1940: "A glorious day for the Squadron with 23 German machines brought down but the loss of the CO has been a big blow for us". A few months later, towards the end of the Battle of Britain, the same diarist wrote: "We are moving to Biggin Hill and the indication of more action. This will be greatly welcomed by the Squadron".

For Roger Bushell a new challenge lay ahead — the desire to escape from the various internment camps to which he was sent. On one occasion he slipped his guards and evaded capture for six months but was eventually returned to Sagan, 90 miles south east of Berlin. Bushell knew he was a marked man and certain death awaited him, if he was found outside the camp again. In 1942 Bushell was transferred to Stalag Luft III where escape activities had grown from a fragmented effort to a highly organised aspect of camp life under the leadership of Harry 'Wings' Day who had been shot down as early as October 1939.

Bushell was invited to become a founder member of a new escape committee known as the X Organisation. With him were Flight Lieutenants John Gilles and Harvey Vivian and an American serving in the British army, Major Johnnie Dodge.

For many months Roger Bushell kept his escape activities to a minimum and the camp commanders assumed the prisoner had resigned himself to captivity. In 1943 'Wings' Day and other members of the escaping fraternity had been transferred to Oflag XXX1B at Schubin and Bushell, as senior officer, found himself in charge.

This was the opportunity he had been planning in his mind for a few years. He wanted to cause the maximum harm to the Reich by arranging mass escapes on a scale never imagined by the Germans — perhaps up to 200 men under the wire at one time. A new escape committee was formed and Bushell revealed his plans.

He wanted three tunnels each descending 30 feet and extending out towards the woods by 300 feet or more. He wanted underground railways and workshops, forged passes, civilian outfits, compasses and maps. The intricate details of the greatest escape plan ever known were in the hands of selected prisoners with Bushell as 'Big X', Tim Waleen as chief forger and Wally Moody as mining engineer. The would-be escapees were enlisted, got to work and the tunnels, originating from barracks 123, 122 and 104 in the north compound of the camp, were christened Tom, Dick and Harry.

On the night of March 24/25, 1944 200 men prepared to break out of Stalag Luft III, as Bushell had always intended. Because of unexpected delays in getting men through the tunnel, Harry, many were in the barracks awaiting their turn when a camp commander discovered a hole outside the wire. Four were captured in the mouth of the tunnel but 76 cleared the camp area including Roger Bushell and another former Biggin Hill pilot Keith Ogilvie who was the last to get free of the tunnel. Inside the barracks the others destroyed the forged papers and maps when they heard shooting.

The Germans issued a *Grossfahndung*, a massive search of the highest priority. Bushell had succeeded in causing enormous turmoil within the Reich, who were now worried about sabotage but even more about the embarrassment the break-out would cause. Hitler was beside himself with rage. Hours and hours would be involved in searching Germany for their whereabouts. He then issued his famous Sagan Order — to capture and then execute those who had escaped.

Hitler was right. The hue and cry over the whereabouts of the escapees and the announcement of the *Grossfahndung* caused massive internal disruption to the Germans in what was to be less than three months before the Normandy landings. The alert included mobilising a Panzer division and diverting a total of 700,000 military police and bureaucrats from their normal duties

Only three of the men, two Norwegians and a Dutchman, managed to reach England. The rest were handed over to the Gestapo, instead of the Luftwaffe as required by the Geneva Convention and 50 of them were ordered to be shot by the Gestapo. Most of the killings took place at Görlitz prison near Dresden on May 19, 1944, arguably the worst atrocity against Britons in the second world war. Only 20 men were sent back to Stalag Luft III.

Squadron Leader Roger Bushell died four days after the Great Escape. He was recaptured at Saarbrucken and ordered to be sent back to Stalag Luft III. On the return journey, during a supposed break for refreshment at Kaiserlautern, Bushell was shot in the spine by Gestapo secretary, Emil Schulz. As he lay in agony on the roadside Schulz ended his life with a single shot to the temple.

Another former Biggin Hill pilot to die was Gordon Brettell, the hero of 92 Squadron, who was court martialled in 1941 for flying from Tangmere with a blonde on his lap. Brettell, though British, was later the first Commanding Officer of 133 Eagle Squadron and it was the result of the disastrous final mission that Brettell led, from which none of the Squadron returned, that Colonel James Goodson was transferred to 133 and became its CO. By 1944 Goodson was also a guest of Stalag Luft III. He didn't take part in the escape but remembered the months of digging and burrowing with sand in the eyes, in the nose and in the hair. He recalled the "boring, uncomfortable process of filling my long underwear with sand so that it could gradually trickle out through the ankles tied with string while I tramped round and round the camp perimeter".

Keith Ogilvie, shot down while leading his Wing over St Omer with 609 Squadron in July 1941, was recaptured after two days and sent to Görlitz. During repeated interrogations by the Gestapo he claimed he was a career officer and later wrote in his diary: "This must have registered with the Teutonic mind, because I was one of eight returned to camp".

In June 1944 Anthony Eden, then Foreign Secretary assured the House of Commons that "His Majesty's Government is firmly resolved that these foul criminals shall be tracked down to the last man, wherever they may take refuge".

The retribution was completed thanks to the efforts of the RAF's own Special Investigation Branch. Although many trails initially went cold the murderers were eventually listed down to the last man. Of the 55 Gestapo officers involved in the killings, six had been killed in air raids and 11 committed suicide. 21 of the remaining men were executed and 17 received long-term jail sentences. Roger Bushell's killer, Emil Schulz was hanged on February 27, 1948 — a memorable day for the Martyrs of Sagan.

Roger's sister Elizabeth, who lived in South Africa, later described her brother as a broad-shouldered rugger player who had dynamism and enthusiasm. "He wasn't a bit like the dour and short Richard Attenborough who portrayed him in the film. We still miss him terribly".

On special anniversaries, survivors of *The Great Escape* gather at St Clement Danes in the Strand to commemorate the slaughter of the 50 Martyred Fliers and on occasions they have been joined by Dame Vera Lynn. On the 50th anniversary in 1994 one of the octogenarian survivors said: "It's not intended to be a sentimental affair. We know that Roger and the ghosts of Sagan would prefer us old buffers to enjoy a wizard-prang reunion, chat about Biggin Hill and the other stations and rub the Krauts' noses into half a century of bloodstain".

In August 1942 an Allied Commando force tried to seize the French port of Dieppe and destroy the German defences. It turned into a massacre. Of the 6,100-strong force more than 4,000 officers and men were killed, reported missing or wounded. *Operation Jubilee* was a disaster. The Squadrons of the Biggin Wing who helped to maintain a fighter "umbrella" over Dieppe was provided by Squadrons Nos 133, 222, 401 and 602 with the 307th Pursuit.

Another CO lost

AS plans for *Operation Overlord*, the Allies' invasion of Western Europe, took shape there were inevitable changes at Biggin Hill. In October 1943 the Alsace Squadron said goodbye and three Canadian squadrons moved in, Nos 401, 411 and 412, equipped with Spitfire Vbs but flying Spitfire IXs before the end of the year. There was also a new station commander in Group Captain H.L. Maxwell, a new Intelligence Officer in Squadron Leader J.W.Hogben and new Wing Commander Flying in the caring Commandant Bernard Dupérier, who had taken over from Al Deere.

As far as casualties were concerned there was no change. American heavy bombers, Marauders, Fortresses and Liberators, were now probing deep into the heart of Germany and it fell to the Canadians of the Biggin Wing to meet them on their return and escort them on the dangerous journey home. Seventeen pilots of 401 Squadron alone were killed and many others flew to the limit of their Spitfire's range and crash-landed or baled out through lack of fuel.

Nearer home there were more fatalities — all recorded (in the briefest detail) in the station record book filed with the Public Record Office. On January 27, 1943 two NCO pilots, both Australian, were killed in collision above Biggin Hill while carrying out cine gun exercise. On March 6, 1943 Pilot Officer George Whitmore and Sergeant Harris Fraser of No 1 Squadron crashed in Kent and were killed. Theirs was a Typhoon squadron and they were billeted at Biggin Hill for less than a month.

It was in the Spring of 1944 that the Canadians left and Biggin Hill was bereft of aircraft for the first time in its history. Too far away from striking at the heart of Nazi Germany the station was still ideally placed for the defence of London — and a new menace was on the horizon. The doodlebug.

In June 1944 Biggin Hill was renamed No 22 Balloon Centre. The station's role now was to establish hundreds of barrage balloon emplacements in an arc from the Thames into deepest Surrey and massive convoys of squadrons arrived to select the ideal sites. The 519 airmen and 177 WAAFs who lived on the station braced themselves for the arrival of Hitler's last-ditch orgy of terror — the VI pilotless plane, later to be christened the doodlebug.

By the middle of July a formidable barrier of 1,750 balloons were floating over the North Downs. With later extensions they stretched from Redhill to Chatham and covered 260 miles of countryside — 31 miles long and 11 miles deep. Smooth and silver against the blue sky the balloons were at their most beautiful by moonlight and produced a mystic, almost magical sound as 6,000 cables stirred in the breeze.

It was not long before Biggin Hill was under bombardment once more as the bombs started falling in or near the station. The married quarters were damaged again and the WAAFs sickroom at Keston completely destroyed. One flying bomb severed the cable of a balloon and crashed harmlessly into an orchard and another injured several members of a balloon squadron. At 5.30 am on July 1 a doodlebug exploded on top of a Nissen hut standing on the airfield. The incident revived the horrors of August 1940 for all that could be seen was a gaping hole in the ground and a few scraps of notepaper on the ground. The rescue party, consisting of more than 100 airmen, were uncertain how many men were sleeping in

GASBAGS: Each day from June 16, 1944 more and more balloon squadrons arrived in Kent in massive convoys. Biggin Hill was the Balloon Centre and the men were quickly christened "gasbag types" by the Canadian pilots stationed there. The station was also given control of all "diver" operations.

the hut. They found three bodies.

There was worse to come. Weald House, Westerham — less than four miles away as a doodlebug flies — received a direct hit and 22 children under the age of five and eight female staff died. At Brasted, not far from the White Hart pub, three WAAFs were killed when a V1 ran down a balloon cable.

Three days into the main thrust of Hitler's new assault the situation looked grim. More than 500 people had been killed and that figure was rising as Civil Defence recovered more and more bodies. As gun, searchlight and balloon defences were organised to mass their strength against the approach route of the bombs across Kent, Biggin Hill was given overall control of all operations. The code name for the doodlebug was 'Diver' and the Ops room was in the large house called Towerfields, two miles north of the airfield.

By the middle of September 1944, with the doodlebug menace abated, all the regular sections that make up an RAF station had returned and a succession of Spitfire Squadrons, including the Frenchmen of 340, were flying again from Biggin Hill. It was all too brief. The battlefront was now close to the frontiers of Germany and Biggin Hill was too far removed. The Spitfires left after a few weeks and No 168 (Heavy Transport) Squadron of the Royal Canadian Air Force moved in to run a regular transatlantic airmail service for the Canadian forces in Europe.

On March 16, 1944 a Henley Page Halifax which had taken off from East Anglia just after midnight for a raid on Stuttgart got lost in the fog and the crew baled out over Biggin Hill leaving the pilot to nurse the aircraft down. He failed. The Halifax crashed in the garden of Bertrey Cottage between Single Street and Berry's Hill and the pilot, Flight Sergeant Harry Walter Hill of 587 Squadron, was killed. The son of Harry and Florence Hill of Lee, he was

The Dutchmen of 322 Squadron who moved to Biggin Hill in October 1944. Left to right: Back row: F/Sgts Bakker, Dijkman, Harms, F/Off van Eijk, F/Sgts van Valkenburg, Janssen, de Vries. Middle row: F/Sgt Bary, Fl.Off Homburg, F/Sgt van Roosendaal, Fl Offs Krediet, Groenveld, Koes, Ditmarsch, Cramerus, de la Bretonière, Speetjens, Maclaine Pont, Vlug, F/Sgt Cramm, Flt Lt van Daalen Wetters. Front row: Flt Lt Arts, Meyers, Group Captain Maxwell, Sqn Ldr O'Neill, Flt Lts van Arkel, Dekker.

buried with full military honours in the Hither Green cemetery, London.

A Dutch Squadron, 322, commanded by Major von Edenburg, moved to Biggin Hill at the end of October 1944 and spend considerable time practising high-dive bombing on the Goodwin Sands. The mascot was a tame grey parrot who used to enjoy drinking in the Officers' Mess as much as the pilots. Group Captain Hugh O'Neill, who took command in November remembers how they used to lubricate the top of the bar and slide Polly from one end to the other. She really enjoyed it.

During their time with the Biggin Wing seven Dutchmen were killed.

322 Squadron had been formed in June 1943 with 28 Dutch fighter pilots and a few Englishmen who were gradually replaced by Dutchmen. Having learned to fly the latest Spitfire they became operational in the Dover area patrolling the coast in an effort to prevent German aircraft making photographic reconnaissance flights over Southern England where the Norman invasion fleets were being assembled. In August they switched their attention to V1 flying bombs and brought down 110 before that campaign ended in September.

Of the 59 Dutch and 33 Englishmen who made up 322 Squadron, 17 were killed and seven of them while flying from the Biggin Wing. One of the survivors later wrote: "Life was lived day by day. You never talked about it and you hardly ever thought about it but subconsciously your pattern of behaviour was aimed at the possibility that the next day might very well be your last. The most important issues were the will to win and to ensure that you remained alive..."

One Dutch fighter pilot, unable to join the Squadron when it was formed, was Flight Lieutenant Bram van der Stok who flew with 91 Squadron from Tangmere. Baling out over

France in 1942 he found himself a prisoner of war at Stalag Luft III where he assisted with *The Great Escape.* Van der Stok was the 18th man to emerge from the tunnel. He walked to Sagan station, waited three hours for a train to Utrecht which took 36 hours. After six weeks in his home town, not even daring to visit his parents, he was fed into the Dutch-Paris Escape Line and smuggled across the Maas and into Belgium. From there he made his way to Toulouse, across the Pyrenees, onto Madrid and down the Line to Gibraltar. A Douglas Dakota Transport took him to Bristol. A few months later he was commanding 322 Squadron — only one of three Allied prisoners to make the "home run" after the Great Escape.

At Biggin Hill the traumas continued. On November 29, 1944 a Dakota flying from the Midlands was seen to be in trouble over South London. The pilot, Wing Commander Pearson DFC attempted a forced landing at Biggin Hill but was killed and his navigator, Flight Lieutenant W.E.Plummer injured. Both men were with 107OTU Leicester East.

Biggin Hill, as ever, mourned the loss of these young men. They were not flying from the Biggin Wing and so were not included on the reredos in the Chapel of St George's. One name that is there is that of Group Captain Gordon Learmouth Raphael DFC and Bar, DSO — the station commander from November 1943.

Gordon Raphael, a Canadian from Ontario, had taken over from Group Captain Maxwell as the station's seventh CO since the outbreak of war. Although he quickly proved himself to be both efficient and popular with his fellow officers he was renowned for his severity and objected to pilots who smoked and drank alcohol in case their reflexes were impaired. Like many of his predecessors he preferred flying to the everyday administrative details demanded by a busy RAF station. On Tuesday April 10, 1945 Raphael's Spitfire (ML 232) collided with a Dakota not far from Lympne airfield and came down in the village of Appledore. He died instantly — the second Biggin Hill CO to lose his life in a flying accident.

Gordon Raphael had run out of luck. Flying Whitleys with Bomber Command in May 1940 he had been forced to ditch down in the sea while making for an oil refinery target near Hanover. The crew were rescued and Raphael, shot in the foot, spent a few days in hospital. On August 16th/17th 1940 his Whitley was again attacked during an attack on Jever but he managed to limp home. Moving eventually to Fighter Command he commanded RAF Castle Camps and subsequently Biggin Hill.

The funeral took place at Cudham on April 16 conducted by Squadron Leader Pellatt, padre of RAF Manston. Among the mourners were Gordon's parents Howard and Pearl Raphael, wife Dorothy and sister, Lieutenant Mildred Raphael, a nurse in Canada. Representing the pilots were Group Captains John Cunningham and R.K. Hamblin and Wing Commanders Mike Crossley and Bobby Oxspring.

Group Captain Gordon L. Raphael D.S.O., D.F.C. & Bar

7
Victory and peace

Peace came to Biggin Hill in May 1945 in the form of several parties — in the Officers' Mess in the White Hart, The Jail and in Whitehall, where several officers cheered themselves hoarse after Winston Churchill spoke. One of the most memorable parties was the VE dinner staged in the Sergeants' Mess where a note on the menu modestly claimed that they had played "at least a small part in the successful termination of the European war and in something which found its beginnings in the earliest days of the struggle..."

That "something" was the Biggin Hill tradition — the indomitable spirit of the most famous fighter station in the world. Among the 453, who lost their lives flying from the Biggin Wing were 131 Sergeant pilots. The cost of victory was high. This final chapter shows how the tradition lived on. The Auxiliary Air Force, the end of flying, the bid to save the station from closure and the annual flying displays rivalling the pre-war pageants. Those who attend in their thousands know they owe their freedom to many sacrifices. Long live the ghosts of Biggin Hill.

Old canvas by a million breezes worn,
Now on some airfield scrap heap to be thrown.
These rents are wounds of war by Germans torn,
A thousand hard strained eyes on thee alone
Depended to be guided in to land
After the fight. Eyes of my friends; and now
Some see no more. All these waiting with hand
On stick and throttle, glanced at thee, made vow
To give a good account, and in that glance
Looked last on England, climbed up into cloud
And flew away for ever. John fell in France,
And Bill in flames, for Simon sea was shroud,
Shall danger-money workmen end thy year?
"Leave it with us!". Their voice is in my ear.

This Sonnet to a Windsock, written in December 1940 by the Station Chaplain Canon O'Hanlon, was placed in the new RAF Memorial Chapel. The windsock was just a few yards away from the shelter where the 39 airmen were killed.

1945 - 2001

July 1946: Auxiliary Air Force reformed. 600 and 615 Squadrons fly in with a mix of Spitfires F14s and F21s and later re-equipped with Meteor 4s.

December: Chapel of St George's catches fire and is totally gutted. Little salvaged from ruins except charred visitors book with just one legible name — Winston S Churchill. Padre Cecil King becomes the driving force behind the appeal for a new purpose-built Chapel. Contributions begin to come in from all over the world.

July 1948 - 1950: Runway 21/03 is extended to service bigger, faster fighter aircraft.

October 1949: The Queen, as Honorary Air Commander, visits 600 Auxiliary Squadron. Winston Churchill has the same responsibilities for 615 Squadron. 'At Home' flying displays are held on the weekend closest to *Battle of Britain* Day, September 15, each year.

July 25, 1951: Air Chief Marshal The Lord Dowding lays foundation stone for new Chapel. It is dedicated by the Bishop of Rochester.

March 1957: Auxiliary Air Force reconstituted. 600 and 615 Squadrons disband. Serious proposals to turn Biggin Hill into a rocket base come to nothing.

Jan 16, 1958: 41 Squadron disbands and reforms the same day at Coltishall and amalgamated with 141 Squadron. The South Camp area is handed over to civilian control as a new home for aircraft from the now-closed Croydon Airport. A new phase in the history of Biggin Hill begins.

April 1959: The RAF opens the Officer Selection Centre at Biggin Hill on the North Camp.

July 1959: 'Sailor' Malan, aged 48, returns from South Africa to Biggin Hill to meet the senior officers. He enjoys a drink with some of his former compatriots in the White Hart, Brasted.

March 1960: Squadron Leader Jock Maitland operates the air field as a civilian airfield and the Surrey Flying Club moves onto the South Camp. Airfield now home to half a dozen flying clubs making it one of the busiest training airfields in the country.

September 15 1969: Biggin Hill fighter aces reunited once more at the premier of the film *Battle of Britain*. Lord Dowding gets a standing ovation as he takes his seat in the Dominion Theatre.

June 1973: The ownership of the airfield, having changed hands many times from the Air Ministry to the CAA, now goes to Bromley Borough Council for the sum of £450,000. They encourage private aircraft and executive jets to use the airport which is now run by the BAA under the subsidiary name Airports UK. Jock Maitland introduces an Air Fair and more than 100,000 visit for a weekend in June to witness hard and fast flying at the cutting edge of aviation technology.

Summer 1974: Two of the three WAAFs, Miss Elizabeth Mortimer and Mrs Elspeth Green (neé Henderson), who won Military Medals for outstanding courage in 1940, return to the married quarters where roads are named in their honour. The third recipient of the medal, Miss Helen Turner died some years earlier.

1980: Fighter aces return for a special flying display and photographic exhibition to mark the fortieth anniversary of the Battle of Britain.

1990: An illustrated history of RAF Biggin Hill entitled *Biggin on The Bump* is published by Froglets Publications supporting the RAF Benevolent Fund. It raises £15,000.

September 1990: Fiftieth anniversary of *The Battle of Britain*. Spectacular flying display from Battle of Britain Memorial Flight.

October 1992: The RAF finally says goodbye to Biggin Hill after an association of 80 years despite Wing Commander Ian Cosby's petition to 10 Downing Street signed by 14,000 people who want the North Camp to become a museum. A lone trumpeter plays the Last Post and the Officer and Aircrew Selection Centre moves to Cranwell.

January 1993: Regional Airports Ltd (RAL) buy the airfield on a 125-year lease from Bromley. The company spends £1.5m resurfacing the runway and improving the apron area. The chairman is Andrew Walters.

Summer 1993: A clifftop memorial for the fallen in the Battle of Britain is opened at Capel le Ferne, near Folkestone, inspired by Wing Commander Geoffrey Page. The flagpole comes from Biggin Hill.

1995: The Viscount Goschen, Minister for Aviation and Shipping opens the new Executive Terminal providing exclusive VIP facilities.

1997: Glenda Jackson, MP opens the new passenger terminal enabling efficient processing of larger aircraft which visit on corporate charters.

Bernie Ecclestone, chairman of Formula One leases part of what is now known as the West Camp (or the original RAF enclave) and receives planning permission to build offices around the hangars. He works from an office in Wireless Road.

After much controversy as to its future use the Officers' Mess is sold. Planning application lodged for a hotel on the site.

The White Hart blackboard

WHEN Dickie Grice, the much-loved and respected Commanding Officer of Biggin Hill during the most harrowing days of its history, requested dynamite and blew up the hangar that he knew German reconnaissance had earmarked for destruction anyway, he was quickly brought before a Court of Enquiry. Group Captain Grice had destroyed Air Ministry property without filling in the correct forms outlining his proposal and, even in the most desperate days of the war, this was a serious offence that carried appropriate punishment.

During that Enquiry it was explained that the hangars were never used in wartime and the Luftwaffe, having destroyed two already, would soon be back to finish the job. It was also reported that Grice was a hero of the Great War, an excellent Commanding Officer and had shown great courage and calm leadership during the bombing of Biggin Hill. Paperwork was certainly not his priority when massed formations of German bombers were bearing down on his beloved airfield.

In the end Grice was given a reprimand and later removed to another post. In December 1940, just before Christmas, he held a farewell party at his favourite pub, The White Hart at Brasted, and his fellow officers gave him a rousing send off. Landlady Kath Preston remembers that party: "Towards the end of the evening", she said, "Dickie was running around with a piece of chalk saying 'I must put my name on the wall'. Put it on the black-out screen in front of the bar door, I said, and let the other pilots sign it too".

They did. By closing time there were 18 names and, on a side panel, the latest score of kills by each of the pilots. Kath said she would encourage more Biggin Hill pilots to sign but would certainly not give permission for the 'brown jobs' to add their signatures. Brian Kingcome, one of the original signatories later said: "Regrettably it later became the habit of any itinerant pilot passing through to add his name until the board became overcrowded, though oddly enough, even today, it is possible to pick out the few signatures from the original gathering. They are bigger and bolder than the rest. Perhaps we used different chalk, or maybe ours was a better party!"

By the end of the war that black-out screen was one of the better memorials from the Battle of Britain but, almost every night in the bar of the White Hart, locals discussed what they should do with it. Eventually came the idea of preserving the signatures in a frame. A local timber merchant provided the wood, Mr Walford Chalk, a resident of the hotel, arranged for the wings to be carved on top and another supplied the glass. The chalk names were sprayed with artists' gum for preservation and an unveiling party was organised with Jamie Rankin detailed to locate the pilots who had signed the board. Some had been killed and he knew that Tony Bartley could not be present as he was on honeymoon with his beautiful wife, the actress Deborah Kerr.

Who should have the honour of unveiling the board? There was only one real candidate — 'Sailor' Malan — and he gracefully accepted the honour. Kath Preston remembers that day just after the war. "The old familiar faces arrived one by one and when the time came to 'unveil' it was difficult for everyone to squash themselves into the bar so the overflow filled the corridor. Just before 'Sailor' spoke two more people managed to push their way in. Tony and Deborah Bartley had taken a break from their honeymoon. They were not going to miss

KATH PRESTON — "pre-war, wartime and post war CO of White Hart". In 2001, in her nineties, she was living in Sevenoaks.

the party".

As the years passed and Biggin Hill lost its status as an operational station the pilots continued to make regular visits to the White Hart with the highlight always being Battle of Britain Day in September. A regular was Bob Stanford Tuck, whose young sons were then at the New Beacon School, Sevenoaks. Tony Bartley occasionally popped in with the two young daughters from his marriage to Deborah Kerr while Pete Brothers, Jamie Rankin, Brian Kingcome, Bobby Oxspring and Paddy Barthropp were more routine visitors. On January 16 1958, Biggin Hill ceased to be a fighter station and Flying Training Command took over. A few days later Jamie Rankin flew his Spitfire to the station and, with a Hurricane, it was placed at the gates of the aerodrome. He was then driven to the White Hart where Kath and Teddy Preston joined him in drinking a silent toast in front of the board to Biggin on The Bump.

The famous Battle of Britain black-out screen remained in the White Hart until Kath Preston retired in 1971. The brewers did not appreciate its true worth so there were various offers from local hoteliers and even one from America. Kath, determined it should remain in Britain, eventually accepted an offer by Group Captain Hugh Tudor from Westerham who 'loaned' it to the RAF Club in Piccadilly. Later it was removed to the RAF Museum at Hendon where it remained, in prime position, in the Battle of Britain section for many years. Today, it's been transferred to the wonderful museum in Shoreham village, run by Geoff Nutkins, a superb aviation artist, and his wife Lesley.

The names of the Battle of Britain board are as follows: The Lord Tedder, Marshal of the RAF, Air Marshal Sir Walter P.O. Pretty, Air Vice Marshals J.E. Johnson and J. Worrall.

Air Commodores A.C. Deere, R. Deacon Elliott, E.J. Morris, P.M Brothers.

Group Captains C.F. Gray, J.A. Kent, G.B.F. Kingcome, A.G. Malan, R.W. Oxspring and J. Rankin.

Wing Commanders P.P.C. Barthropp, J. Checketts, Rupert Clerke, M.N. Crossley, D.H. Grice, J.I. Kilmartin, J.R. Milne, M.L. Robinson, J. Rose, D.H.S. Rusher, H. Russell, H.M. Stephen, R.R. S. Tuck.

Squadron Leaders A.C. Bartley, D. Clive, N.F. Duke, P.M. Gardner, R.S. Gilmour, G. Harris, E. Mayne, D.W.A. Stones, J. White, J. Zurakowski.

Flight Lieutenants G.F. Buerling, A.F. Eckford, J.B. Loudon, J.C. Milner and Sandy Sandeman.

Teddy Preston, landlord of the White Hart (centre) surrounded by the aces. Left to right: Jamie Rankin, Paddy Barthropp, Bobby Oxspring, 'Sailor' Malan, Brian Kingcome, 'Tubby' Mayne, Tony Bartley and Bob Stanford Tuck. Mayne of 74 Squadron was, at 40, the oldest pilot in Fighter Command to fly in the Battle of Britain.

Adolf Galland, commander of Germany's elite Fighter Squadron 26, was the Luftwaffe ace who wined and dined Bob Stanford Tuck at the JG26 headquarters on January 28 1942, the day he was shot down. In the early 1960s he was a surprise visitor to the White Hart where Tuck repaid the compliment and spoke about the extraordinary chivalry which existed between the two adversaries. This picture was taken at the book launch for Tuck's biography, 'Fly for your life'.

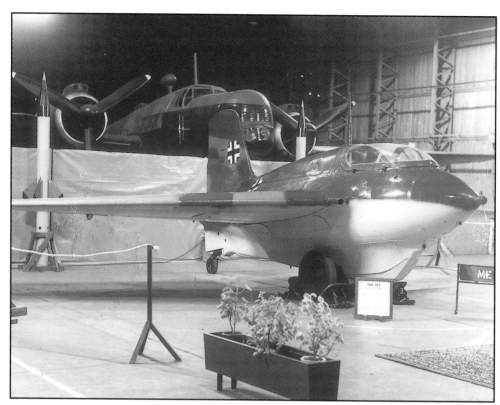

In November 1964 this Messerschmitt Me 164 Komet which had been captured and restored at Biggin Hill was handed over to the Deutches Museum, Munich. The presentation was made by Air Commodore Robert Deacon-Elliott on behalf of the RAF.

Lord Dowding laid the foundation stone to the St George's Chapel in July 1951. The Hurricane and Spitfire — the gate guardians — were later put in place and dedicated by the Bishop of Rochester.

Towards a civilian airport

POST war peace at Biggin Hill was accompanied by the re-formation of the Auxiliary Air Force, the billeting of two exceptional Squadrons — 600 (City of London) and 615 (County of Surrey) — and a mix of modern Spitfires, later to be replaced by Meteor FIVs and then FVIIIs. In 1950 the Auxiliaries were joined by 41 Squadron and Biggin Hill, to the delight of all who worked at The Bump, became a fighter station once more — but not for long.

A regular visitor was Queen Elizabeth (later the Queen Mother). As Honorary Air Commander of 600 Squadron she was often invited to meet the officers, inspect the men and watch the most spectacular flying displays. In October 1949 she addressed the squadron from the control tower and a few years later visited the station on St George's Day for her first ever helicopter flight. She knew the commanding officers of the period, Wing Commanders A.H. Donaldson, W. Pitt Brown and D.G. Smallwood and she agreed with Winston Churchill that this manned fighter station, whose people had refused to lie down and be beaten when facing the most desperate crisis, should never close.

Imagine her shock on June 18 1951 when two of "her boys" — pilots of 600 Squadron — and one from 41 Squadron were killed within seconds of each other in a tragedy that surpassed almost anything that had gone before. In a dramatic and horrifying chain of events three Meteors crashed within an area of 100 yards. Two Biggin Hill residents were taken to hospital after their homes had been hit and an ambulance overturned on a sharp bend on its way to the scene. An hour earlier Winston Churchill had been at the aerodrome inspecting 615 Squadron.

The first crash occurred as a Meteor VIII of 41 Squadron was taking off from the main runway piloted by Flight Lieutenant Gordon McDonald, aged 28, of Bickley. After becoming airborne, the aircraft faltered in mid air and then corkscrewed with pieces of superstructure shredding off. It plunged earthwards, skimmed the perimeter fence and crashed onto the roof of a bungalow on the other side of the road belonging to Mr Harold Harvey. It is believed that the pilot had failed to allow his leader sufficient time after take-off and followed into a turbulent slipstream.

Within seconds of the tragedy two Mark IV Meteors of 600 Squadron, circling over the wreckage and preparing to land, collided about 2000 feet above the scene. Both crashed in the valley. Sergeant Kenneth Clarkson, 21, a National Service pilot was killed in his aircraft while the more experienced Squadron Leader Philip Sandeman, 28, managed to bale out but his parachute failed to open. The first fighter came down on The Homestead, Victoria Gardens where Mr Frank Buley was just finishing mowing his lawn when it was dramatically wiped away in a welter of wreckage. The rear portion of the house was shorn clean off and he was taken to hospital with minor injuries and shock.

One week after the triple tragedy another Meteor overshot the runway, narrowly missed passing cars and came to rest across the main road less than 100 yards from the demolished bungalow. Several nearby residents immediately said they would be "selling up" while others called for traffic lights to be installed on the Bromley Road and operated whenever aircraft were landing or taking off.

Following emergency meetings of the Biggin Hill Ratepayers' Association the Air Ministry was told that "to locate manned fighters in such a heavily populated area was sheer madness". They would not have known that the days of RAF jets at Biggin Hill were numbered anyway. With the reconstitution of the Auxiliary Air Force in 1957 the station said goodbye to 600 and 615 Squadrons and, less than a year later, the decision was made to end all operational flying. The first fighters had been the Brisfits of 141 'Cock' Squadron. The last, just 40 years later, were the Hawker Hunters of 41 Squadron which was amalgamated at Coltishall with 141. The irony did not go unnoticed.

The Ground Officers Selection Centre moved to Biggin Hill from Uxbridge in 1959 followed, a few years later, by the Aircrew Selection Centre. The third major component — the Aircrew Selection Board — was added in 1964. RAF Biggin Hill remained operational for just one day a year. The hugely popular 'At Home' displays, similar in format to the Empire Day pageants of the late 1930s, were staged before massive crowds who watched the Bristol Fighters, Sopwith Pups and Tiger Moths give enthralling displays of synchronised aerobatics — but reserved their greatest cheers always for the Hurricane and Spitfire.

As Biggin Hill became a thriving civilian airport and home to numerous private flying clubs under the management of Squadron Leader Jock Maitland, so the ownership of the airfield passed from the Air Ministry to the Civil Aviation Authority and then finally to Bromley Borough Council who paid less than half a million for the site in 1973.

Three years later, in 1976, the Ministry of Defence made the decision to scrap the annual At Home display and in September of that year the Battle of Britain Memorial Flight reduced grown men to tears with a momentous farewell performance that included a series of victory rolls low over the old station. But it wasn't goodbye to the veterans. In a bid to maintain Biggin Hill's historic contribution to aviation folklore, the summer Air Fair was already well-established under the skilful eye of Jock Maitland, and his International Air Fairs company was operating successfully from an old pavilion on the South Camp. The 10th anniversary in 1974 attracted crowds of more than 100,000 rivalling both the At Home displays and the pre-war pageants at Hendon as the most popular two-day summer event in the country.

The 14th year of the Air Fair saw the first major tragedy. On Sunday May 13, 1977 spectators watched in horror as a Ferranti helicopter taking passengers on a 10-minute joy ride, collided in mid-air with a Tiger Moth killing all five people on board. An Inquiry was later told that the Tiger Moth was coming in to land as the helicopter, piloted by Captain Hugh Lovett of Taunton, began to lift off. It rose rapidly for 100 feet and the rotor blades sliced off the wheels of the Moth which crash-landed inches away from a parked Cessna belonging to King Air. The pilot of the Moth, Captain Ian Taylor and his co-pilot Stephen Bates, were uninjured.

Three years later, on September 15 1980, a second world war Douglas Invader bomber crashed into the valley hillside beyond the airfield after the pilot failed to pull out of a barrel roll. Four British passengers, two American serviceman and the pilot were killed.

It emerged that Captain Don Bullock, an experienced pilot but renowned as a dare-devil had asked the organisers for an early take off. He wanted more time to perfect a barrel roll in front of 40,000 spectators — a stunt he had performed only once before in the 37-year-

Thewreck of the Meteor which crashed into The Homestead, Victoria Gardens in June 1951. Three pilots died in a horrifying chain of events.

old Invader. The request was refused.

Spectators described how, two minutes into the eight-minute display, the pilot began the fatal roll and then appeared to hesitate. The bomber sheared through power cables and nose-dived just yards from a row of houses in Oaklands Road, Biggin Hill. One wing separated from the aircraft and went through the front garden hedge of number 90.

It was in 1992 that the RAF finally pulled out of Biggin Hill with a farewell dinner in the Officers' Mess, a march past in Bromley town centre and a decommissioning service in St George's Chapel. The Last Post and the lowering of the Standard commemorated the final act in the life of the station.

By then the Battle of Britain was just a distant memory but, encouraged by those with vivid memories of wartime crash sites, enthusiasts across the south-east were continuing with their fascinating hobby of digging up the fighters of both sides and placing Rolls Royce Merlin engines, fuselage, propellers, parachutes, maps and even personal belongings as museum exhibits. These museums exist today in such places Manston, Brenzett, Chilham, Hawkinge, Headcorn and London. One of the smallest is in Shoreham village where Geoff Nutkins' converted barn serves as a poignant tribute to those who fought on both sides. "I've never met a Roman soldier", he said. "We're about living history. Half the fun for us is talking to the pilots who jumped out of these aircraft".

Some of the oldest surviving veterans are still flying thanks to the Battle of Britain Memorial Flight and groups like the Medway Aircraft Preservation Society who have many members older than the aircraft they are restoring. Recently they brought a Mark 1 Spitfire, K9942, back to pristine static condition and delivered it to Hendon Museum. Pilots who flew that fighter included Flying Officer J.B.Nicholson, the only RAF pilot to be awarded the Victoria Cross in 1940. It flew 50 sorties with 72 Squadron from Gravesend.

Five were killed in 1973 when a Ferranti helicopter and a Tiger Moth collided in mid air.

Ambulancemen extract bodies from the smouldering remains of the Douglas Invader which crashed on Battle of Britain Day, September 15, 1980.

Three aviators died and two war planes were lost during the weekend of June 2-3 2001, leaving a question mark hanging over the future of the annual Air Fair at Biggin Hill. On the Saturday evening a Vampire, piloted by Sir Kenneth Hayr with Jonathon Kerr as co-pilot, inexplicably lost control and crashed in open ground at Keston, not far from nearby homes. During the Sunday show a King Cobra, piloted by Guy Bancroft-Wilson came down to the south of the Control Tower. The picture above shows the Cobra just a fraction of a second before it hit the ground. After local inhabitants called for the Air Fair to be stopped, Biggin Hill Airport chairman, Mr Andrew Walters said he was impressed by the commitment of Air Fair International to safety.

610 Squadron   **Fighter Command**   **No 11 Group**

Stained glass windows of St George's Chapel —

SIX of the 12 stained glass windows in the St George's Chapel of Remembrance at Biggin Hill, designed by Hugh Easton, are featured on pages 22 and 23 in the first chapter of this book. Here are the remaining six, starting with 610 Squadron whose pilots served at the station during the Battle of Britain.

The badges of Fighter Command and No 11 Group is accompanied by portraits of the immortal Spitfire and

Hurricane. Finally comes the Station crest with its motto *The Strongest Link*. This shows a sword ringed by a circlet of chain. The sword unsheathed, with point upward, is symbolic of the famous part played by the station during the Battle of Britain. The blood red colour is symbolic of fighting and of the warriors who took part in the Battle.

In the St George's Room adjoining the Chapel is a

Hurricane

Spitfire

RAF Biggin Hill

— a unique tribute to the 453 airmen who died

Battle of Britain Memorial Window illustrating the symbolic victory of St George over the forces of evil. At the top are the badges of the Squadrons at Biggin Hill during July to October 1940 and of the army, a reminder of its invaluable support. Four smaller stained glass windows depict ground support, parachute packing, rescue services and ground control. The three Military Medals awarded to WAAFs serving in 1940 are shown on the Ground Control Window.

Today services are held regularly, the highlight being the annual Battle of Britain memorial service on the Sunday closest to September 15th. The Chapel is visited by people from all over the world and remains a deeply moving reminder of the men, women, machines and indomitable spirit which made Biggin Hill the most famous fighter station in the world.

Where 1940 used to be

ON the far side of the airfield, close to the old crumbling dispersal pens, it is not too difficult to find out where 1940 used to be. But you have to be prepared to tramp through thick undergrowth, where brambles show no mercy and the Virginia creeper is some 60 years old, to discover what is left of that unforgettable summer.

The contrast between the abandoned, forgotten area just beyond the perimeter fence and the cluster of shining, white, privately-owned aircraft lined up outside the massive hangars nearby is notable. Most of the buildings here are post-war in construction and, of course, so are the runways and approach roads.

A public footpath runs just outside the airfield boundary but the woods to the east are rarely used. In fact they look hostile. Deep in this overgrown area are the remains of two surface shelters built in early 1940 to a specific Air Ministry pattern. The first shows signs of age but there is an entrance at each end and, inside, the rotting framework for about 18 bunk beds. No-one knows if the ghosts of Biggin Hill still lurk in this area. It is not a place for night-time sojourns.

The second shelter, completely hidden in the undergrowth, is in good condition and another symbol of a different world. It is not impossible to imagine mechanics of a night-fighter squadron sleeping here, a game of cards perhaps, before turning in, wondering who would return safely and who wouldn't. This shelter does not show up on English Heritage's "thorough" survey of Biggin Hill. They couldn't find it!.

Back on the airfield are the remains of three dispersal pens — concrete blast protectors that once afforded a degree of shelter to grounded Spitfires and Hurricanes. Today they are full of weeds and used only for the parking of light aircraft. All three have their own shelters with a front and rear exit and the original solid iron doors, bomb proof and gas proof. An elderly man lives in one of these shelters — he has done for years. In the middle of one of the dispersal pens is a rusty iron ring, embedded in the concrete, to which the tails of the fighters were tied to keep them down.

92 Squadron used one of these dispersals pens and its old hut was nearby. It was from this area that the pilots were so frequently scrambled and, in 1940-41, the grass would have been worn down by the constant tread of airmens' boots hurrying towards their machines. The Spitfires — 12 at a time spread across the widest part of the field — would have been warmed up and ready. 92 Squadron always took off on grass, going line astern immediately after take-off. They would use the runways for landing only.

One old dispersal hut does remain and, according to English Heritage it is the genuine article. It does not show up on the aerial photograph of Biggin Hill taken in 1948 so was perhaps moved from elsewhere. It could have been 92's much-loved home. The ghosts will know.

Nearby, among the trees inside the airfield boundary, bleak and forlorn, is an extant brick-built pillbox (known as type 22), of hexagonal shape and designed to an Air Ministry pattern around a large tree (now dead). The wooden framework outside would have held wire mesh in place to stop grenades being thrown in. Inside it smells (and almost sings) of 1940. There are hooks in the tree for hanging hurricane lamps and iron pivots below two slit windows

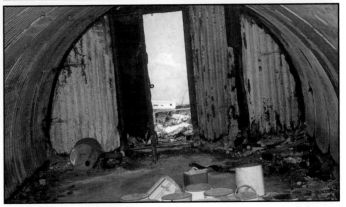

CLOKWISE from above: A dispersal hut which has been removed from its 1940 position, a gunpost to the west of the Bromley Road and the interior of a dispersal shelter.

for the mounting of Lewis bren guns. The shelter door, now detached, is bomb and gas proof and the original locking catch still survives.

There would have been about 20 such pillboxes and 12 dummies at Biggin Hill in 1940 but they were abandoned in 1941 in favour of underground battle headquarters, a must, according to English Heritage, for all well-defended airfields. Does one exist at Biggin Hill?

In another corner of the airfield, pranged so badly in 1940, is the area once known as "the Belgian quarter". Very convenient for them. Through the hedge at the back of the dispersal hut, onto the footpath towards Jail Lane and there was their pub.

Next to the Windsock is the site of a Pickett-Hamilton Counterbalance Fort, designed by Francis Pickett of Tenterden, constructed exclusively for use on an airfield. Below ground, are the original hydraulics which once operated the raising mechanism. The fort, circular in shape, could be lifted from its location flush with the surface of the ground into an exposed position for action and provided a garrison with room for about five men, one of whom would have been the commander. The fort could be lowered in about 10 seconds, thereby offering no obstruction to aircraft taking off or landing.

Not only a fighter airfield, Biggin Hill was on the direct bomber path to London.

CLOCKWISE from left: The iron ring, embedded in concrete, to which the tails of the fighters were held down, the brick wall of a dispersal pen, the remains of a surface shelter in the woods and a hexagonal extant pillbox built around an old tree

The Spitfire flown by Wing Commander Michael Robinson, who commanded 609 Squadron and then led the Biggin Wing between July and September 1941. During the summer sweeps over Occupied France in 1941 his claims mounted rapidly and by 1942 he had a total of 16 destroyed, five 'probables' and nine damaged. He was shot down and killed over the Channel in April 1942. The painting is by Trevor Lay and is produced by courtesy of Spitfire Art, Ditchling, East Sussex

The old Sergeants' Mess. Released by the developers for a possible Heritage Centre.

Heritage Centre in the Sergeants' Mess?

ENCOURAGED by Winston Churchill's insistence, some years before his death in 1965, that RAF Biggin Hill "should never close" and angered by the decision by the Secretary of State for Armed Forces that the site was to be sold and the Selection Centre moved to Cranwell, Wing Commander Ian Cosby delivered a petition to 10 Downing Street urging the Government to reconsider.

The petition was signed by 14,000 people including many pilots. It was to no avail. The camp closed in 1992 and only the Chapel of St George's was retained as a symbol of the historic role played by RAF Biggin Hill during the war.

With the battle lost the Friends of Biggin Hill immediately promoted the idea of a permanent exhibition centre to celebrate the station's heritage and urged Bromley Borough Council, owners of the airfield, to take action. A Working Party, under the chairmanship of Bob Shekyls, was formed to study the concept of a museum and more than 1,000 signatures were collected at an Open Day in 2000 to celebrate the 60th anniversary of the Battle of Britain.

As the interest for a Heritage Centre grew, with letters of support from all over the world, the development company, restoring homes in the former RAF married quarters, offered to make the old Sergeants' Mess available. The Working Party accepted the offer and said they wanted to create a Trust, under the chairmanship of Dennis Barkaway, to raise funds, restore the building and, in the meantime, apply to the Lottery Heritage Fund for financial help.

By September 2001 many doubts had been expressed about the feasibility of such a project. Some prominent people were uncertain about the popularity of a permanent exhibition given that the Battle of Britain was more than 60 years ago and that interest was being diluted by time.

This is not the case and never will be. Generations of children born after 1940 grew up to admire and respect those brave men who became involved in what we all hope will be the last great war against world domination. The pilots, the WAAFs, the fitters, the mechanics, the drivers, the caterers, the plotters and the controllers of Biggin Hill were at the forefront of that struggle.

What better place than the former Sergeants' Mess for a Heritage Centre?

Air Chief Marshal Lord Dowding

HAD I thought of writing this book before February 1970 then I would almost certainly have sought an interview with the one man who collectively knew the fighter pilots better than anyone — Air Chief Marshal Sir Hugh Dowding. But Dowding died that month at his home in Tunbridge Wells, giving historians a timely opportunity to assess his greatness in masterminding Britain's victory exactly 30 years earlier in the summer of 1940.

Robert Wright, Dowding's personal assistant for some of the time during his period as head of Fighter Command, remembers him saying: "One of the worst features of the battle from my point of view was the continuous anxiety for the lives of my fighter boys and the wish that it might be possible in any way to ameliorate their lot".

It was concern for those young men, who had been so suddenly and violently killed, that aroused his interest in spiritualism. Dowding realised there were many dimensions of experience beyond the physical and he approached the subject in a practical and scientific way by writing a book called *Many Mansions.*

The Air Chief Marshal knew Biggin Hill well. He visited the station in 1936 soon after he became AOC to talk about its pioneering experience of ground-to-air contact and to meet the pilots of 32 Squadron. He personally chose Biggin Hill to be a senior sector station of No 11 Group. He accompanied the Prime Minister on several occasions soon after war was declared and sent frequent messages of condolence to Group Captain Grice as the bombing continued and the toll increased. He visited the makeshift control centre in the butcher's shop where he found the controllers and plotters working with a school blackboard and chalks and was deeply impressed by the determination of everyone to overcome all the odds. He used all his influence and authority to ensure that a new Operations Block was opened at Towerfields in nearby Keston. In November 1940 when Biggin Hill became the first "600 station" he sent his personal congratulations to "The Bump". By then he was, alas, no longer at Fighter Command to enjoy the triumph. He had been succeeded, controversially, by Air Chief Marshal Sir Sholto Douglas.

Dowding also knew about the "ghosts of Biggin Hill" and never disguised his confidence that in the after-life he would meet again the hundreds of young pilots who died under his command. During his last few years, when crippled with arthritis, he renewed his close association with The Few through the making of the *Battle of Britain* film and was able to talk about those who flew into the heat of battle never to return. He watched the shooting at Pinewood Studios and had a series of happy reunions. On September 15 1969 he was wheeled into the Dominion Theatre to attend the premier and 1,500 people rose to their feet and gave him an ovation he thoroughly deserved.

In 1951 Lord Dowding, who had been a widower for 31 years, received a letter from Muriel Whiting. She told him how her husband, Max Whiting had been killed on operations in a Lancaster bomber in 1943 and wondered if she would ever see him again. Dowding replied that she would and suggested they meet to discuss his belief in the after-life.

Muriel Whiting and Hugh Dowding fell in love and were married. He was 68 and she 43. They bought a house on the Great Bounds estate at Southborough called Oakgates. It was to be their home until Dowding's increasing infirmity prompted them to move to a more manageable house in Calverley Park, Tunbridge Wells.

While at Oakgates they enjoyed the visits of many ex-fighter pilots and military leaders and Biggin Hill was often on the "agenda". Group Captain Grice called on them and so did 'Sailor' Malan, then crippled with Parkinson's disease. While at Oakgates Dowding wrote several books about spiritualism. In one of them he said: "My plan of operations, in so far as I have a plan at the present stage, is to try and throw some light on the conditions of human life after death while the persons concerned are still not too far removed from earthly conditions for us to be able to follow their progress.

"The mass of material available on this subject is enormous but the volume of evidence available, so far from facilitating the task of producing an ordered picture of the future life, has a contrary effect, because of the fantastic inconsistencies and contradictions with which it abounds.

He then wrote that this was one of the chief stumbling blocks of spiritualism — one of the chief reasons why educated and intellectual people who have had their attention attracted to a study of the unseen, either through phenomena or by personal experience of communication, fell away, lost interest and returned to materialism.

Like Hugh Dowding, but from a much earlier age in her life, Muriel Whiting also developed an affinity with other orders of existence and levels of consciousness. Her mother had amazing powers as a healer, seer and exponent of other psychic abilities and this influenced Muriel to study, and strongly believe in, astrology, spiritualism and Theosophy.

Muriel had many spiritual adventures and one very alarming one. In 1949 she was looking after her father's former housekeeper who had lost her husband some years earlier and was preoccupied with thoughts of suicide. On one particular occasion she heard the sound of knives being sharpened in the sitting room and found the lady about to take her own life. "Please", said Muriel, "Don't kill yourself. You will be lonely if you do". The housekeeper replied: "You have been so kind to me. I am taking you with me".

Muriel managed to escape from the room and ring her friend, the healer, Dorothy Kerin who lived at Burrswood, Groombridge. "This is an attack by dark forces," Dorothy said. "Don't be frightened. I will go into the Chapel and hold you and this poor woman in the Light. Go back without fear and try to calm her down".

Muriel had great faith in Dorothy's spiritual awareness so she re-opened the door of the sitting room, sat the lady down on a sofa and gave her a hot drink. She then took her to the doctor's surgery at Tunbridge Wells. Dr McDowell took Muriel immediately outside and said: "Do you know I certified that woman for trying to murder her sister. I cannot leave her alone with you and your little boy!".

Famously, as Lady Dowding, Muriel founded the *Beauty Without Cruelty* movement — an organisation dedicated to curtailing the indiscriminate exploitation of wildlife for such items as perfume, fur coats and cosmetics. It became a world-wide movement and Lord Dowding made many speeches in the House of Lords in support of her campaign against cruelty in slaughterhouses. He even followed his wife's example and became a vegetarian. Air Chief Marshal Lord Dowding's soul slipped away from his body on Sunday February 15, 1970. He was 87. His death prompted commentators throughout the country to describe him rightly as the principal architect of the Battle of Britain. At a private service in Tunbridge Wells Father Geoffrey Nixon echoed the feelings of many when he said: "No crown is won without suffering and it fell to him (Dowding) to bear the cross of seeming ingratitude and perhaps, too, misunderstanding from many of those whose standards were not his own...We offer Muriel the consoling hope, that as her affinity with the spirit world knows not the barrier of physical distance, so even in the pain of bereavement she may find herself in communion with him..."

Three weeks after his death Muriel and Hugh Dowding met again — in a dream. "We were driving around", she said, "not in a car but in a chariot, seeing a lot of friends and we were so happy. So realistic was the experience that I thought I must get through to the Air Ministry and tell them how well Hugh is and that his Memorial Service must be cancelled. It was a spiritual, uplifting, psychic experience and it certainly helped get me through the Service at Westminster Abbey on Thursday March 12, 1970".

It is unlikely that Hugh Dowding is a ghost of Biggin Hill although there is a road there named after him and, with the likes of Debden, Northolt, North Weald, Kenley and the other senior sector stations of Fighter Command, it remains one of his spiritual homes.

No, Dowding had spent too many years probing the mysteries of life and its relationship with the spiritual world and the universe to want to hang on to an earthly existence. Today he's with his beloved boys of Fighter Command — not directing them against the mighty Luftwaffe, not telling them about the bitterness he felt when rejected by the Government but explaining how God rewarded him.

"He gave me Muriel".

Lord Dowding with a few of his 'chicks' preparing for the inaugural Battle of Britain Memorial Flight, September 15th, 1945, taking off from North Weald. Left to right: Squadron Leaders John Ellis, Tim Vigors and Denis Crowley Milling (background), Air Chief Marshal Lord Dowding, Wing Commander Douglas Bader, Squadron Leader 'Hawkeye' Wells and Wing Commander Peter Brothers.

SUBSCRIBERS

The following kindly gave
their support to this book

Charles Armitage
E R Arnold
Vic Ashlee
Margaret Aspinall
Frances Austen
Mr & Mrs Austen
Jonathan & Sally Balcon
Robert Barham
John Beadle
Francis Bellingham
H Belsey
David Blundell
Sheala Blundell
Marjorie Borner
Paul M Boulton
Miss S M Bourne
B. Bowman
Geoff Boxall
Ruby & Mary Breeds
W J Brenton
Mr & Mrs M A Brett
Mick Bridge
Doris Britten
Violet Brook
Derek Brown
Mrs B J Buchanan
Raymond Bullion
Stephen Bungay
Stan Burchett
Florence Causton
Rob Champion
Barbara Clark
Mr Maurice Clue
Marjorie E Cocker
Sebastian Coe
Steve Coe
Josephine Cole
Dr John W Comper
J M Cook
David Coombs
Mark Coombs
Simon Peter Cosham
Maxwell Creasey
Margaret Crerie
E M Crosse
Peter W Currie
John Dawson
Dorothy Deaney
Monica De Garston
Val Dennett
Simon Denney
Rosemary Denton
Jennifer Dexter
Les Dickson
John F Dorling
Mark Dutton
David William Easton
Douglas Harold Elks
Colin & Angela Elliott
Mr Dominic Ellis

Rachel & George Elvery
Richard R D Ewing
Sue Fairchild
J J Farrar
M Fearne
Edgar Fitzgerald
Bill Foster
Michael G A Foster
Colin Henry Fox
Mrs Emerald Frampton
Pauline Freeland
Maurice Austen Fry
Bernard L Fuller
Ray Garner
Stuart & Lydia Gay
Michael Ginn
H A Glover
R Godsalve
Peggy Gosling
Tom Goulding
Peter & Eileen Gray
Trevor Green
Harold Greenup
Ken Gregory
R B Griggs
Eileen Gunnell
Mary Hackney
Marion Hall
Barbara Hammerton
Kendrick Harding
R T Hattrill
Ken Hayes
Paul Heasman
Marjorie Hewes
George R Higgs
Neil Hilkene
Ruth Holdaway
Ken Hooker
Mrs Edith Hopkins
Mrs D A Hopkins
Mary Hover
David R Hull
Sally & Alan Humphrey
Maureen Humphrey
Wing Cmdr D S G Jackson
OBE DL
Ken & Margaret James
Maria Jarvis
A Jeffreys
Mr & Mrs F W Jenns
Tony Johns
Rob (Johnny) Johnson
Mrs J Johnson
Derek Kemp
Roger King
Mr S Kinnes
Edward, Robin & Mavis
Kitchingham
Victor Lake
Mr O C Lambert
T A Lampard
The Langridge Family
Tony Lathey

Miss G M Law
Norah Leggatt
David Lewis
Iris Lilley
David & Christine Lillo
Jean Lindsey
Peter Lloyd-Davies
Martyn Longstaff
Audrey Lucas
Jean Luckhurst
Leslie Lyne
Ron Machen
Jack Macro
Joan Marsh
Jean Martin
Peter Martin
B L & J F Matthews
Colin Philip Matthews
Pete Matthews
Wg Cdr Joe May
Timothy F P McGrane
Bill Meridew
Keith Miles
Chris Miles
Chris Miller
Gerald Mills
Raymond Mills
Pat & Lal Mineham
Sam Morgan John
Queenie Mortimer
Bill Morton
Alan & Anne Mount
Tony Nicholls
Richard Nobbs
Betty Oades
Dick Olive
Ron Pankhurst
H A & R Parkes
James E Peall
Gwen & Reg Pearce
Lucy Peatfield
Peter Persighetti
Ray & Betty Phillips
Don Phillips
Victor & Joan Philp
Cyril & Vera Pile
Chris Porteous
Jan & Chris Powis
Hugh R Pryke
Janet & Alec Ramage
Esme Irene Rand
Paul & Denise Rason
Kevin John Reardon
Chris Reardon
Roy & Iris Reardon
Geoff Reardon
Pam Reed
Mark Rees
Wendy Reynolds
Ivy Rhodes
Dennis Ridler
Peter Rogers
Clarence Rose

Mick Ruberry
Mr Dale Rush
The Ruston Family
Joan Evelyn Sale
Mary Sampson
Eileen L Sands
Evie Saunders
Ian Scott
Michael Scott
Paul Scott
Mike & Tessa Sheeres
Flt Lt W G A Shepherd
Maurice G Short
Coral Simpson
Maria Sinclair
Alan Smith
Steve Smith
Sydney Smith
Tom & Debbie Smith
Ian Smith Watson
Roy & Freda Spivey
Mick Springate
D G & C Stevens
Jeanne Stevens
Maurice Stocker
Ronald H H Stokes
Mrs Phyllis Streets
Derek Sutton
Dave Sutton
Maureen Thatcher
Mrs Hilda Thickins
Troye R Thomas
P Thompson
Paul Thompson
Angela Thorn
L W & J G Thorne
Mr E A B Thorneycroft
John R Toms
Eunice D Towersey
Colin Towse
Vivienne & Brian Tremain
Eve Tucker
David W Twining
Miss B Twinn
Cyril Van Beers
Marielle Van Dalen
Ced Verdon
Ray Wagner
Trevor Wales
Bruce Walker
Patricia E Walsh
Philip Wanstall
Geoff Warne
Christine Webb
Alan Weeks
Eileen & Ian Whitehead
D R Willis
Sidney G Willson
Brian Wingate
S M & P F Winton
Mrs Sarah-Jane Wood
Mick Worrall
John Edward Wratten
Ivor Youngman

This painting by Brian Petch of Kingsdown, Deal shows a Spitfire pilot of 610 Squadron about to be rescued by Air Sea Rescue High Speed Launch HSL122 in 1941. This launch, based in Dover, was sunk in August 1942 by FW190s. High overhead can be seen the contrails of German bombers pressing on to their target while Stukas attack shipping around Dover Harbour. A Bf 109E flies low over the scene.

Please note: The rank is consistent with the pilot's first mention. In the case of most of those who lived promotion would have followed as the war progressed.

BIBLIOGRAPHY

IN writing this book I have referred to pamphlets, newspaper articles and Squadron diaries and combat reports kept in The Imperial War Museum, Public Record Office and Bromley Borough Library. Prominent among these is *Aces High* by Christopher Shores and Clive Williams, which is a tribute to the most notable fighter pilots of the British and Commonwealth Forces in the second world war.

I have also referred to the following books: *Battle of Britain Now and Then,* edited by Winston Ramsey, *Men of the Battle of Britain* by Kenneth Wynn, *Air Battle Over Dunkirk* by Norman Franks, *The Few* by Philip Caplan and Richard Collier, *A Willingness to Die* by Brian Kingcome, *I Fear No Man* by Doug Tidy, *Pure Chance* by Dame Felicity Peake, *Inn of The Few* by Kath Preston, *Bograt* by Donald Stones, *Tumult in the Air* and *The Last of the Knights* by James Goodson, *Luftwaffe in the Battle of Britain* by Armand van Ishoven, *The Blitz Now and Then* edited by Winston Ramsay, *Many Mansions* by Hugh Dowding, *RAF Biggin Hill* by Graham Wallace, *Biggin on The Bump* by Bob Ogley, *Polish Wings in the West* by Bohdan Arct. *Kent at War* by Bob Ogley, a *Schoolboy at War* by Peter Halliday. *Unexplained Kent* edited by Brian Paine, *Ghosts of Kent* by Peter Underwood, *VCs of the Air* by John Frayn Turner, *601 Auxiliary Squadron* by Hugh Dundas (Evening Standard July 1960), *609 Squadron* by Frank Ziegler, *Invisible Brother* by Nick Gilman and Thea Keeler (to be published 2002).

THE first edition of Bob Ogley's book, *Biggin on The Bump,* published in 1990 for the 50th anniversary of the Battle of Britain, sold out within a month of printing and duly became a collector's item. Since then it has been reprinted five times and continues to be in great demand, having raised £15,000 for the RAF Benevolent Fund.

Bob is a journalist by profession and an author by courtesy of the greatest storm of the century. *In The Wake of The Hurricane* sold almost 250,000 copies, remained in the top ten bestseller list for eight months and changed his life. Many of his other books about Kent and the south-east have been county bestsellers. They include *Doodlebugs and Rockets, Kent at War* and *Surrey at War.* He also found and edited an unpublished manuscript by the novelist, H.E.Bates, whose widow, Madge, donated her royalties to the RAF Benevolent Fund. *Flying Bombs Over England* raised more than £15,000 and that, for Bob and Froglets Publications, was the continuation of a wonderful partnership.

Today, Bob travels extensively in pursuit of information and is in great demand among clubs to tell his unique story.

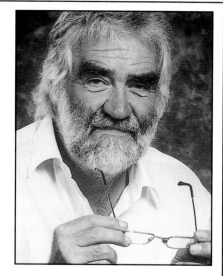

Coming soon:
Kent in the 19th Century
by Bob Ogley

Books available from Froglets Publications, Brasted Chart, Westerham, Kent TN16 1LY Tel: 01959 562972 Fax: 01959 565365

COUNTY WEATHER SERIES
By Bob Ogley, Ian Currie and Mark Davison

The Kent Weather Book
ISBN 1 872337 90 2................................£10.99

The Sussex Weather Book
ISBN 1 872337 13 9................................£10.99

The Norfolk and Suffolk Weather Book
Paperback ISBN 1 872337 99 6.................£9.95
Hardback ISBN 1 872337 98 8...............£16.95

The Hampshire and Isle of Wight
Weather Book
ISBN 1 872337 20 1................................£9.95

The Berkshire Weather Book
ISBN 1 872337 48 1................................£9.95

The Essex Weather Book
ISBN 1872337 31 7................................£10.99

HURRICANE SERIES

Surrey In The Hurricane
by Mark Davison and Ian Currie
ISBN 0 9513019 2 6................................£8.95

Eye on The Hurricane (Eastern Counties)
Paperback ISBN 0 9513019 6 9.................£7.95
Hardback ISBN 0 9513019 7 7...............£11.95

WAR AND AVIATION SERIES

Biggin On The Bump
the most famous fighter station in the world.
by Bob Ogley
Paperback ISBN 1 872337 05 8.................£9.99
Hardback ISBN 1 872337 10 4...............£16.99

Doodlebugs and Rockets by Bob Ogley
Paperback ISBN 1 872337 21 X.............£10.99
Hardback ISBN 1 872337 22 8...............£16.95

Kent at War (1939-1945) by Bob Ogley
Paperback ISBN 1 872337 82 1...............£10.99
Hardback ISBN 1 872337 49 X.............£16.99

Surrey at War (1939-1945)
Paperback ISBN 1 872337 65 1..........Temp o.p.
Hardback ISBN 1 872337 70 8...............£14.95

Westerham and
Crockham Hill in the War by Helen Long
ISBN 1 872337 40 6................................£8.95

OTHER LOCAL HISTORY BOOKS

Underriver: Samuel Palmer's Golden Valley
By Griselda Barton and Michael Tong
ISBN 1 872337 45 7................................£9.95

Tales of Old Tonbridge
by Frank Chapman
ISBN 1 872337 55.4................................£8.95

Tales of Old Tunbridge Wells
by Frank Chapman
ISBN 1 872337 25 2................................£14.95

Sevenoaks Chronicle of the Century
by Bob Ogley and Roger Perkins
ISBN 1 872337 26 0................................£14.95

FLOOD — the weather that ravaged Britain in
October and November 2000
ISBN 0 86367 998 6................................£9.99

CHRONICLE SERIES

Kent: A Chronicle of the (20th) Century
by Bob Ogley

Volume One (1900-1924)
ISBN Hardback 1 872337 24 4...............£16.99
ISBN Paperback 1 872337 19 8.............£10.99

Volume Two (1925-1949)
ISBN Hardback 1 872337 84 8...............£16.99
ISBN Paperback 1 872337 89 9.............£10.99

Volume Three (1950-1974)
ISBN Hardback 1 872337 16 3...............£16.99
ISBN Paperback 1 872337 11 2.............£10.99

Volume Four (1975-2000)
ISBN Hardback 1 872337 06 6...............£16.99
ISBN Paperback 1 872337 01 5.............£10.99

Boxed Set Hardback 1872337 15 5.........£60.00
Boxed set Paperback 1872337 75 9........£45.00

e-mail address: *frogletspublications@bobogley.co.uk*